FORCEFULLY ADVANCING

saints to boldly and forcefully advance the kingdom of God! Written in study-book format with each chapter ending in powerful self-examination questions, *Forcefully Advancing* is a great tool for homeschooling parents committed to training up their children as world-changers for Christ. If you've ever wondered what really happens when you think, "Well, somebody else will do it," then read on!

—John Codispoti
Former Director Region 5 North Carolina Home Educators

In *Forcefully Advancing* Wes Moore has produced a biblical, insightful, and interesting fictional account of Carter Fitzgerald's journey thirty years into the future and his discovery of how the United States has degenerated into a thoroughly pagan society. While at first blush this may seem far-fetched, if you think about the degradation we have experienced over the last fifty or so years, the state of things the book projects is not at all unlikely.

But Wes does not leave the reader floundering hopelessly. He presents a detailed analysis of current church growth and cultural change approaches, and critiques, each using biblical standards. If the book ended here, readers would be discouraged, but we are not left downcast.

Wes next presents a model for promoting truth to the lost, a practical approach anyone can use in friendly conversations. Taking it beyond the individual, Wes also shows how to develop a support system in your church or small group.

Finally, readers are encouraged in the book's last section where Carter Fitzgerald is taken back to the future and sees what America could become if the *Forcefully Advancing* strategy were implemented by Christians across the country.

Buy it. Read it. Take it seriously.

—T. C. Pinckney
Editor, The Baptist Banner

There is the clear ring of authenticity to Wes's writing. The principles for which he advocates are ones that he has practiced across the years. I can vouch that he is the real deal because I have personally watched him flesh out a bold and loving witness for Christ. May his challenge result in Kingdom advance!

—Jeff Ginn
Executive Director
Southern Baptist Conservatives of Virginia

Leadership requires change and change requires risk. Risk requires sacrifice and sacrifice requires cause. There is no greater cause than the "Great Commission," and there is no greater risk than the 'Great Commission' in the lives of individual Christians who desire to change the future and hope for America. In a time when there is a clarion call for a "Great Commission Resurgence," this book comes with a lightning bolt realization that we can in fact change and impact our world and our culture. "Sacrifice, it seems is the fuel in the engine of God ... " is a profound statement that has enormous implications in our daily approach to reaching our world. Time is short and the need is great.

—Don Matthews
Director, Church Health and Revitalization Office
South Carolina Baptist Convention

Forcefully Advancing takes us on a clear walk through the state of Christianity in America. Wes uses Carter's life story and states the current issues, resources, and strategies clearly. He gives hope that God can use the church to further His plan to reach, love, and train Christians to live, walk, and serve Him with confidence. FCA joins Carter on this quest to abide in Christ, boldly standing for the one true faith and one true God.

—Damon Fogal
Director, Central North Carolina Region
Fellowship of Christian Athletes

America is never again going to be a Christian Nation unless the Christian, young and old, passionately pursues the Great Commandment–love God and love others, and aggressively advances the Great Commission–to go and share Jesus and teach everything He commanded. *Forcefully Advancing: The Last Hope for America and American Christianity* is a must read for teenagers, young adults, middle aged, and seniors. A revolution must take place that revolts against Satan and seeks to further God's kingdom. Wes Moore's book challenges the reader to do just that! This book will be a required reading for all of the students in my ministry who desire to be on the Leadership Team.

—Jim Scott
Youth Pastor
Cornerstone Baptist Church

FORCEFULLY
ADVANCING

Wes Moore

FORCEFULLY ADVANCING

The Last Hope for America & American Christianity

TATE PUBLISHING & *Enterprises*

Published by Tate Publishing & Enterprises, LLC
127 E. Trade Center Terrace | Mustang, Oklahoma 73064 USA
1.888.361.9473 | www.tatepublishing.com

Tate Publishing is committed to excellence in the publishing industry. The company reflects the philosophy established by the founders, based on Psalm 68:11,
"The Lord gave the word and great was the company of those who published it."

Book design copyright © 2009 by Tate Publishing, LLC. All rights reserved.
Cover design by Kandi Evans
Interior design by Joey Garrett

Published in the United States of America

ISBN: 978-1-61566-730-7
1. Religion / Christian Ministry / Evangelism
2. Religion / Christian Church / Growth
09.12.30

To my wife, Dana, who has stood faithfully
with me during my struggles, and to my God,
Yeshua, who has sent them faithfully to me.

ACKNOWLEDGMENTS

I must begin my acknowledgements by thanking my heavenly Father. Not only did he pour his creativity, organizational skills, and writing ability into my mind as I wrote these words, but by his providence through many years taught me its principles when I would have preferred to do something else. He kept me where I didn't want to be, so I could learn things I didn't want to learn, so I could write a book I didn't know I needed to write. Though my life has been filled with struggles, I cannot thank him enough for what those struggles have produced on these pages. Indeed, he has given me "a crown of beauty instead of ashes, the oil of gladness instead of mourning, and a garment of praise instead of a spirit of despair" (Isaiah 61:3). Thank you, Father.

Secondly, I thank my wife, Dana, for her loyalty and faithfulness to me, not only through the writing of this book, but also through our sixteen years together. During that time, God has placed us on an interesting and sometimes very difficult path together. But, through it all, she has remained steadfast in her love and support for me. Humanly speaking, she makes it possible for me to devote time to projects like these, and I am so thankful to God for giving such a rich gift to me in her. Thank you, Dana.

On the family front, I am also grateful to my four children, Madi, Asa, Corbin, and Silas. They share in both my excitement and frustrations and, through their smiles and hugs, give me unending joy and encouragement. What would I do without you, my little critters?

Finally, I offer thanksgiving to those who have prayed for me and pushed me on through the months of this project. Let me mention a few of them by name: Sarah, Andy, Lisa, Mike, Kyle, Chris, Reid, and Dean. You each serve as my Titus and Aaron, and I am humbled by your enthusiasm and blessed by your love. Thank you, my friends.

TABLE OF CONTENTS

INTRODUCTION

Why should you read this book? *Because you want to change America.* Don't you? That's why you picked this book off the shelf and started flipping through its pages or clicked on the hyperlink and peeked inside for the Table of Contents or Introduction. You saw the title with the words *Last Hope for America,* and somewhere inside of you, deep down in the secret places, you know we're getting dangerously close to our last chance, our last chance before the gavel of God's judgment falls not only on the culture at large, but on his own people as well (that's you and me).

You know this. You watch the television, you follow the elections, and you read the papers and the blogs. You're no biblical scholar, but you know evil and perversity when you see it. You cringe as our culture bathes itself in orgies of lust; you step back in fear as the average citizen spits in disgust at the law of God; you burn with anger as our youth parade their atheism and godlessness before the world; you stand—mouth gaping—as our so-called leaders defile the holy Creator by reforming him into a passionless, lawless wimp. You know the time of reckoning is quickly approaching.

But you want to do something about it. You want to see it change.

Not only this, but you are beginning to see the pathetic state of the church in America as well. You don't remember the last baptism at your church, and you aren't sure when you had your last visitor. You know the "mega churches" are growing, but something tells you it's not mainly through new conversions. You've seen the church buildings for sale and know of others not far from the auction block. As you've visited other churches, you've felt the chill of death and smelled the stench of irrelevance. Once again, in that secret place in your soul, you know our days are numbered. It won't be long now.

But you want to do something about it. You want to see it change.

More than anything, you want to see your friends believe. You hurt because they reject all you hold dear. You mourn as they dismiss Christ without even hearing him out. It saddens you that your invitations to church fall on lifeless ears. You want to talk to them, but you don't know how; you don't even know where to start. And that frustrates the life out of you. When you do talk, they hit you with a stone wall of questions and objections. You don't know what to say, so you've learned to say nothing at all. But you know this is not God's will for you. You feel helpless, overwhelmed, defeated.

But you want to do something about it. You want to see that change too.

That's why you need this book. This book is about America and American Christianity and how you—yes, *you*—can do something that will bring lasting, biblical change to our land. How does that sound?

I must warn you. Some of your idols may be dashed along the way. The first will be politics. We live in a land of political action, and that action has become the modus operandi of the Christian community these days. Just today I was listening to a political radio program, and a caller called in praising the host for his conservative views. This caller said he had received a lot of resistance to his efforts to promote conservative ideals in his sphere of influence. What's the problem? *This man was a Christian minister who was taking his "gospel" into the pulpit of his church.*

As good and helpful as Christian political action can be, you won't find that solution presented here. The politicized faith of the average believer is not found on the pages of the New Testament. Red and blue Christianity has failed us in the past and will continue to fail us in the future. Ballots, judges, laws, elections—these are not the answer.

You may also have to say good-bye to your popular notions of church growth and personal outreach. Many models of church growth exist today, from growing through transfers to growing by relaxing the "unacceptable" parts of God's Word. However successful at filling seats, these models fail miserably in biblical terms. The same is true for common approaches to personal outreach. Some think the church will grow automatically while others hold to a "museum" outreach technique (displaying a holy lifestyle without directly engaging others). None of these are found in the Bible, however, and, consequently, none have worked as methods of extending the kingdom and changing the culture.

So what will work then? What can you do to turn all of this around? Well, I don't want to give away the end at the beginning, but, in simple terms, you can accept a very old directive: the Great Commission. What will save our culture and our churches and provide God the applause his perfections deserve is when you and I adopt *a personal commitment to the Great Commission.* Churches grow and cultures change when the hearts of people are transformed. And the only instrument that can do this is the gospel of Jesus Christ—the gospel you and I are called to promote aggressively with our own lives. In other words, a forcefully advancing kingdom is the last hope for America and American Christianity.

WHAT DOES THIS BOOK DO?

To this end, this book will do the following:

1. *Shock you* with a clear picture of the future of our nation if things continue on their present course.

You'll go on a journey with a man named Carter Fitzgerald as he receives a vision of the future of America. You'll be stunned at the perversity, idolatry, and godlessness of our once promising nation as you see what Carter sees in a small town thirty years in the future.

2. *Educate you* with a detailed analysis of church growth and cultural change philosophies that exist today. Each model will be critiqued against biblical principles to determine its validity. Through this process, the single, scriptural answer to our pressing concerns will be deduced and outlined.

3. *Equip you* with a natural, widely applicable (meaning the average Joe Christian can do it) approach to promoting truth to others. This model, called the Forcefully Advancing strategy, is built around a genuine friendship with the lost and will give you a low-pressure way to engage others with God's truth. You'll learn how to make friends, start conversations, transition to spiritual topics, answer questions and objections, and share the message of Jesus with relevance and impact.

4. *Show you* a way to organize your church or small group to engage the lost around you in an ongoing, consistent way. Many strategies fail because they don't create a system that brings believers together for ongoing training, communication, and accountability. To overcome these weaknesses, you'll learn how to implement a Forcefully Advancing Action System (FAAS), a detailed plan to create teams in your church or small group for not only ongoing training, communication, and accountability within the team, but also for communication with church leadership for planning and resource allocation.

5. *Encourage you* by taking you back to the future with Carter to see what America could be like if the *Forcefully Advancing* strategy is implemented across the nation. You'll be inspired by what he sees on his second visit to this small town. The transformation

you will observe, built on biblical principles, will give you hope for the future and good reason to be bold and courageous as you adopt your own personal commitment to the Great Commission.

THE OUTLINE

To accomplish these important objectives, the book has been organized into four sections. In "Part 1: The Core Issues and Their Real Solutions," we'll be introduced to Carter's first vision, analyze church growth and cultural change philosophies, and take a hard look at our failure to keep the Great Commission within our own land. Then, in "Part 2: The Necessary Foundation," we'll work through three issues that will undergird our success in transforming the church and culture: hypocrisy within the church, sacrifice and risk as principles of kingdom advancement, and a biblical view of the conversion process. Laying out the detailed Forcefully Advancing strategy is what part three is all about. Here we'll review befriending the lost, discovering and overcoming objections to faith, and presenting the gospel. Finally, in "Part 4: Claiming the Future Now," the FAAS will be explored in detail, and we'll join Carter again for his second, powerful vision of America.

One other thing before we get started. This book has been designed and written to facilitate group study. There are a total of thirteen chapters, which easily fits into a typical church semester, and each chapter ends with discussion questions that can be used to facilitate dialogue in a group setting. So start thinking about how you can use this book as a resource in your group or church.

Well, it's time to get started. Turn the page, and start making a difference in America and American Christianity.

PART ONE

The Core Issues and Their Real Solutions

CHAPTER 1

CARTER'S VISION: AN AMERICA WITH NO CHRISTIANITY

L ight—blazing, white light—came from every direction, surrounding me, blinding me. I was paralyzed instantly, frozen in place like a statue. *What just happened?* I wondered. *Where am—?* But before I could finish the question, a horn blared just in front of me, and my instincts took over. *Move!* my mind cried—so I did, diving as hard as I could to my left, toward the curb. I stood to watch a clean, black Mercedes dart into the night, my hair disheveled, course gravel layering my palms. I brushed them on my pants. *Close,* I thought. *Too close.*

Where am I? I pondered, finishing my thought from a microsecond before. *A moment ago I was... Well, I think I was at home. Was I in bed or working in the garage? I can't remember.*

So I walked.

Judging from the line of buildings just in front of me, I was in a small town somewhere. They were short, brick buildings, no more than two or three stories tall. I was on one end of the procession moving toward them. It was late fall; the smell of dry leaves and crisp evening air confirmed it. *There's something familiar about this place,* I thought. As I walked, I noticed the year "1939" carved into a cornerstone of one the buildings. *But this isn't 1939, or even what I would call the present. I think this is the future.*

But I kept walking.

I passed an old service station. A Chevy blazer, probably forty years old, sat in the parking lot with the hood propped open. But nobody was working on it; it just sat there, silently, like an old man on a porch. Then I noticed the railroad tracks to my right. Slightly above street level, they ran parallel to the line of buildings. In fact, there were no buildings at all on the right side, just the tracks. Several crossings dotted its length for the next several blocks, like rungs on a ladder. I heard the *thump-thump* as cars crossed.

Look at all the people, I thought. *They don't look like my kind of people; this isn't like any small town I've ever seen.* Apprehension hit me without my even realizing it. *This place gives me the creeps.* But I kept going. There was something for me to see here—I could feel it—something for me to learn.

The sidewalk was brighter now. Street lamps poured their light on glass windows, tall, wooden doors, and pedestrians huddling in shadows. As I passed the first brick building, I realized how spiritually dark this place really was. A faceless guy sitting cross-legged with a needle falling from his arm, an old man leaning against a wall, talking to himself and shaking uncontrollably, a woman dressed in sleazy clothing and thick, cheap makeup leaning into a car window—each told me that God was not to be found in this place.

I don't like this. I'm a Christian. I shouldn't even be here. Turn around, call someone, and get out of here, I ordered myself.

Then he spoke to me. I didn't even see him coming, but suddenly he was staring me right in the face. "Hey," he said, breathing alcohol on my skin. "How 'bout you loan me a buck?"

"I—I don't have any money," I responded. He was thin, black, looked to be sixty, skinny with a rough, sunken face and blood shot eyes, scruffy white beard. Over camouflage overalls, he donned a thick, winter coat.

"Oh, come on, now. I know you got money. Help me out, man." He stumbled, almost falling. I reached out to steady him.

"No, really, I don't have anything, man." At first he scared me, but then I realized he was just a harmless old man with some sad story. Maybe he's somebody's dad or grandpa; he raised his kids and then something terrible happened; he didn't start on the streets but was driven there by life's unfortunate circumstances. A pain welled up from inside.

"What's your name? Do you live around here?" I offered.

"I'm Ed. No, I don't live here. I got me a condo down at the beach." With that he laughed and turned away, back into his world of shadows.

I slowed to watch him and then continued on my way.

Eventually, I came to a street crossing. Apparently I was on Center Street. Center was intersected by several smaller side streets. This one was Clay.

At the intersection I noticed two signs in the ground just before the sidewalk ended, the kind real estate agents use to get you to their open house, rectangular with thin, metal rods that stick in the ground. When I read the words, I did a double take. One was purple with pink, reflective letters: Girls—See Before You Buy. The other was equally as perverse, but with a plain, white background and black, square letters: Gay Love—Cheap and Discreet. My stomach curled. *Oh, my, you can't be serious. What kind of place is this?*

There was no way I was going down that street. I wouldn't dream of dishonoring God or Eileen by being seen in such a place. But then I heard a voice, as mysterious as anything I had experienced thus far. The voice said simply, "Go." I don't know if it was audible or just inside my head. I'm thirty-eight years old and have never heard God speak to me in a voice before—and perhaps I never will again—but tonight I was sure. This voice was God's.

So I turned left and walked.

Within a few seconds, I entered the most degenerate strip of ground I had ever seen. As before, there were people everywhere, walking up and down the sidewalks: men in business suits and cardigans smoking cigars, couples leaning against the walls kissing, young men in dark trench coats walking in ominous packs. Then the women in the windows appeared. Dressed in sordid lingerie, they danced behind glass windows, prostitutes on display like manikins in a department store, their bodies unreachable, yet their power all around. With the simple motion of a finger, they called in their prey like a puppet on a string.

I can't believe my eyes. Tell me this is some big city, some foreign land! Oh, God, what is the meaning of this? I pleaded. *I've got to get past this; I feel sick.* I tucked my head and pushed through the crowd. Finally, after a few blocks, I could breathe again.

But my lesson was not yet over. I had more to learn.

I reached the end of the block and turned left. Church Street.

The scene was less outwardly corrupt here, but no less disheartening for a man raised in a land—and a time—of Christian influence. As part of the quaint, clean, Christian subculture, I went to church every weekend, never spent time in bars, and carefully avoided the "dirty" people and parts of town. I read my Bible (occasionally) and prayed with my son, Jeff, every night.

This street must be more of a business area than pure pleasure. As I walked, I became more and more curious. What types of businesses would rent in this district? And what about the church? There must be a church around here somewhere. A bulletin board on a nearby wall caught my attention. I stopped to take a look. Pinned erratically were ads for used furniture and a plea or two for lost animals. Then I saw it—an ad for a new church stapled toward the bottom. I shifted to get a clear look. It read:

New Temple Opening in April
   The nation's newest spiritual phenomenon is coming to you!
   With Temples in every state in America, the Atheon is a secular temple devoted to scientific worship, delivering spiritual fulfillment through exposure to the latest research in fields ranging from cosmology to quantum mechanics. Our

credo is to make faith rational. The Atheon offers an alternative to theocentric religions such as Christianity—now banned by the Edict of Freedom Act of 2034.

The Atheon seeks to free its adherents from the tyranny of God and deliver them to the freedom of scientific discovery and man's independent conscience.

So, this is America. I can't believe it. And science is our newest religion? I read something about this a long time ago but never thought it would come to this.

2034? Oh, no—I'm in the future. What's going on here?

Edict of Freedom Act? Christianity banned? What? Our constitution says the government can't do this; it's illegal. Then it hit me. *They changed the constitution; that's the only answer. Wait, there's got to be a church somewhere in this town.* I ran from door to door, bumping into people, pushing past them, checking the signs at the entrance of every office, open or closed. There were clothing shops but no soup kitchens, taverns but no youth houses, sex clubs but no inner-city sanctuaries. I ran across to the other side. A restaurant, a security company, a lingerie store. Still, no sign of life.

Then I found it. A small church building tucked between the common brick facades. It looked to be a hundred years old. *Yes, I recognize this place. Christ's Community church. My church when I was a kid. Oh, God … this is my hometown!*

I ran up the steps, jerked the front door open, and, in an instant, was stopped cold. This was still a church building, all right, but not a *Christian* church. Various statues were neatly arranged in what was the pulpit area. At center stage, where Pastor Ken used to preach the Word of God, was a beautiful stone statue of a naked woman, a pagan goddess. Smoke filled the air, and the scent of spices and herbs was overpowering. From behind a curtain, a woman emerged, dressed like some kind of belly dancer, with a bowl of incense in her hands. "Are you here to worship?" she asked seductively. I didn't say a word, just slowly backed out the door.

Maybe the church moved to one of the open spaces in another building; old buildings are hard to keep up, after all. I returned to my search and in a few moments found something promising. The sign said The Best Life Clinic. *Maybe this is some kind of "underground" way of saying "church."* I read on. "We ensure society can purify itself of unwanted or unhelpful life, strengthening the genetic health and long-term happiness of the culture." Wait a minute. *That sounds like a fancy way of saying, "We get rid of the babies and old people and invalids you don't want."* When I read the "services offered" bullets, I knew I was right. "Services include abortion on demand, euthanasia (without doctor's consent), and mercy terminations for low-IQ adults and children. Medicaid and Medicare accepted."

"This is no clinic of *life*," I whispered. "This is a clinic of *death*, right here in the open—and the government foots the bill!" *Oh, God, what has happened to my nation? What has happened to my home . . . and what about my son? What must it be like for him?*

I felt dizzy. The lights started spinning. I was going down. All went black.

My eyes opened and started to focus. I was lying on a couch with several people huddling over me, concern on their faces. One of them spoke up. "I'm J.R. We found you on the street. Apparently, you passed out and laid there for some time before my people found you. You're lucky you're not dead." Probably in his late thirties (like me), his face was slender and pleasant, his voice calm and comforting. For a moment, I thought I recognized him.

"Can you sit up?" he asked.

"I think so." My feet slipped off the edge as I slowly sat up. After a pause to look around and orient myself, I spoke slowly. "I'm really not sure what happened. I think I was a bit overwhelmed, and then the lights just went out."

"Well, you seem to be all right now," he said.

I think I was in an office on the strip, though probably a basement (no windows). The floors were checkerboard black and white overlaid with a few couches and chairs here and there, and a whiteboard was mounted on one wall; about half way down the room a bar angled out into the room.

J.R. sat down in a nearby chair and waited for a moment then prodded me for more information. "You said you were 'overwhelmed.' About what?"

How do I explain this? I thought. "Well, I ... grew up around here and just came back to visit," I started. Then I noticed something on the bar, sitting cockeyed toward the end, a worn, dark brown form. The words *Holy Bible* were barely visible on the sleeve. I glanced quickly to the whiteboard. Though it was erased, the faint remnants of handwritten text remained: "John," "righteousness," "God."

"Are you guys Christians?" I blurted out.

Heads turned quickly back and forth. After a second, every eye focused on J.R., apparently their leader. His eyes filled with confidence; his heart, courage. "Yes, we are. Are you ... ? Sorry, I didn't catch your name."

Adrenaline filled my veins, out to my fingers and toes. "Yes, yes, I am!" I cried. "Man, am I glad to see you guys! And my name is Carter." It was Carter Fitzgerald, but I was too much in a hurry to waste words on details. J.R. had a curious look on his face. I continued. "I was wandering around downtown and noticing the incredible changes. This used to be such a, well, 'Christian' town, but now it's one of the most disgusting places I've ever seen. What happened?"

With that innocent question, the mood became much more serious, even sullen. It felt like one of those times when your doctor was about to tell you you've got a fatal illness or your boss was about to fire you. J.R. leaned forward in his chair, interlaced his fingers, and tried to explain.

"Well, looking back on it, it's easier to identify the causes. As you probably know already, in the late twentieth century and beginning of the twenty-first, we started to lose our foothold in America. I've found study after study documenting the disintegration of the church. Youth were leaving, baptisms declining, and churches closing. A bloodbath before our very eyes. Some were trying to show the people what was happening, but nobody wanted to hear the bad news." He shook his head and glanced down at his worn shoes.

"The church had been living on borrowed time from earlier years when people were more receptive to the gospel, back in the days of Billy Graham and D. James Kennedy. I guess they thought if they kept the doors open, people would continue to come in. But that wasn't the case."

He went on to tell how Satan had changed his strategy, not going after the cross directly, but after the foundation of the cross: the Bible. The enemy had created so much skepticism about the validity of the Scriptures that in just a few generations, most Americans wrote off the Christian faith as mythology.

"In response," he continued, "the Christian community—fat and happy with our nice little fellowships, sweet sermons, and comfortable Sunday school classes—turned inward. Instead of taking on the lies and aggressively pushing the truth, we hid in our churches and ignored the world around us. Yes, in spite of our disobedience, God saved some during that time as well; however, once they were saved, we taught them to hide from the culture instead of going back and changing it. We abandoned the Great Commission within our own borders. Average Joe Christian relieved himself of any responsibility for the lost around him.

"Failing in a scriptural approach, we chose politics. We still had a large voting block and political influence, so we tried to use them to *force* the culture to be 'Christian.'"

By this time, many of the young people had gathered around, creating a standing-room-only mass on our end of the room. I looked around at their faces, tense and focused.

"We had some success for a while, but eventually, as fewer people truly surrendered to God's will, our political influence eroded, and the laws and judges we once were able to influence were changed or replaced. When our enemies gained control of the political power, they ran us underground, taking our rights one at a time."

I interjected. "You mean the Edict of Freedom Act?"

"Yes, that Act was the final nail in our coffin, but we were all but marginalized even before that," he said, shaking his head. "The result of our failures is what you see on the streets today." He leaned back in his chair again. For a long moment, his eyes looked away. It was as if he had never really said it out loud before. A weighty silence descended on the room.

Eventually he spoke again, almost in a whisper. "Now we meet in secret and try to keep a low profile. As long as we do this, they leave what few of us remain alone. But I know one day they'll come for us."

I tried to say something, yet nothing came out. Questions formed faster than I could process them. My mind locked up. When the clogs turned again, thoughts overwhelmed me. *I had no idea. I thought things were okay. I feel so foolish, so convicted. I've had my head in the sand.* Then my mind turned toward them, toward a response. *But we—they—can't just let things continue. They've got to do something.*

"So why don't you do something about it?" The words flew out. "Why don't you learn from the past and do what they *didn't* do?" It was then I saw the defeat in his eyes—in *all* their eyes. Like whipped pups, they were too discouraged—too scared—to fight back.

J.R. didn't even bother to defend himself or offer a justification for giving up. "My friend, I admire your spirit, but it is too late for us. I only wish someone had done something thirty years ago. I wish I could go back in time. I wish I could show them what was going to happen. I wish I could open their eyes to the road they were on. But I can't. May God have mercy on us."

With those words, our discussion ended. J.R., obviously too upset to continue, got up and walked away. A moment later, a nice, white-haired lady named Betty brought me a cup of coffee. I drank a couple of sips in that awkward space of time when no one knows what to say or do.

Then somehow I knew it was time for me to go. My lesson had been learned. So I said good-bye and thanked them for saving me from the street. As I started up the stairs, I glanced down the long room to J.R., sitting on a couch by himself, deep in meditation. There was something about him. I knew I would never forget him. *Oh God, please give him courage,* was all I could pray. Then I pressed up the stairs.

I stepped out onto a side street called Dover, just as the sky was starting to brighten. I turned left and headed back toward the main drag, my mind racing with thoughts and implications and lessons from the intense and sobering experience God had just given me.

"There must be something I can do to change this," I whispered emphatically. As I reached the corner, I realized I was back where I'd started. *I will do something about it,* I committed to myself. *I'll start with my son.*

And then the light was back, and I was gone.

COULD CARTER'S DREAM ACTUALLY COME TRUE?

It already is.

Carter's vision is only the logical extension of what is *already happening* in America. Maybe you don't think the church will become so impotent in the future. If so, let me share some sobering statistics with you. According to one expert, 80 to 85 percent of churches in America are failing with little hope of revival.[1] And how about this one: up to 88 percent of children raised in conservative Christian homes leave the church after their eighteenth birthday and never come back.[2] You don't have to go far to find a church with no youth, only gray hair, and empty pews.

And if you don't think the sexual perversions will reach the heights of Carter's scary small town, you're right. It won't be as bad as his vision—*it will be worse.* The broad goals of this movement are laid down in a document known as the 1972 Gay Rights Platform. In this document, goals are identified for changing federal and state laws where sexuality is concerned.[3] Here are four of their stated goals from the state law section[4]:

3. Repeal all state laws prohibiting solicitation for private voluntary sexual liaisons; and laws prohibiting prostitution, both male and female.

6. Repeal of all state laws prohibiting transvestism and cross-dressing.

7. Repeal of all laws governing the age of sexual consent.

8. Repeal of all legislative provisions that restrict the sex or number of persons entering into a marriage unit; and the extension of legal benefits to all persons who cohabit regardless of sex or numbers.

Read these carefully. Goal three means legalized prostitution (including homosexual prostitution); goal seven, pedophilia (legalized child sex); goal eight, polygamy. Many of these radical goals have been accomplished in various places around the world, including the Netherlands, where prostitutes *actually dance in store windows today.* And in America, courts and legislatures are accomplishing these radical goals with increasing speed. As I write, another court just overturned a state law banning homosexual marriage. According to the article, "Iowa's highest court unanimously ruled … that a state law barring same-sex marriage is unconstitutional."[5] Still think Carter's vision is off?

Perhaps you don't buy the whole Atheon science-temple thing. "No way!" you say. Sorry to disappoint, my friend, but the first Atheon *has already been built.* It recently opened in California, and the plan is that "one day there will be an Atheon in every town."[6]

If you have trouble with "The Best Life Clinic," you may want to read an article entitled "Marvelous Suicide and Beneficial Abortion: Worldviews Matter" by Albert Mohler.[7] This article takes you into the perverted thinking of pro-suicide, pro-abortion advocates, Ludwig Minelli and Bonnie Erbe. In their view, not only are abortion and suicide good in a moral sense, but they are also *good for the economy.*

Finally, do I really need to prove that the culture is putting all of its energy into intellectually discrediting the Bible and the tenets of Christianity? From every outlet available—24–7–365—the enemy undermines the existence of God, the veracity of the New Testament documents, the reality of truth, the creation account, and the deity of Jesus (to name just a few). This message of doubt and skepticism rings through public school and university classrooms, through the pages of bestsellers, and through the television airwaves. It is inescapable, and it is devastating to the promotion of truth in America.

Yes, Carter's vision is not only *possible;* it is *in process.* So, the question before us isn't whether or not it will happen, but what will we do to stop it? How do we bring about sustainable church growth and genuine cultural change in modern, secular America? Unfortunately, many have answered this question in the wrong way, in ways that are not biblical, in ways that are failing us. For church growth, our approach has ranged from doing nothing to building through transfers. For changing the culture, our weapon of choice has become politics.

Can these in the end save us? To put it bluntly, no. And that's what this book is all about—understanding the weaknesses of our present approaches to church growth and cultural change and presenting the correct, biblical antidote: aggressive, persistent, and organized promotion of God's truth in America.

So lets get started. In the next chapter, we'll take up a detailed review of contemporary church growth methods and compare them to the Bible's teaching.

GROUP DISCUSSION QUESTIONS

If studying the book in a group, break into teams of three to five people and work through the questions listed below. Pick a spokesperson, and be ready to discuss your answers with the group.

If studying on your own, work through them independently.

1. Is Carter's vision of America on target? Why or why not?

2. Were you aware of the statistics quoted in the chapter about the percentage of churches failing and the number of youth leaving? How does this make you feel?

3. When you think about how to turn things around in the *church*, what ideas come to mind? Elaborate.

4. When you think about how to turn things around in the *culture*, what ideas come to mind? Elaborate.

CHAPTER 2

EXPANDING THE RIGHT KINGDOM: CHURCH GROWTH ACCORDING TO THE BIBLE

P astor Shaun was so excited. Having just taken over as lead pastor of Middle America Church, he was full of fire and energy and ready to move the church ahead. For most of his adult life, this was all he had wanted to do—take a struggling church and lead it to prosperity. Today was especially important because of the big 10:00 a.m. meeting. His church hired a consultant to help them develop a growth strategy, and the big kick-off meeting was about to begin. *We're going to be like one of those big churches one day,* he thought.

Like most churches in the U.S., Middle America's growth was stagnant. Baptisms were few and far between, and morale was sinking quickly. The few youth they had were discouraged, and things didn't look like they would turn around soon if they didn't alter course. But Shaun was determined to change all that.

After some preliminary discussions with the consulting firm, they decided to form a focus group of various members of the congregation, folks from different backgrounds, social classes, and ages, in order to get input on the growth plan. After all,

Pastor Shaun believed in the wisdom of the body. He just knew they were going to get some great ideas on the table today.

One by one, the panelists, consultants, and church staff members filed down the long, bright hallway to the large conference room in the church office building. Slowly, the rectangular, finely furnished room filled to capacity. As Pastor Shaun closed the door behind him, he couldn't help but smile. *Now we're getting somewhere,* he told himself. *Now we're* really *getting somewhere.*

After the staff members and consulting team made their introductions, Pastor Shaun asked the focus group panelists—Suzie Rogers, John Morgan, Fred Gates, Todd Hancock, and Barry Cox—to introduce themselves. In turn, they gave their names and shared a little of their history with Middle America. They were your average Christian people. Some were married, some divorced; some were professionals, some retired. But all had this in common: they loved Jesus and Middle America, and they all wanted to play a part in moving the church forward.

"Now that we're done with the pleasantries," Shaun began, "let's get down to the purpose of our meeting. We're here to develop a strategy to grow Middle America. Each of you has had a few weeks to think of the best way for us to do this. What I'd like to do now is turn the floor over to you, one at a time, and hear the ideas you've developed. How does that sound?"

"Fine," they all replied in unison.

"Now, why don't we start with you, Suzie? You have the floor." And they were off.

WHAT WILL THEY SAY?

So what do you think they'll say? Odds are you're a Christian not unlike these five panelists, and you attend a church something like Middle America. You've been around to witness the dwindling of our congregations across the nation, and you've read the Bible and given some thought to how the church can grow again. If you had to guess the common responses of American Christians to Pastor Shaun's inquiry, what would they be? But, most importantly, how would their recommendations stack up *in a biblical sense?* Would God's Word affirm them wholeheartedly or condemn them swiftly?

You see, it isn't good enough to have a "new" church growth strategy. You can make an organization grow in a myriad of ways, many of which are not biblical at all. What we want, as people of the book, is to approach building Christ's kingdom *as Christ modeled and commanded.* Ultimately, this is the only approach that will win his approval and produce results that last in time and eternity.

So, let's peek back into the conference room and listen as our friends share their thoughts. After we hear from each, we'll step out into the hallway and open the Bible. How do their ideas jive with the principles of Scripture? Will this group really get anywhere, as Pastor Shaun hopes?

SUZIE "WAIT-AROUND" ROGERS

Suzie loved to be the center of attention. In her mid-fifties, she'd been around Middle America as long as anyone could remember, and she was sure to let everybody know it. Lately she hadn't been attending as regularly because her husband, Carl, was struggling with cancer. When she did come, she sat in the back pew with Carl and reviewed everything with her infamous, critical eye. Her short, graying hair and thin-rimmed glasses hid a very forceful, opinionated personality.

She piped up without hesitation. "Well, Pastor, I've given this a lot of thought, and—I hate to rain on the parade here—but I really don't think we need a 'strategy' as such. The church has been on the earth for two thousand years, and I don't think it's going anywhere soon; we just need to keep preaching the truth and praying, then the Lord will add to the church as he sees fit."

At the other end of the table, Pastor Shaun sunk slowly into his seat. *Maybe this isn't going to be as easy as I thought.*

Sadly, Suzie's excuse for sidelining the Great Commission is not uncommon in the church today. It can appear as Suzie expressed it: "We just need to keep preaching the truth," or, "We just need to pray more." Or, it can appear as the spiritually sounding, "We just need to live godly and people will be saved," or, "We just need to preach through this or that book of the Bible," or, "We need to go through this popular Christian book." In the end, whatever the wording, it boils down to *the assumption that the church will grow by itself.* According to this view, there is no need for a strategy or organized effort; all that needs to be done is what is already comfortable, and things will turn out just fine.

Now, no one is saying that preaching the truth, praying, godly living, and Christian books are bad for the church. But is this all the New Testament requires of us where kingdom growth is concerned? Is this really the way to change Carter's vision? Let's take a look and see for ourselves.

problems with the church-will-grow automatically approach

This view of kingdom growth fails to recognize at least two fundamental realities taught on the pages of Scripture. The first is this: *The growth of the kingdom of God is resisted by violent men and spiritual powers.* Church growth is not like a ball rolling down a hill; there is no natural inertia that takes over after the ball begins to tumble. In fact, the opposite is true. Growing the kingdom is like pushing a ball up a hill... *while twenty men with clubs and sticks fight against you.*

Bloodthirsty resistance to the redemptive efforts of God is everywhere and continually present. Consider one often overlooked statement of Jesus from Matthew 11:12: "From the days of John the Baptist until now, the kingdom of heaven has been *forcefully advancing,* and *forceful men* lay hold of it" [emphasis mine].

The words translated *forcefully advancing* are from a Greek word meaning "to force, crowd one's self into, press, or suffer violence."[8] In other versions, it is translated as *suffers violence* (NKJV) and *suffered violence* (RSV). The phrase *forceful men* comes from this same Greek word and means "a forceful person" or one who is "violent."[9] Again, other translators have rendered this as "violent" (NKJV) and "men of violence" (RSV). Through these terms, you get the picture of a kingdom that is forcing its way into the world while violent people fight against it. D.A. Carson captures the essence of Jesus' expression with these words: "From the time of John the Baptist until now, the kingdom of heaven has been forcefully advancing; and violent and rapacious [ferocious or furious] men have been trying to plunder it."[10]

Of course, nothing ultimately can stop the forward movement of the purpose of God, but that does not mean his work will be consummated with ease or without price. One need only think through the life of Christ himself or the experiences of the apostles and early disciples to see Jesus' sobering affirmation in action. Just imagine in your mind the resistance Jesus found as he taught and ministered on the dust-laden streets of the Middle East, resistance that would ultimately end his life. Think of the stoning of Stephen and the beheading of James (Acts 7 and 12). Remember the floggings of Paul and the day he was left for dead outside Iconium and his grave charge, "We must go through many hardships [pressure, anguish, trouble, persecution[11]] to enter the kingdom of God" (Acts 14:19, 14:22).

Saying that the kingdom will grow automatically (if we just keep playing "good" Christian) is equivalent to shredding 80 percent of the New Testament, writing off the crucifixion as bad luck, and blaming Paul and the apostles for their suffering. And, of course, no one wants to do that.

The second fundamental reality this viewpoint fails to recognize is that *the Spirit of God vigorously promotes the kingdom through the instrument of people.* Jesus promised the kingdom would forcefully advance in the midst of violent men who opposed it. But how was that going to happen? What would God use to accomplish that advance? In one word, *people.*

When Jesus had finished his work and launched the kingdom

of God, he handed the continuation of this task over to his disciples, whom he then empowered by the Holy Spirit. This passing of the baton was expressly set forth in Acts 1:8: "But you will receive *power* when the Holy Spirit comes on you; and you will be my *witnesses* in Jerusalem, and in all Judea and Samaria, and to the ends of the earth" (emphasis mine).

Jesus' remaining followers may have been anxious to share the remarkable things they had seen and heard over the last forty days (and the last three years for that matter). After all, they had seen a man come back from the dead. But knowing the truth of our previous point—that incredible difficulty lies ahead for them—Jesus commanded them to put their excitement on hold and wait for the only person who could ensure their success: the Holy Spirit.

Luke records Christ's words: "Do not leave Jerusalem, *but wait for the gift my Father promised*, which you heard me speak about" (Acts 1:4, emphasis mine). To say it another way, "Guys, you aren't aware of this, but you just don't have what it takes to do what I'm asking you to do. You're getting ready to enter a storm like you've never experienced before, and it will tear you to shreds. I'm not going to allow you to fail. So, I'm sending you someone—in fact, the only one—who can guarantee your advance, my Spirit."

The Holy Ghost was given to satiate the believers with *power*, a word meaning "force, ability, might, or strength."[12] And what is the book of Acts but a confirmation of what they received to carry out their Herculean task? Nevertheless, the point here is that, though God could have used angels or even carried out his work directly, *he has chosen to use us.*

As further evidence, consider the experience of Cornelius as recorded in Acts 10. Think about all the trouble God went to just to prepare Peter and get him to Cornelius to share the good message. First, Jesus trained Peter personally for three years; then, God gave him a vision to convince him to speak to non-Jews (Gentiles); and, after all of that, he sent three men thirty miles, from Caesarea to Joppa, to bring Peter to Cornelius's house.

Now, God did all of this *even though he had an angel at Cornelius's house the day before* (Acts 10:1–8). God could have avoided all the trouble of bringing a man to Cornelius simply by having the angel—who was already there—tell the gospel to Cornelius. But he didn't. Why? Because he has chosen us for this task, plain and simple.

Like it or not, it is God's will to put us on the front lines of his work, empowering us to get the job done, letting us receive the deep joy of overcoming darkness, and himself being glorified in the process. So, as much as we might love Suzie and as right as she may be in some aspects of her statement, from a biblical perspective, her central argument is dead wrong. And to the degree we harbor and apply her thinking, we will fail in our task of expanding this kingdom.

Before we peek back into the room, however, let's ask ourselves a revealing question. Here we've shown how the kingdom advanced—*forcefully advanced,* to use Jesus' words—in the first century. When you reflect on the actions, boldness, and success of these early Christians and then compare that to what you see in American Christianity, would you say *we* are forcefully advancing?

Far from it. Whereas they forcefully advanced, we slowly retreat; whereas they fearlessly preached, we sheepishly hide; whereas they boldly risked all, we shamefully risk nothing.

What has happened to our once great kingdom? When did we lose our courage, our fire, our warrior's edge? What happened to the apostles' brand of Christianity, the kind that caused riots, converted thousands at a time, and turned the world upside down? Isn't it time we found it again? I believe it is.

JOHN "GIVEN-UP" MORGAN

Sensing the tense moment and hoping to move on to more productive comments, Pastor Shaun politely stepped in. "Well, thank you, Suzie, for your thoughts. We … appreciate your ideas." After scribbling down a few notes, he looked up again. "So, who would like to be next? Anyone?"

The heads pivoted nervously left and right as the panelists waited for someone to speak up. Finally, John raised his voice. "I'll go ahead, Pastor."

John was a simple man of God. Now retired, he lived in a small house in the city with his wife of thirty-nine years, Mildred, whom he loved very much. John enjoyed watching television preachers and reading his Bible. He was at every Bible study the church had, whether on Sunday night or Wednesday evening; he always sat quietly toward the back and took it all in. On occasion, he offered a comment or answer, if it was something he felt strongly about. His voice was quiet; his face, thoughtful.

"Well, Pastor," he offered, "first of all, let me say that I don't think I'm the best man for this type of thing. I'm not as educated as the others in this room, I'm sure, and I don't pretend to be wise in the ways of this world. But I appreciate you inviting me to this meeting, and I'll do my best."

Pastor Shaun really loved John. He smiled at him and said, "Thank you, John, for stepping up and being here today. Your best is all we can ask for." With these kind and encouraging words, John relaxed a bit and continued.

"Pastor, the way I see it, I've lived in my little house for over thirty years. I remember a time when this was a beautiful, bedroom community. I remember a time when people used to push their strollers down the sidewalks and talk with each other. I remember a time when we all felt safe and at home. But things have changed. Mildred and I can't go out anymore because the gangs have moved in. Just a few nights ago there was gunfire in our neighborhood." A few others in the group were nodding their heads. "And, you know, I invite people to church from time to time, but they don't seem interested. They always get this look on their faces like I'm crazy or something.

"The Bible says it's going to get this way at the end, Pastor. Heck, I saw a preacher on television the other night who was talking about the end times and how evil people would get."

Shaun listened intently. *I don't think I've ever heard John say so much,* he thought.

"Well, I guess what I'm saying is that trying to grow the church today may not be what we should be doing. The people are so bad, they just won't listen. It's useless to try. Maybe what we need to do is just hunker down and wait it out."

Not exactly what Shaun wanted to hear.

where does this view stand when compared to scripture?

Well, it's certainly hard to argue with John about the moral degradation of America. The evening news is proof enough of the increasingly evil society in which we live. Whether it's the power of the homosexual movement, violence in schools, drugs, sexual promiscuity, or pornography—take your pick—the land of the free and home of the brave is quickly becoming the land of the perverse and home of the corrupt. Furthermore, John is right about evil growing worse as we approach the end. Paul stated it very bluntly in his correspondence to Timothy. "Evil men and impostors," he declared, "will go from bad to worse" (2 Timothy 3:13; see 3:1 for Last Days context).

However, as much as Scripture would affirm John's conclusion about righteousness in America, it would not support his corresponding application to advancing the kingdom. The mistake John is making (and many of our people make this mistake today) is to conclude that because things are getting worse morally and because people seem more apathetic and antagonistic toward God's message, we should run and hide and give up on the forward movement of the kingdom of God in our time. This conclusion does not naturally follow.

To prove this, let's take a big-picture view of the Roman world of the first century, the world in which Jesus labored and the world into which the church was sent with the good message. The question I want you to ask yourself is this: Is the nation in which we labor worse than the world into which the first century Christians were sent? If it isn't, how can we refuse to carry out the Great Commission in our nation?

First, consider Christ's own words describing the people of his generation. Jesus openly condemned the people of his time. "A wicked and adulterous generation," he accused, "asks for a miraculous sign" (Matthew 12:39). The word translated *wicked* here describes their actions and can also be translated as "derelict" or "vicious."[13] *Adulterous* is a common Jewish expression for people who are unfaithful to God. On a later occasion, he calls them an "unbelieving and perverse generation" (Matthew 17:17), meaning "without faith in God" or "heathen," and "crooked, distorted, and morally corrupt."[14]

The apostles differed little in their estimation of their contemporaries. Paul picks up on Jesus' words in Philippians 2:15, calling them a "*crooked* and *depraved* generation." These two adjectives are the same Greek words Jesus used in Matthew 12:39 and 17:17 for *wicked* and *perverse*. Not to be outdone, Peter gets in on the public condemnation in his sermon at Pentecost. "Save yourselves," he pleaded, "from this corrupt generation" (Acts 2:40).

But were Jesus and the apostles on track with their evaluation? What did these folks do to draw such righteous fire? Well, a long list of dirty deeds, I'm afraid. They openly worshiped idols (think of Paul at Athens). Their judicial system was controlled by despots who, at the slightest agitation and without cause or accountability, could sentence a righteous person to death (I refer you to the beheading of John the Baptist by Herod). Remember also the brutal punishments of the time, like stoning, beheading, and crucifixion; recall the violent prejudice against Christians, sometimes leading to imprisonment, torture, and death; reflect on the worship of political leaders, such as kings and emperors; and let's not forget the blatant homosexuality that infested every corner of the empire (Romans 1).

Now, my friends, we have our problems in America. Without question, our moral foundation erodes daily and our penchant for debauchery grows by the hour, but let's not imagine for a single moment that our contemporary, American landscape is in the remotest sense as dark, violent, and malevolent as that of the first century Roman Empire. In comparison, we are immersed in blankets of silk.

Back to my point. If God would send his precious people into such a world as the first-century empire to forcefully advance his kingdom, what makes us think he would allow us to hide out, away from the fire, in such an easy place as modern America? The answer, obviously, is that he wouldn't. The evil actions of the nation in which we labor do not change the will of the Father. So, we appreciate John Morgan's viewpoint and empathize with his sadness at watching his bright neighborhood turn gray. Yet we must point him back to the Scripture he loves to see that, far from a reason to turn away, these realities should give him more determination than ever to push Christ's good kingdom forward.

FRED "TRANSFER" FITZPATRICK

So far, Pastor Shaun didn't like what he was hearing. What he wanted was a plan of *action*, not *inaction*. He loved these people dearly, but nothing they had offered so far had resonated with him. *Maybe it will get better as we move along*, he thought, trying to lift his spirits.

"Well, John, you've clearly given this a lot of thought," Shaun replied. "And I know you're right about what's happening in our community. So, thanks for your input." Shaun looked around the room. This time he would pick the next person himself. *Let's see*, he mused. *Who will help us get on the right track? Yes, Fred. He's a man of action.*

Fred was a businessman in his forties and really looked the part. His neatly cut, black hair was slicked back, revealing a slightly receding hairline. His short, soft turtleneck and sport jacket made him appear as the one professional in the group. In fact, he really was in the professional field. He was a business development manager for a large, local computer company.

He sat in meetings virtually all day, developed to-do lists, and worked with his staff to make things happen. More than that, Fred was a man of integrity and a serious follower of Jesus. With this combination, it was hard not to want his input, especially on the subject of church growth.

"Fred," Pastor Shaun said energetically, "why don't you jump in and give us your ideas."

After a brief pause to look down at his notes and collect his thoughts, Fred began. "Pastor, you know as well as I do that there are many Christians out there who are unhappy with their present church. They are either not being fed, or they don't like the music, or the youth group is too small. Now, one of the purposes of the church is to feed the flock and provide discipleship programs that help them grow. And here at Middle America, we have a great foundation in these areas. Yes, we have some room to improve, no doubt. But, with your preaching and the new music minister we've brought in, we could be a real draw to the Christians around us." At this, several heads nodded, including one of the consultants and Todd Hancock, one of the remaining panelists.

"Besides, think about those big churches on television or down off the interstate. How do you think they got so big? They did the things that Christians liked and wanted to see in their church, and the people flocked in by the hundreds. That's what you want to see, isn't it?" Pastor Shaun nodded, though he had his reservations.

"So, what I propose is a three-fold plan. First, we make the changes we need in our worship services and programs to meet the needs of the Christian community in the area. Two, we really invest in our youth department. A lot of people will come if we have a great youth department. And, third, we advertise, get the word out about the type of church we have here at Middle America. We could say something like, 'If you don't have a church home, please come visit us.' This will not be too in your face, but it will get across the message that if you're not happy where you are, come give us a try. What do you think?"

so, how about this get-them-to-transfer attitude?

Fred lays out a very organized and common sense approach. It is, after all, one of the roles of the church to feed its members, and no one can question the failure of many congregations to keep up with the times in terms of worship style, music, and youth. Furthermore, Fred has hit on a very practical and effective strategy for growing a local congregation. His words remind me of that famous phrase from the movie *Field of Dreams:* "If you build it, he will come." Many churches are building "it," and many Christians are coming. Who can argue with numbers?

Well, maybe this is it for Pastor Shaun. Perhaps it's time to bring the meeting to a swift close and adopt Fred's three-point-plan as is, or maybe not. While Fred's ideas are very pragmatic and efficient, they have some serious biblical weaknesses.

First, keep in mind the Great Commission is to make *new* disciples, not draw existing ones. It almost seems silly to point this out, but the entire context of Jesus' mandate is to push the gospel to people *who have never heard or do not believe.* "Go and make disciples of all nations," he charged. Of course, the text does not mention or even imply that we should have as a priority drawing other Christians into our fellowships. Now, don't misunderstand me. I'm not saying transfers are wrong; they are natural and healthy in many cases. But don't allow yourself to be deceived into thinking they amount to genuine kingdom growth. They don't.

Imagine you have a deck of fifty-two cards and you deal them into four equal hands of thirteen cards each. Now, find a way to swap the cards around in the four piles in such a way that, in the end, you have more than fifty-two cards. So, how long will it take you to do it? Right, you can't. No matter what you do with those fifty-two cards, you still have only fifty-two. It's the same with redemptive work. When I trade Christians around between churches in my community, I still only have the number with which I started.

Our priority, ultimately, is not to add members to "our" church or to "our" denomination; it is to *expand the coast of Christ's rein and kingdom,* to grow it by reaching *new* souls, not ones already added. When we do this, transfers will take care of themselves.

Of course, Jesus, the apostles, and the first-century Christians witnessed to this truth by their actions. How did they interpret the Great Commission? Read it for yourself. On practically every page you see them reaching *new* people in *new* places with the rescuing message of the crucifixion. They were unstoppable in their forward momentum to *new* cities and *new* faces.

On this point, Paul made an interesting comment in his correspondence with the Roman church. Toward the end of his letter, he explains why he hasn't been able to get to Rome as soon as he had wanted:

> It has always been my ambition to preach the gospel where Christ was not known, so that I would not be building on someone else's foundation. Rather, as it is written, "Those who were not told about him will see, and those who have not heard will understand." This is why I have often been hindered from coming to you.
>
> Romans 15:20–21

In other words, given Paul's desire for the godless and inasmuch as the church at Rome was already founded and organized, he continually found it difficult to visit them. Though he desired to see them intently, he was overcome with other priorities. His mind was always on those who "were not told about him" or "have not heard." "His statement about 'not ... building on someone else's foundation,'" writes Everett F. Harrison, "requires no more explanation that that he was impelled by the love of Christ to reach as many as possible. He felt deeply his obligation to confront all men with the good news (1:14)."[15] Certainly, many pastors and churches today could benefit from a large dose of Saint Paul's single focus and ambition for the unsaved.

Sometimes I wonder whose kingdom we're really building: Christ's or ours? At the end of the day, are we laboring to build

Messiah's work, Messiah's way, or are we just erecting our own little kingdom while plagiarizing Christ's name and more acceptable teachings in the process?

Jesus told a story that can be applied to many places in the American church today. There was a landowner who was betrayed by his workers (Matthew 21:33–46). As the story goes, a rich man planted a vineyard and built a winepress and watchtower to support that vineyard. After getting things off the ground, he rented it to some tenant farmers to work until harvest, at which time he would send other servants to receive the fruit of his land. The farmers, however, started to like the vineyard a little too much and wanted the fruit—and, in fact, the entire vineyard—all for themselves. So, when the landowner sent his servants to take the harvest, the tenant farmers beat them all, killing one of them. Eventually, they even murdered the landowner's son.

The point is, these people had been given a great blessing that was not their own, charged in good faith to steward that blessing and provide the owner with the return he expected in good time. Instead, they violated his trust, murdered those important to him, and received his righteous wrath for their treachery. Of course, Jesus told this story to illustrate how the Pharisees had taken over God's kingdom and made it their own, killed his prophets through the centuries, and eventually killed his own Son, Jesus. So while it doesn't apply to us directly (we are not the Pharisees of the first century), I believe there are important parallels that can be drawn between their acts and ours.

There is enjoyable fruit in Christ's kingdom today, his church. Wonderful people, exciting events, useful facilities, good jobs, the rest of familiarity and ritual—such benefits litter his kingdom. But if we are not careful, we can grow to like these benefits too much, so much, in fact, that we fight against the owner of the kingdom. We can, in effect, take it as ours and deny God the power over it and fruit from it he justly deserves. When we resist his will to make his house a place where the lost are welcome, when we oppose and crucify his servants sent to bring the change he demands in our congregations, when we hold our tongues when we see indifference, Pharisaism, and downright evil within our fellowships, what are we doing but making his kingdom our own?

After all, we don't want to stain our "nice little church" with the messiness of reaching "those sinners"; we can't possibly pollute our beautiful, "holy" sanctuary with that modern video screen, even though it helps us communicate the message of the gospel; we can't stand the thought of replacing our hymn books with a praise band because "that's not how we were raised"; we don't dare risk our cushy church jobs and good salaries by calling out the Pharisees in our churches or preaching against the sin of the people or our secular age. "Let's just build a nice, clean, little church," we quietly tell ourselves, "where only 'good' Christians are welcomed, enjoy the fruits of our Master's efforts, and keep telling ourselves he approves."

With such an attitude, should we expect Christ's blessings or, like the evil tenant farmers in Jesus' parable, to have the kingdom taken away from us and given to someone else? I think you know which. So, how about you, fellow Christian? Whose kingdom are you building? Yours or his?

I'm afraid our brother Fred must be taught the way of God more adequately; we must show him that, though we are happy other Christians are encouraged and attracted to what we are doing, our focus cannot be on enticing them to join our church, but on aggressively building the kingdom of God with those who have not yet received it.

TODD "THE PLACATER" HANCOCK

Shaun briskly scribbled notes on his new, yellow legal pad as he mulled over Fred's ideas. *Well, I guess we made a little progress— at least we're talking about an actual* growth *strategy this time,* he reflected. But there was something about Fred's comments that made him feel a little uneasy. He refocused his mind. *Well, it's time to move on.*

As he looked at the two remaining panelists, he could tell

that Todd had waited about as long as he could. Spurred on by some of the things Fred had said, Todd was anxious to speak up. "Todd, you look like you've got a few things to add to our discussion," Shaun observed. "Why don't you go next?"

Todd Hancock was in his late twenties. About average height, he was a trim, handsome man. His jet-black hair was spiked with hair gel, coming to a peak at the center of his scalp. His black T-shirt—with the words "Radical Christian" written in sloppy cursive—said a lot about both his personality and approach to the faith. Shaun recalled that sometime in the last year or two, Todd had graduated from a seminary out west. His degree was in "Church Growth Strategies for the Twenty-First Century" or something like that.

Confidently, Todd looked around the table, making eye contact with everyone, and then leapt in. "You know, guys, as some of you have mentioned already, things are changing in our culture. The things that used to work for the church just aren't working anymore; that's one of the reasons we aren't growing overall. We just aren't as relevant as we used to be. Now, we've made some great strides forward with changes in worship styles and music, but we've got a long way to go.

"Here's the deal—and somebody just needs to say it—we aren't going to reach our culture by offending everybody in America. I mean, people just don't respond that well today to things like sin and truth and judgment. The average guy in America will just write you off if you start saying that Jesus is the *only* way to God, or if you go around condemning homosexuals and stuff like that.

"You see, I think Fred's really on to something with reaching out to Christians, doing the things they like in order to draw them. I like that. But I also think, in order to reach non-Christians, we need to preach to them in a way that doesn't offend them so much. You know, emphasize the more culturally acceptable teachings of the Bible. Focus on love and doing good and not all the things that make people mad. If we do that, I think we'll see the lost come out in droves."

Now, if Fred's comments gave Pastor Shaun heartburn, Todd's pushed him into full-blown cardiac arrest. *How in the world am I going to respond to this?* Shaun asked himself, completely bewildered.

so, what about the placate-the-world strategy?

As with most of the approaches mentioned already, there is some validity to Todd's thinking. Indeed, we must strive to be relevant to the lost world, speaking to issues that affect them, contextualizing the gospel message so that it has real meaning to them, adapting some of our cultural practices (music, for example) to keep up with the changing norms of the day. Our methods must change with the culture—of this there is no doubt. And many of our people need to embrace this truth in order to be more "relevant," as Todd mentioned.

But can we take this valid principle and apply it to every part of Christianity, including the parts of truth we preach? Can we, with scriptural approval, "emphasize the more culturally acceptable teachings of the Bible ... and not all the things that make people mad," to borrow Todd's words exactly? Now, on this point, we cannot offer so easy an affirmation. Let's analyze this thinking and see how it compares to Scripture.

The basic idea here is that people will accept Christ more easily if we leave off certain aspects of the truth, the aspects that offend them. By and large those aspects boil down to four elements: hell, judgment, sin, and non-politically correct truth (like homosexuality, exclusivity of Jesus, and so on). What does the Word say about this idea?

First, *these elements are not lacking in the preaching of Jesus and the apostles.* In other words, though they desired to make the gospel relevant, they didn't do this by pulling theological punches. Far from a man-pleaser, Jesus revealed a fiery, cutting edge to his words to the lost. A vivid example of this is his response to the people's complaints about Pilot's attack on "innocent" Jews in Jerusalem (Luke 13:1–8). If you believe in the impotent Christ preached in many pulpits today—and the one espoused by the world—you would have to believe Jesus would show only sympathy and understanding for the sufferings of the lost in this situation. But his actual words demonstrate his concern for telling them the truth over soothing their egos. Note his response:

> Do you think that these Galileans were worse sinners than all the other Galileans because they suffered this way? I tell you, no! *But unless you repent, you too will all perish.* Or those eighteen who died when the tower of Siloam fell on them—do you think they were more guilty than all the others living in Jerusalem? I tell you, no! *But unless you repent, you too will all perish.*
>
> Luke 13:2–5

Without question, Jesus felt sympathy for those who suffered these tragic circumstances, but he sought to make a broader, more important point from this situation. In a fashion that would stupefy our politically correct culture, he nailed them with the harsh truth about their own future if they didn't change course. Obviously, in this case, he didn't place too much emphasis on taking out those parts of the truth that could offend a lost person.[16]

Similarly, the apostles would have to take a politically correct timeout if they preached to our delicate generation. Examples abound of their incendiary discourse. From the beginning of Acts, the apostles held nothing back from their hearers: a frank discussion of their sins and the need for repentance and the stark reality of God's judgment. Peter, in his first two sermons in Jerusalem, sets the standard for proclaiming the complete gospel. With breathless courage, he accused his hearers of operating in conjunction with the Romans to put Jesus to death (Acts 2:23–24), an accusation that cut them "to the heart" (Acts 2:37). Not long after this, he accused the unbelieving Jews of handing Jesus over to be killed, disowning the "Holy and Righteous One," and killing the "author of life" (Acts 3:13–15), for which he was promptly thrown in jail.

Now, these don't sound like men who made a priority out of placating the sinful consciences of lost men, do they?

Secondly, *it is good for mankind to hear the things that offend them.* God desires the entire spectrum of truth be preached to mankind not because he desires to verbally slap them around (maybe he does), but because they need to hear these truths for their own good. The truth about hell, judgment, sin, and non-politically correct topics brings benefits to its hearers that cannot come otherwise. Setting these topics aside simply because they are uncomfortable does the entire race a disservice. Here is a brief overview of some benefits of these harder truths:

> *Hell:* Hell teaches us about the holiness of God. It, through a stunning photo negative, measures the heights of the righteousness of our Creator. So morally pure and transcendent he is that all who violate his character must suffer banishment from his affinity…*forever.* Furthermore, hell shows us the greatness of our salvation (Hebrews 2:3); his love for us is quantified fully only when we come face-to-face with what he has delivered us from. If we never hear of this very real and frightening place, how can we receive these two benefits?
>
> *Judgment:* This concept also is a teacher. It reveals for us a real aspect of our Maker's personality and role in the universe. He is the judge of all. Modern man comforts himself by suggesting that truth is relative and mankind has no real, objective standard for weighing his actions. But God slices through the fog of this deception with not only a clear, moral code, but also by the proclamation that a divine judge will measure every man *against this code* in due time. This inescapable reality lays a requirement at the feet of every person: to honor their judge. "Moreover, the Father judges no one," declares Jesus, "but has entrusted all judgment to the Son, that all may honor [revere, value] the Son just as they honor the Father" (John 5:22–23). Judges are to be revered and valued, and so, Jesus, as the Father's appointed judge of human-

ity, must also be honored. Indeed, a valuable lesson for all to learn, regardless of how it affects their consciences.

Sin: Sin is an integral and basic element of the gospel; in fact, you can't really preach the gospel without eventually getting to the place of sin (see 1 Corinthians 15:3). To take it one step further, without mournful acknowledgement of personal sin, one cannot be saved. Furthermore, battling against sin and doing right is the recipe for pleasing God and experiencing his closeness and friendship (John 8:29). On the contrary, treating sin as inconsequential puts one's salvation at risk (Hebrews 12:14). It is essential, given these truths, that sin remains—no matter how many rage against us for so doing—a steady part of the message of the church.

Other Non-PC truth: People today reject virtually every truth the Bible puts forward. Whether it's unpopular moral teachings (like cohabitation, abortion, homosexuality, or any one of a thousand other degenerate acts) or claims about truth in general, Jesus, or God, secular man will tolerate none of Scripture's strong stands. However, this type of declaration—the declaration of biblical truth—is the only way to release someone from the damaging and painful bonds of sin.

We are all very familiar with Jesus' words, "Then you will know the truth, and the truth will set you free" (John 8:32). But from what does it free me, Jesus? From slavery to my sin. "I tell you the truth, everyone who sins is a slave to sin" (John 8:34). To put it another way, the only way I can see someone freed from the bondage of homosexuality (or any other sin) is to confront them with the truth about it. Now, do you really want to deny them the opportunity to be free?

And, finally, consider this: *what kind of a disciple do you really have if a person accepts not the Jesus of the Scriptures, but the politically correct Jesus?* Keep in mind, it was Jesus himself who told his earliest followers to teach new disciples *"everything* I have commanded you" (Matthew 28:20). He didn't say, "most" or "whatever is popular," but "everything." So, Jesus defines a genuine disciple as one who is on the course of learning *the entire scope and span of his teachings,* something that cannot be done if parts of the truth are left out.

Besides, when we chop Jesus up into so many small pieces and remake him into the culture's image, have they actually believed in the real Jesus at all? I met a guy a few weeks ago who said he believed in the same Jesus I do. However, as I talked with him more, I realized his Jesus and my Jesus were miles apart. He believed there was a man who lived two thousand years ago and was a prophet of God, but that was where the similarities ended. He didn't believe in the resurrection; he didn't believe in hell; he didn't believe in sin or judgment; he didn't believe in the Trinity.

So, how can you believe in Jesus if you don't believe in his major teachings? That would be like saying, "I believe in the ideals of America," but at the same time saying, "I don't believe in life, liberty, or the pursuit of happiness." The answer is simple: He believed in the Jesus *he had created,* the one he liked that fit his views of truth. But he didn't believe in the *real Jesus.*

The point is, when we take out the parts of the truth that the lost don't like and they accept the gospel shell that's left, they really aren't becoming disciples at all and remain lost, condemned, and without the real Jesus to save them. So, far from making it easier for them to be saved, we keep them from salvation altogether.

So, we must firmly object to Todd's attempts to grease the skids of redemption by altering the uncomfortable, complete message of the gospel found in the New Testament. Though we admire his willingness to become all things to all men, we must resist his efforts to persuade us to rewrite the Bible in order to do so.

BARRY "SIMPLY-BOOK" COX

Well, time was running out for Pastor Shaun. The meeting was scheduled to stop at noon, and it was now twenty till. So far, he gave the focus group a weak *C;* they had brought to light some important issues and were open and honest about what they thought—and that was good—but none of the responses really hit home with him. From the looks on the consultants' faces, they seemed a bit more pleased than he was at the moment, but that didn't overcome the nagging feeling in his heart that somehow they just weren't on the right track.

"Maybe God has saved the best for last," he repeated under his breath. Pleading with God, Shaun offered a silent prayer, *Oh, God, please give us your wisdom before we leave.*

"Well, thank you, Todd. You've definitely given us a lot to think about. Now, let's wrap up our discussion with you, Barry. Thanks for waiting so patiently. Why don't you go ahead and share what's on your mind."

"Sure," Barry said as he leaned forward and folded his hands on the table.

Barry Cox was a usual-looking man. In his mid-thirties, his face was still youthful, though his bald head would argue differently. Barry had always been a wise and level-headed young man, even before his conversion to Christ. That conversion had been a radical one, a sort of Paul-like experience twelve or thirteen years ago. Since that time, Barry had been a serious student of the Bible, studying Scripture in detail with the help of commentaries and lexicons and concordances. His home library was quite extensive. Pastor Shaun respected Barry a lot and considered him, from a biblical standpoint, one of the most knowledgeable men in the church.

"Pastor Shaun," he began in his baritone voice, "let me first say how happy I am that we are actually talking about *growing the church.* Of the churches I've been involved with since I came to know Christ some years ago, this is the first time I've ever heard a church talk about growing. For that, I am extremely thankful.

"My brothers and sisters have raised important issues this morning, and I respect each of their views and appreciate them bringing them to the table today. As most of you know about me, I believe we must start our thinking with Scripture. God is wiser than we are, and I believe his Word can show us not only *what* we are to do, but in most cases, *how* we are to do it."

Something inside of Shaun yelled, *Amen!*

"We are here today, really, to talk about how we keep the Great Commission in our local setting. How does Middle America make new disciples for Jesus? That, of course, comes from the Bible. What I want to ask you all is this: How did Jesus and the disciples do it? What principles did they implement that we too can put into practice as we try to be obedient to God in this way? It seems to me that if we do this, we can't possibly go wrong because we are doing what we do as a people anyway, following the teachings of this book." Barry tapped on his maroon-colored, leather Bible just under his hands.

Yes, yes, Shaun thought, without even realizing it. *Everybody needs to hear this.* "Barry, I agree with you wholeheartedly. In your study, have you found any principles that you can share with us now?" *Keep it coming, Lord. Don't stop now.*

"Yes, I have, Pastor. Let me hit on a few just briefly before we end our meeting." Though they had been going for a long time at that point, every person in the room was attentive and focused on Barry's words. "Now, there really are a great many principles in the gospels and book of Acts; these books are basically books about promoting truth. But here are three briefly from Acts.

"First, it seems to me that the disciples went out into the world to keep the Great Commission. In other words, they didn't just huddle together and wait for people to come to them. They went out into all kinds of different areas where all kinds of different people lived and worked. If you'd like, take a look at Acts 8:1 where the Scripture says, 'On that day a great persecution broke out against the church at Jerusalem, and all except the apostles were scattered throughout Judea and Samaria.' There's another interesting passage in Acts 11:19, if you want to look over there." The room was immediately filled with the sound of rustling pages. "Luke says, 'Now those who had been *scattered* by the persecution in connection with Stephen traveled as far as Phoenicia, Cyprus and Antioch ...'" Now, in these cases, their spreading was the result of a persecution—maybe because they weren't going as fast as God wanted—but, nevertheless, it shows us that the principle of going out into the culture is valid and worth our consideration.

"A second principle is that the disciples engaged people aggressively. God may have had to push them out the door at first, but when they got to where they were going, they weren't shy about talking to people. Going back to the Acts 11 passage, notice that one group was 'telling the message only to Jews' while the other group was going after the Greeks, 'telling them the good news about the Lord Jesus.'" Barry looked up with a smile.

He's really passionate about this, isn't he? Shaun noted.

"This very same thing is said back in Acts 8. Notice verse four: 'Those who had been scattered preached the word wherever they went.' I could go on with the passages that show how aggressive the early disciples were, and I believe this is something we must be in order to keep the Great Commission.

"And that leads me to the final principle, they were organized. If you recall the Great Commission itself, it lays out an organized, methodical approach to taking the gospel global. Jesus told them that they would be his witnesses in ... "

The group finished the phrase for Barry, " ... Jerusalem, Judea, Samaria, and the ends of the earth."

"Yes," Barry affirmed; they were starting to get it. "Think back to the Acts 11 passage we've just been reading. It says that some took the 'message only to Jews,' while others 'went to Antioch and began to speak to Greeks also.' Why? Maybe because they planned it that way. It made sense given their backgrounds or skills or passions.

"Then there's an interesting passage in Romans where Paul shares a thought that gives us some insight into his mind. He says, 'I plan to [visit you] when I go to Spain. I hope to visit you while passing through and to have you assist me on my journey there, after I have enjoyed your company for a while.' That's Romans 15:24. So, what is Paul doing? He's planning where he wants to take the gospel next, to Spain.

"I believe this is an important principle for us today. We are very organized in discipleship; we need to be equally organized for promoting truth to others.

"As I said a moment ago, there is a lot more that we should talk about, but these can help you see that the Bible does have the answers to our questions about how we grow the church. Maybe at some point in the future, you'd allow me to talk to you about some others."

Pastor Shaun knew Barry had nailed it. At the bottom of his last page of notes he wrote, "Must base plan on biblical principles." With an amazed look on his face, Shaun said, "Barry, thank you for bringing the Bible into our discussion. I think we can all agree that we must set aside our wisdom and the wisdom of the sages of our day and base our plan on God's Word." As he finished this statement, every head nodded in affirmation.

"Well, it's time for us to wrap up. It's been a good meeting." After a brief prayer, the group dismissed. As they slowly filed out of the room, Shaun reached over and caught Barry by the arm. "Barry," he said, in almost a whisper, "maybe you could put together a few more of those principles and review them with me and the consultants soon."

"I'd love to, Pastor," Barry replied joyfully.

It didn't go just as I had planned, Shaun thought. *But, we really are getting somewhere now. We are* definitely *getting somewhere.*

Table 1

Summary of Common Church Growth Strategies		
Approach	*Weaknesses*	*Passages*
The church will grow automatically	Fails to recognize that kingdom growth is resisted by men and spiritual powers	Matthew 11:12
	Fails to recognize that the Spirit promotes the kingdom through people	Acts 1:4; 1:8; Acts 10:1-43
The world is too evil	The evil of a nation does not change the command of God to make new disciples	Matthew 12:39, 17:17, and 28:19-20
The church should grow through transfers	The Great Commission is to make *new* disciples, not draw existing ones	Matthew 28:19-20; Romans 15:20-21
The church should take offensive elements out of its message	These elements are not lacking in New Testament preaching	Luke 13:1-8; Acts 2:23-24 and 3:13-15
	It is good for mankind to hear things that offend them	Hebrews 2:3 and 12:14; John 5:22-23; 1 Corinthians 15:3; John 8:32-34
	The person doesn't accept the real Jesus and may not be saved	Matthew 28:20
The church should use biblical principles to grow	When we follow the principles of the gospels and Acts, there are no weaknesses	Acts 8:1, 8:4, 11:19; Romans 15:24

Who gave the best advice? What do you think? As you reflect back on the answers given and the biblical reviews, where do you fall? Maybe you were in Suzie's camp before, or even Todd's, or maybe you weren't sure what position to take. In this brief chapter, I hope you've been given a lot to think about where biblical church growth is concerned.

Now, how do we change the culture? What's the biblical approach for this task? The answer to that question is the subject of our next chapter.

GROUP DISCUSSION QUESTIONS

If studying the book in a group, break into teams of three to five people and work through the questions listed below. Pick a spokesperson, and be ready to discuss your answers with the group

If studying on your own, work through them independently.

1. Which of the five views did you hold before you read the chapter?

    - Suzie "Wait-around" Rogers–The church will grow by itself

    - John "Given-up" Morgan–The times are too evil to promote truth to others

    - Fred "Transfer" Fitzpatrick–The church should grow by transfers

    - Todd "The Placater" Hancock–The church should avoid subjects that offend

    - Barry "Simply-book" Cox–The church should use biblical principles to grow

2. Did you disagree with the analysis of any of the first four approaches? If so, why? Can you think of a biblical reason to object?

3. What approach prevails at your church? Name them (it can be one or more, or none at all).

4. What are some other growth principles Barry could have mentioned from the book of Acts or the gospels. List and elaborate.

CHAPTER 3

REMAKING AMERICA: HEART CHANGE OR POLITICAL CHANGE

It was late Sunday night, and Jeremy was checking his e-mail one last time before bed. The study was almost dark except for the two computer screens sitting opposite each other on desks on opposing walls. The flat screens glowed like weak street lights in the dim, quiet room. Just behind him, his wife was checking her Facebook page on the kids' computer. *Funny,* he thought. *They used to think it was something when every home had just one computer. Now we have three. Sign of the times, I suppose.*

A few seconds after entering his password, a window popped up. Four unread messages in his inbox. He scanned them quickly. Two were junk. *How'd they get past the SPAM filter?* he wondered. Two were legit. One he had been expecting from a friend in Maryland; he'd catch it in the morning. The other had a title that caught his eye: "FW: Judge orders home-school family to send their children to public schools."

He felt a wave of adrenaline and fear as he hurriedly double clicked the icon. The forward was short and to the point, with a link to read the entire story; he clicked the link and read the report. An unnamed divorce court judge had ruled some lady's children must be sent to public school because the science curriculum they were being taught at home didn't include "modern science," as the judge put it. Although Jeremy and his wife didn't even home school (their kids attended a Christian school in town), he found himself irate. "How can they do this?" he cried out loud.

"Do what?" his wife replied, jerked unhappily out of her *Facebook* trance.

"This judge—a divorce court judge, no less—tells this woman she must send her kids to public schools to be indoctrinated in evolution when the laws of this state expressly give her the right to teach them at home if she chooses!" Jeremy, though tired, was now getting fired up. "Unbelievable!"

Over the last few months, Jeremy had been passing through some kind of personal awakening. He'd been noticing the great losses Christianity was taking on the political front. Just the other day, he read where another state legislature passed a law expanding abortion "rights"; with great frustration, he saw how most politicians and the liberal media ignored America's Christian heritage (this especially perturbed him when, on a recent trip to Washington, he saw the many references to God and the Bible carved into the nation's monuments); and, though he never really cared that much before, he was now completely enthralled with the upcoming elections. He talked about them with his coworkers—which he had *never* done before—and followed the issues closely, especially the spiritual ones.

Jeremy was reaching the age where these things were becoming more important to him. He had his own children now, three in fact, and he couldn't help but imagine what America was going to be like when they were his age. After all, he had seen with his own eyes the incredible change sweeping America over the last twenty-five years. *I remember when we actually prayed at school,* he thought, almost with a chuckle. *My, how times have changed.*

What will they do to us in the future? he worried. Would they pass laws that would forbid reading the Bible to children or taking them to church? They would probably call it "child abuse" to "indoctrinate" children in religious training. Maybe they would even take them away because the parents were no longer "fit" to raise children ready for our modern, scientific world. Too much to bear, he pushed the thought from his mind.

He was fearful, and he was frustrated. *America used to be such a different place,* he lamented. Pastors used to be respected members of the community; they served on boards and advised government leaders. There was a time when you could use Jesus' name at the end of a public prayer, and what wonderful words of faith in our founding documents. No, the founding fathers weren't all committed Christians—though many were—but they did not use the power of the government to silence the faith and rip God from public life either. *How far we have fallen,* was all he could think. Though it didn't really apply, his mind immediately recalled Jeremiah's words from the first verse of Lamentations, "How deserted lies the city, once so full of people!"

Quietly, he turned the computer off and walked through the dark to the stairs. *I just can't stand idly by while the culture goes to hell. I must do something,* he demanded. As he placed his foot on the first step, he paused. *I can't sleep now. I've got to pray for a few minutes. Whenever I feel this way, I know God is speaking to me in some way. Isn't this how it started with Nehemiah?*

He slipped over to the couch and turned on the lamp. *Let me look this up. Yes, Nehemiah 1.* He read how the men had come from Jerusalem and told Nehemiah that the wall was broken down and the people were in deep trouble. Then he read Nehemiah's response aloud. "When I heard these things, I sat down and wept. For some days I mourned and fasted and prayed before the God of heaven" (Nehemiah 1:4).

Yes, this is how I feel! he exclaimed to himself. Most of the time, Jeremy prayed silently, but tonight he was too troubled; he didn't even realize he was praying out loud now. Almost in a whisper he started, "Oh, God. I am so troubled inside. I know that America is not Israel, and I know I am not Nehemiah. But I am hurting because of what I see and hear and read." He paused briefly. "I believe you still give men burdens today, burdens to do something about what they see in your world. I see bad things coming for your people. I see a nation that has forgotten you and, more than that, is trying to erase you from existence. I am so troubled." Tears coming to his eyes, he felt his hands slide up the sides of his face. His breathing getting deeper, he started to cry, silently cry.

"God, please show me what to do. Do you want me to get involved in some kind of political action? Should I organize your people and petition the courts and politicians for change? Or, do you have another way, another plan? Please let me know. I am scared, but I am here. I will do whatever you tell me."

MANY JEREMYS IN AMERICA TODAY

America is full of Jeremys. Christians—men and women, young and old—who care deeply about the moral and spiritual direction of our beloved country. The babies' lives cut short on abortion tables, the decadence and violence of our youth, the corruption of our business leaders—all these bring them great pain. Though they haven't had a vision like Carter, they sense the future all too well anyway. Instead of hope, they have fear; instead of peace, they feel apprehension; instead of security, they find alarm. And they want to do something about it. There is something within them pushing them forward, toward action, though they feel inadequate and hesitant.

While many stand on the sidelines wondering what to do, masses have jumped headlong into the fight, choosing as their weapon political action. The Christian faith seems more like a political movement than a redemptive machine these days. We give millions to campaigns, organize ourselves into all kinds of political action groups—to get prayer back in school or restore the Ten Commandments or petition the school board to throw out evolution. E-mail forwards on every conceivable moral and political issue speed back and forth across the Internet like millions of electronic tennis balls. "Forward this to ten friends if you love Jesus," or, "Sign this petition or you'll be sorry," or, "Donate to this cause before it's too late," they say; yet the problems grow worse, and the enemy takes more ground with each election, ballot initiative, or high court decision. And, as Jeremy did, we ask God, "What should we do?"

God's reply, as it has always been, is in one place: the pages of his book. The answer to Jeremy's inquiry, and to ours by extension, is there, if we are willing to look hard enough to find it. So, let's take a moment together and find that answer. What would God have us do in times like these? Is politics his answer, or is it something else, something harder and more costly, something better for us and for our nation?

Before we set out on this task, let's first ask ourselves another question, one we need to answer before we can fully mine from Scripture a direction for Jeremy. That question is this: What changes do we desire to see in our land in a moral and spiritual sense? We know we are dissatisfied with the American moral and spiritual situation, but exactly what things distress us? Delineating these will help us step back and find their ultimate solution—a solution present since the kingdom of God began.

WHAT CHANGES DO WE WANT IN AMERICA?

With the way things have been going in the U.S. for the last couple of decades, we could probably list a thousand things we'd like to see changed from a biblical perspective. However, for time's sake, let's distill the list down to five broad issues.

relinquish idols and turn to the true god

Properly speaking, an idol is any god worshipped other than the true God. Though many idols throughout the world still take physical form, an idol does not have to be a statue or even go by the designation "god" to qualify as an idol. Anything a person positions in the place of God, something that rules a person's life other than God, something that receives the reverence only God is due—all these fit the definition of a false god. In this broader sense, America is truly a nation of idols.

Ours take many forms. We idolize money, Wall Street, and prosperity; we bow down to sex, looks, and celebrities; we sacrifice on the altar of government, business, and science. But more than anything, our real idol is as old as our race. We are *our own idol*. In the end, our idols demonstrate that what we really want is to be *our own god*. Regardless of what we call our gods, in America we are immersed in them, and you and I find ourselves like Paul in Athens: lone biblical theists among a museum of beloved, but lifeless, deities.

God, of course, hates idols and desires to be known and acknowledged for what he, in fact, is: the single, real God, our Creator. "I am the Lord," cries the Father, "that is my name! I will not give my glory to another or my praise to idols" (Isaiah 42:8). So then, we, as his faithful people, share his pain as we watch our nation slip into more blatant and guiltless idolatry.

value life

Like many before us, as we have rejected the biblical God, we concurrently have rejected the value of human life, young and old. We embrace more and more brutal types of abortion (as if any type of abortion is not brutal) and technologies that can make "good" use of an aborted fetus. We euthanize those, in our judgment, in too great a misery to continue to live or, perhaps, of too great a burden to our already overburdened medical system. Where will our evolving definition of life take us next?

As Christians, we don't deny the great complexities and heart-wrenching decisions forced upon us by the ethical issues of life, but we long for a return—or a turning anew—to the sober concept of "made in the image of God" and its weighty applications to the ethical issues of our time.

marriage and sexuality

Perversity. It's a word that defines our age. Every billboard, magazine cover, Web site, and mall window in our land is evidence of this truth. Sex dominates our every medium and invades our every thought. Our pagan brothers are bent on removing any barrier that prevents them from calling "good" every debauched relationship, sexual practice, and marital arrangement possible, no matter how obscene. Adultery, pedophilia, prostitution, homosexuality, cross-dressing, gay and lesbian marriage, pornography—take your pick. It's all on the table in modern America.

We haven't simply rejected God's standards for sex and marriage, saying, "No, thank you," politely to our Maker. We have thrown them to the ground and spit on them in contempt. As God's people, we are not prudes, but we recoil at what we see today and are alarmed beyond words at what the future may hold if something doesn't change.

heart-level righteousness

Righteousness. It's a concept lost on most Americans today. We lie for a living. We cheat on our taxes. We watch porn and think nothing of it. We gossip; we complain; we curse; we give thanks for nothing. We—and I hope you aren't one of these—even call atheists *good* in America these days.

Average Joe has no integrity to speak of; his word means nothing. He smiles at his neighbor while (behind closed doors) destroying him. He looks down the shirts of the women at the office and listens with great interest to the dirty jokes at the coffee pot. Ironically, after all of this, he thinks of himself as a *good* guy. He's no saint, mind you. But he's in the top 20 percent for sure. God's standards, unfortunately for him, are not as low, and he has absolutely no idea.

Though no one is saved by their good deeds, God places a high moral standard upon all mankind and will judge our lives by that standard when time has ended. We, as Christians, do not seek perfection from our fellow citizens. What we do desire, however, is for the law of God to be known throughout our land once again and for our fellow man to respond to it, from a heart-level, with a great desire to keep it.

protection of christian rights

Jeremy hits on a real concern for many of us: our rights as Christians. While we recognize persecution is a reality in the Christian life and pray for God's grace to endure it when it comes, we don't want to sit idly by while evil men bring it about uninhibited.

A concern for a great many is the freedom to raise their children according to biblical guidelines. Therefore, the right to home school, enroll children in Christian schools, and opt out of patently ungodly courses and instruction at public schools represent important liberties for the Christian family. Freedom to express the Bible's condemnation of sin without the threat of being jailed for hate crimes, the freedom to worship and give without penalty, and the freedom to share the gospel in the work-place and public square. These are all serious concerns within the Christian community today.

Table 2

Summary of Our Desires for America	
Desire	Explanation
Relinquish idols/turn to the true God	Acknowledge and worship the God of the Bible while turning from all other idols
Value life	Turning anew to the concept of 'made in the image of God' and a renewed value for all human life
Marriage and sexuality	Rejection of perversity and a commitment to sexual purity in the bonds of one man, one woman marriage
Heart-level obedience	A knowledge of the law of God and a consequent sincere desire to keep it
Protect rights of Christians	Upholding of laws protecting the rights of Christians to raise their children, worship without interference, and share their faith

Protecting these rights is so important to us, not only because of the liberty they afford us today to "live peaceful and quiet lives in all godliness and holiness" (1 Timothy 2:2), but also because when these basic rights are lost, the door is open to take more and more from us in the future, eventually leading to outright physical persecution. So, while we don't desire to strip others of their rights (except for the right to do evil), we do desire to preserve our present freedoms in the face of a society retreating quickly from our convictions and values.

HOW DO WE CHANGE THESE THINGS?

Making a list of grievances is pretty easy, but how we bring about changes to this list in a lasting, biblical way is a different story. The answer, however, begins with a simple realization: *enduring moral and spiritual change only come from a change in the human heart.* The change we desire in our culture—rightly desire—can only be brought about if the people's hearts change first.

Jesus taught this on several occasions. One especially clear example is from Matthew 15:19: "For out of the heart come evil thoughts, murder, adultery, sexual immorality, theft, false testimony, slander."

In the first half of this chapter, Jesus is teaching his disciples about the importance of focusing on the inner person as the fountain of life's actions. Erecting an outward code for the people and themselves, the Pharisees had neglected the inner motivation to keep such a code. Jesus pointed out how, though they often kept the outward rule, they had failed the inward test of the heart (Matthew 15:3–11). "What goes into a man's mouth," he cried, "does not make him 'unclean,' but what comes out of his mouth, that is what makes him 'unclean'" (11). Forthwith, the disciples showed their ignorance of this simple spiritual rule, and Jesus rebuked them for not already understanding it (12–16). Then he explains himself, expressly stating the heart-level principle in verse nineteen.

The word *heart* here means "the thoughts or feelings of the mind"[17] and is used by Jesus many times to refer to the innermost self, the deepest part of a person. He says only the pure of heart will see God, your heart is always with your treasure, and the heart is the source of evil actions (Matthew 5:8, 6:21, and 9:4). Further, out of this deep well of the soul come things like evil ("hurtful and calamitous") thoughts, murder, sexual immorality, stealing, and blasphemy (translated as "slander" in the NIV). Showing he did eventually learn the lesson, James taught later that all temptations to sin ultimately start in our evil *desire* (James 1:14), a word whose root means "to set the heart upon."[18]

As the heart represents the real battlefield for cultural change, our efforts to effect this change must center there. And herein lies the problem with using politics as our de facto approach to bringing change in America: *It cannot change the heart.* In the realm of the invisible capital of the soul, politicians, elections, laws, political action committees, judges, and the political process in general have absolutely no power. You and I can change the laws and leaders from dawn until dusk, and not a single ounce of one stony heart will be affected. Political action, as good and necessary as it is in many ways, will not change our land.

but what about "salt and light"?

So often the call to Christian political action is connected to Jesus' commandment to be salt and light as recorded in Matthew 5:13–16. Since salt is a preservative, many argue, Christians must seek to preserve the culture by aggressive political action. The problem with this connection, however, is that Jesus' teaching really doesn't have anything to do with political action but the positive influence of righteous living.

In our modern setting, it is difficult for us to picture the compliment Jesus was paying to believers when he called them "the salt of the earth." According to J.H. Bratt, salt was a very valuable and versatile commodity in the biblical Middle East. Not only was it a seasoning and preservative for food, it was also used to clean new born babies (Ezekiel 16:4), was given as a gift to seal a friendship, and represented "loyalty and perpetuity" in God's covenant with Israel (Numbers 18:19). Furthermore, in the teachings of Jesus and Paul, salt represented "the wholesomeness and vitality of the Christian."[19] But how were they to be this salt and bring about this wholesomeness and vitality? Simple—by *living by and for the will of God while the pagan world looked on.*

In Mark 9:50, Jesus used a similar expression to that of Matthew 5:13, and the context once again points to righteousness, not politics. "Salt is good," the Savior explains, "but if it loses its saltiness, how can you make it salty again? Have salt in yourselves, and be at peace with each other." This passage occurs in the broader context of a discussion of sin in verses 42–50. Here Jesus warns against causing others to sin (42) and the radical measures that should be taken to keep from sin (43–49). The phrase "loses its saltiness" is also translated "lose its flavor" (NKJV) and means "to lose taste," or, figuratively, "to make or act as a simpleton, become a fool, make foolish"[20]; it comes from a root word which can mean "dull or stupid, heedless [careless], or morally blockheaded."[21] So, as when salt decays it loses its power to bring about good in its many applications, so when a believer slips into sin he loses his power to influence the world.

Also, you can see the direct tie to righteous living in the second metaphor of Matthew 5: the "light of the world." These two metaphors, salt and light, are directly connected; they are saying the same thing in different ways, a common teaching technique of Jewish rabbis. This "light" of the believer is analogous to a city built on a high hill that everyone can see. With candles burning in the evening, you can imagine the sight of such a city as its collective light illuminates the sky above. The light that is the "good deeds" of those who believe, the light that leads mankind to praise the Father, this is the light that shines before men. Jesus, obviously, is talking about righteousness, not politics.

Let me make one more point about the salt and light passage as it relates to political action. In the Sermon on the Mount, where the salt and light passage is found, Jesus is constantly contrasting the character of real salt with fake salt, good salt with that which has lost its effectiveness. Interestingly, much of the contrast has to do with the tendency of people—religious people—*to approach righteousness as an exterior-only exercise.*[22] Ironically, this is in effect what we seek to do through our political efforts: use the law to attach an outward moral covering to an inwardly wicked people.

We, in essence, are trying to place our moral code on the world without a corresponding change of heart and motive. We say, "We don't care if you love God or not just so long as you obey *our* rules." How, then, are we any different from the scribes and Pharisees whom Jesus condemned for doing the same with their power (Matthew 23:25–28)? By more and more pressing our agenda through the political system, are we not, in effect, becoming the Pharisees?

other weaknesses of the political process

Lacking the power to change the heart is a catastrophic weakness of the political process; however, it is not the only weakness worth mentioning. Let me bring three more to your attention before we move on.

First, *political action of the scale and scope of Christians today is unheard of on the pages of the New Testament.* The disciples were present at the Sermon on the Mount and were direct eyewitnesses to the rest of Jesus' teaching, yet they almost completely left off political action to accomplish their work. If they had interpreted the salt and light teaching—or any other teaching—as political in nature, would they not have implemented it when their ministry began? However, very little (if any) of their activity was invested in this way, except for the use of their rights to further their outreach work (like Paul's appeal to Caesar). Overlooked by us this should not be.

Next, *today's political gains can be quickly lost tomorrow.* With the next election cycle, court ruling, or session of Congress, significant steps forward can be completely erased. We all have experienced the frustration of watching as a stroke of the president's pen—a single stroke—dashes our hope of lasting change. The Christian community is constantly frustrated by "their" candidate when he or she doesn't stand up for what "they" want, or when "their" political savior loses the election or is voted out of office. For this reason, putting our faith in politics is a losing game.

Table 3

Weaknesses of Politics as an Instrument of Change
1. It cannot change the heart
2. Political action of modern Christianity not found in New Testament
3. Gains today can be quickly lost tomorrow
4. If the people are not righteous, the leaders will not be

Finally, *if the people are not righteous, the leaders they chose will not be righteous either.* The people will always pick leaders that reflect their character and goals. Why would you expect a nation whose biblical, Christian population is shrinking every year to vote for Christian candidates or those who espouse Christian values? And why would you expect that same nation to support initiatives that are Christian at heart? Furthermore, those same leaders must come from the population itself. If 80 percent of the people are unrighteous, what kind of leaders do you think will end up in the elections? Well, you've got an 80-percent chance of getting a pagan. Once again, politics fails and we are forced to focus on the heart.

am i against political involvement?

Based on these comments, you may think I'm saying that Christians should simply forgo the political process altogether. I can see how you might get that feeling, but that is not what

I'm advocating. The Bible encourages us to be good citizens, taking advantage of the rights we have to vote and participate in our government, and some prominent Christians in the New Testament were politicians or officials of some type. The Bible teaches it; how could I stand against it?

Furthermore, we need to be involved in the political process to protect our rights and the rights of the innocent—the right to proclaim the gospel freely, the right to raise our children in accordance with Scripture, the right of the helpless to life. For this reason, I am thankful to God that organizations exist that do just that. I encourage you to support these groups, donate to their ministries, and pray for them. Moreover, if you feel so led, run for office and be a godly politician.

However, what I am saying is that *this cannot be our number one priority.* We can't get so afraid of the inroads of the evil one that we put our eggs in the wrong basket by overemphasizing political avenues to change. In the long run, this will be counterproductive for the culture and devastating to the gospel. Furthermore, we *cannot allow this to be our primary method of influencing the culture.* In my opinion, for every ten of our people who are in some way involved in the political process, only one of those is aggressively promoting the gospel and trying to advance the kingdom in the lives of the lost. This is our real failure—one we cannot allow to continue.

Now, let's move on and talk about the one thing that has always changed the world: the Great Commission.

WHAT REALLY CHANGES THINGS?

When you think about the influence of Jesus and the early church, do you ever long for that kind of radical impact in modern America? Does it excite you to read how they moved so quickly to so many places and brought so much godly revolution to the culture of the empire? I don't know about you, but it fires me up when I see what they were able to do. It must have been a breathtaking time to be a believer. I've often said the one thing

I want to see, the one thing I pray for, the one thing I work to accomplish is the book of Acts taking place in my lifetime, in my nation. You feel the same, I'm sure.

So, how did they do it? What's the magic formula? We know it wasn't politics. Was it money, technology, business? We both know it wasn't any of these either. So what was it? Well, in reality, it was very simple: *They did what Jesus commanded them to do.* They went out and forcefully advanced his kingdom. He said, "Go be my witnesses," and they went; he said, "Go make disciples," and they did.

The chief instrument for the transformation of the entire world was *people aggressively engaging other people with the truth of God championed by the Holy Spirit.* That's it, nothing more. And this formula has not changed today. We can still see the book of Acts in our time if we are willing to do the same.

Earlier we enumerated the types of changes we desire to see in our culture. What I would like to show you from the pages of the New Testament is that these changes *actually came about in the first century* through the obedience of God's people to the Great Commission. Let's list the five again and look at a few texts.

1. Relinquish idols/turn to the true God
2. Value life
3. Marriage and sexuality
4. Heart-level obedience
5. Protect rights of Christians

first corinthians 6:9–11

This passage shows not only the depravity of the first century culture but also the power of God through his Word, people, and Spirit. Pay close attention to the last few words:

> Do you not know that the wicked will not inherit the Kingdom of God? Do not be deceived: Neither the sexually

immoral nor idolaters nor adulterers nor male prostitutes nor homosexual offenders nor thieves nor the greedy nor drunk-ards nor slanderers nor swindlers will inherit the kingdom of God. *And that is what some of you were.*

1 Corinthians 6:9–11

The believers in Corinth were once some of the worst sin-ners you could imagine. They worshipped idols and slept around and sold themselves as prostitutes; they were drunks and conmen and thieves and homosexuals. Interestingly, several of the words Paul uses here *are the same words* Jesus used when he described what comes out of the human heart (remember Matthew 15:19?). So, what happened? God's Word was pushed into Corinth by a fire-breather named Paul, and the Spirit—through Paul's work—changed their hearts. And when their hearts changed, their lives changed, and when their lives changed, the culture around them began to change.

Now, let's briefly reflect back on our list of five changes. In this passage alone, we have at least four being fulfilled. *First, there was a relinquishing of idols.* Not only is there a direct reference here to idol worship, but people were also giving up greed, which, according to Colossians 3:5, is a form of idolatry (think people in our culture could benefit by giving up greed?). Furthermore, some of these Christians may have actually earned their living at pagan temples (male prostitutes and homosexual offenders) but now had given up the service of idols for allegiance to Christ.

Secondly, there was a change in their views on sexuality and mar-riage. As noted above, some had turned away from sexual per-versions like homosexuality and prostitution. Others, notes Paul, had been adulterers in the past but now, presumably, had restored marriages or were looking forward to faithful relationships in the future.

A third change—*a heart-level righteousness*—is shown here as well. Drunks gave up drinking, and thieves gave up stealing—not for any outward reason but because they had experienced a change of heart: "But you were washed, you were sanctified, you were justified in the name of the Lord Jesus Christ and by the Spirit of our God" (1 Corinthians 6:11).

Finally, there was a renewed value for human life. Some had been "slanderers" and "swindlers." A *slanderer* is someone who uses words or language to abuse other people. The NKJV translates this word as a "reviler." A reviler tears up others with insults or demeaning language. Then there was the swindler. One who preys on others in order to manipulate and steal from them, a human predator, a con—this is a swindler. Now, some of these Corinthians were these types of people, but no longer. Why did they change? Because Paul taught them the value of every human being—that all were prized by God, made in his image—and, therefore, deserving of respect and fair treatment.

acts 17:1–9

The Spirit took his work to another part of the Roman Empire as well, and the change he wrought there inspired some of the most famous words in the Bible. In Thessalonica, Paul walked into a synagogue of lost Jews and walked out with Jesus freaks. "Some of the Jews were persuaded," writes Luke, "and joined Paul and Silas, as did a large number of God-fearing Greeks and not a few prominent women" (4). Not bad for three weeks work.

But not everybody was happy. Stirring up trouble for the apostle and dragging a new convert before the city officials, the Jews shouted, "These who have *turned the world upside down* have come here too" (NKJV, 9). In Greek, the phrase means "to disturb, trouble, turn upside down, or make an uproar."[23] Apparently, word had gotten around that wherever these Jesus-people went, things were never the same. But why did they say this? What kinds of changes were taking place that caused so much emotion in them? Well, it isn't hard to see.

First, *the devil was losing his converts.* As verse four states, people's hearts were changed, Jews and Greeks, men and women, and, in short order, this would result in changes in the way they lived. This was happening all over the world, resulting in chaos to the old order. Not only this, but *the power of the elite was being broken.* "The Jews were jealous," the Scripture declares (5). These men—unsaved men—held sway over the people and loved their power. The ministry of the believers was a direct challenge to this power. They simply couldn't stand for this type of upheaval.

In terms of the changes we'd like to see in our land, we see at least one: *the turning from idols to the true God.* The many converts Paul won in Thessalonica were convinced that Jesus was the Christ, "the anointed One," and that he had been resurrected from the dead (17:3), demonstrating his deity. When they were convinced, the Scripture says they "joined Paul," obviously leaving their former allegiances and whatever idols they worshipped, visible or invisible, behind.

acts 2:42–47

From the very first sermon in Acts, the culture started to change because hearts changed. After the first big conversion of Jews in Jerusalem at Pentecost, the Scripture records the new culture the Christians had adopted.

> They devoted themselves to the apostles' teaching and to the fellowship, to the breaking of bread and to prayer ... Selling their possessions and goods, they gave to anyone as he had need. Every day they continued to meet together in the temple courts. They broke bread in their homes and ate together with glad and sincere hearts, praising God and enjoying the favor of all the people. And the Lord added to their number daily those who were being saved.
>
> Acts 2:42–47

Let me highlight some of the changes in the people demonstrated here.

1. *There was a change in devotion* (42). Their loyalties had changed. Instead of devoting themselves to the teachings of the world, they were now devoted to

the teachings of the apostles (Christ's teachings); instead of fellowship with their worldly friends, they chose fellowship with the righteous; instead of putting their faith in themselves, they prayed to their new source of faith, God.

2. *There was a radical transformation in their value system and priorities* (44–45). Once so important, their material things were now shared with their new brothers and sisters. They even sold much of what they had to help others. Wouldn't you like to see this in America?

3. *They now acknowledged and valued God* (47a). They were "praising God" now instead of ignoring or blaspheming him.

For some time, this powerful witness impressed even the unsaved. They were "enjoying the favor of all the people," as Luke records it. Shocked by these changes, the lost around them were deeply affected and many were saved in the process (47).

Here we also see our desires for our nation coming to pass. Clearly there was a turning to the true God as these new converts not only devalued material things, but also valued anew the God who made it all. Their constant fellowship and giving to meet one another's needs showed a new value for human life, and there was heart-level righteousness demonstrated by their forsaking property and possessions—what outward motive would they have?—and the declaration that they had "glad and sincere hearts" (46).

WHY CULTURAL CHANGE AT ALL?

So, we have shown Jeremy that, while he should continue to be a good citizen and participate in the political process as he feels led, if he wants to see long-term, biblical change in America, he must invest his energy in aggressively promoting truth to those around him; in other words, taking personal responsibility for the Great Commission. We have laid out before him the biblical case for cultural change and shown him the practical and significant weaknesses of politics in this area. And that leads us to a final question.

When we opened the chapter, we noticed Jeremy was very upset about the way things were going. He was fearful for the future for his family and for Christians in general and frustrated that a nation once so full of biblical influence was now sprinting away at warp speed. Because of these feelings, he desperately wanted to be used of God to make a difference. He wanted to take action. For this, we applaud him and praise God.

But is Jeremy in this for the right reasons? Is pushing cultural change just to make us feel safer and to restore the "glorious" past good enough reason to pursue it? Not that these are bad things or unworthy goals, but are they the *central reason* we, as Christians, should seek to influence the culture? I'm sure if Jeremy gave this a little more thought, especially as the biblically centered man he has shown himself to be, he would see that these ambitions can't be the ultimate goal for our efforts. What is, you ask? The same goal for all of our actions: the glory of God.

Of course, you and I, as committed Christians, don't need a Sunday school lesson in the glory of God. But it is helpful to be reminded that our entire lives and all of our actions—whether successful or not—ultimately aim at glorifying God. *Glory* or *glorify* comes from the word *doxa* in Greek and relates to how someone is viewed by others, their opinion or regard for another.[24] When applied to God, it means that he is to be held in the highest of opinion by his creatures; he is to be thought of as excelling the value and merit of anything created; his character and characteristics excel, or go beyond, that of anyone or anything else; he is marvelous, splendid, rightly deserving of accolades and acclaim.

Our efforts to influence those around us and bring biblical change to our nation ultimately must be rooted in our desire for mankind—by their thoughts, words, and actions, whether alone or in community with others—to increasingly value and applaud their glorious God. As each person comes to see the glory of God in Jesus Christ and submits their will to the will of their Maker, he is given glory and our utmost goal is being fulfilled—all other motives, however biblical and good, must take a back seat to this single goal. When our thinking is grounded here, we can be assured of God's full help in all our efforts and of real success whether our culture changes in the way we desire or not.

DO YOU BELIEVE THIS?

Sometimes there is a mental disconnect between what the Bible teaches and what we believe is possible in real life. We believe in the miracles, but not that they can happen today; we revel in Paul's bold and glorious life of faith, while we ourselves live in the safe shadows of unbelief. "That was back then," we tell ourselves.

You may be tempted to do this with the powerful pictures of transformation this chapter has revealed. "A thing of the past, that's the kind of Christianity you're talking about," you think. But where is your faith? Is God not still the God of the Resurrection? The Red Sea? The Lion's Den? Is he not still the one who summoned Lazarus from death's darkness, or lifted his arms and quenched the mighty gale?

What is missing in our time is not the willingness of God to act in biblical ways, but the willingness of his people to believe *he is still the God of the Bible*—and to act on that faith. To throw away fear, to stride against common wisdom, to risk all that we have and all that we are so we may follow only our simple belief that the God of the Scriptures is still alive and that he will still do what he says in his Word.

The powerful, exciting, and glorious days of New Testament Christianity, days when people were saved by the thousands and entire cities were swept away with gospel power, are not a thing of the past. If you and I will simply believe in the great power of our God—and act in accordance with that belief—we will see even greater things than these in our lifetime.

GROUP DISCUSSION QUESTIONS

If studying the book in a group, break into teams of three to five people and work through the questions listed below. Pick a spokesperson, and be ready to discuss your answers with the group.

If studying on your own, work through them independently.

1. Have you ever felt like Jeremy did at the beginning of this chapter? If so, in what way?

2. Do you agree with the following assessments regarding the cause of cultural change? Why or why not?
   - Real, lasting cultural change must start with the heart
   - "People aggressively engaging other people with the truth of God championed by the Holy Spirit," not politics, is the only way to change the heart

3. Which other weakness of politics as an agent of cultural change do you think is most significant? Why?
   - The level of political action by American Christians is unheard of in the New Testament
   - Gains won by the political process can be quickly lost
   - Political candidates ultimately must come from the people and are chosen by the people

4. Were you surprised that the types of change we want in our culture were actually accomplished in the first century Roman Empire? Why or why not?

CHAPTER 4

OUR GREATEST SIN: ABANDONING THE GREAT COMMISSION

L et me tell you a sad story, the story of a man named Taylor. Taylor lived just outside the city in a poor neighborhood with his younger brother and mother. His father having abandoned them early on, his mother was left to raise the boys alone. She worked long hours, paid the bills, and kept a roof over their heads; however, for all the good she did, she never taught Taylor about God.

As he grew into his teen years, Taylor's life grew darker. By the seventh grade, he was watching porn; by the tenth, he was drinking heavily; by his senior year, he was doing drugs. While once a promising student, Taylor barely graduated.

After a few dead-end jobs and a couple of semesters in the local community college, Taylor joined the army. His life of debauchery and godlessness only increased while in the service. What little money he had, he spent at the bars outside the base— and on the women. God was very far from his thoughts, and the name Jesus was just another curse word in his ever-increasing, dirty vocabulary.

After his days in the service, he went back to his hometown and got a job at the local tire plant, a job he had for the next thirty years. In that time, he lived with several women, none of whom he really loved; they were just a means to an end for him. As the years passed, he became more and more bitter—bitter at the government, bitter at the "rich folk" on the other side of town, bitter at his father who left him, bitter at the world in general.

His temper, bad enough in his younger years, only got worse as he grew older. He became a violent man, beating his live-in girlfriends on a whim and blowing up over the smallest thing at the plant. Over time, everybody just learned to leave him alone.

When he was fifty-three, he was diagnosed with liver cancer. As with everything else in his life, he had to fight it all by himself. Toward the end, he was hospitalized for several months, but no one came to visit and no one called. He was a bitter and angry man, ending his life with tubes and pills and ventilators, and without God.

He died on a Tuesday morning just before the sun came up. There was no funeral.

THE SADDEST PART OF TAYLOR'S STORY

Taylor's story is a sad one, especially to those of us who know the power and joy of God. We see in Taylor's life a great opportunity for Christ to transform him—his anger, his bitterness, his loneliness—into something beautiful. We know this because many of us have been like Taylor in our past lives. We've seen the depths of alcoholism, experienced the frustration of bitterness, and fought the darkness of depression.

"If only someone had reached out to him," we say. Indeed, *if only.*

And that's the saddest part of the story. You see, *Taylor had Christians around him his entire life.* His uncle Monroe was a deacon in the church; his favorite teacher in high school, Mr. White, was a dedicated believer; his baseball coach, Travis and his wife were evangelicals. Later, his first sergeant, Sergeant Martinez, taught Sunday school; two of his neighbors, Paul and Kim, and Troy and Lisa, led life groups in their homes. His boss for many years, Glen, went to church every Sunday, and his nurse, Beth—the last person he would see in this world—had been a Christian for twenty years when he came to her floor to die.

This is the real tragedy: none of them stepped into Taylor's world to actively preach Christ to him. No one took the risk to promote God's message to this virulent, lost man. Yes, they were nice people and great neighbors. They were loving teachers and faithful coaches. They set a good example—their speech was clean and their words were kind. But they danced around him for fifty-three years and, in the end, failed him as much as anyone in his life. God opened doors to them one by one, each in succession, but they all refused to walk through and save this sad man for whom Christ died.

And I'm sorry to say, Taylor's story is not uncommon in America today.

OUR GREATEST SIN

"One of the greatest sins of the Church that often goes unnoticed is the lack of evangelism."[25] I was struck by this statement while reading D. James Kennedy and Jerry Newcombe's book, *What if Jesus Had Never Been Born?* This is a book that demonstrates the world-altering influence of Jesus and his disciples throughout the centuries. (I recommend it as a counter to the objection that all Christians are hypocrites.) Toward the end of the book, the authors deal with the sins of the church like the Inquisition, slavery, and fallen televangelists. In the middle of this list of sins, you'll find the sentence at the beginning of this paragraph.

Today, the American church is plagued with many sins that are crippling her. Spiritual immaturity, unrighteous lifestyles, busyness, legalism—these are our besetting sins. However, as the authors point out, one of our greatest sins is often overlooked: we have abandoned the Great Commission. The average Joe in the pew has given up his responsibility and duty to personally carry out Jesus' last commandment. Like those surrounding Taylor all his life, we live a silent Christianity, and the world around us (not to mention the kingdom) is suffering the terrible consequences.

Yes, we talk a lot about it (sometimes), we take up offerings for foreign and domestic missionaries (which is good), and we occasionally have a six-week series in our small group about it. But we *don't do it ourselves.* The vast majority of American Christians know very few lost people, and of the ones who do, most are not engaging them for the sake of the gospel. Fat and happy on our pews and in our Christian small groups, we are safely insulated from the world around us and the lives of troubled, dirty people, like Taylor.

Now, I know what some of you are thinking. You are remembering some study you read that talked about how many Christians share their faith each year. I've read these studies myself. You are thinking maybe I don't really know what I'm talking about, making these serious allegations without proof to back it up. However, before you write me off, let's look at these statistics a little more closely.

Recently, I found an article online that talked about the "large" percentage of people who "shared their faith" in the last twelve months. This particular one was on the Barna Web site, www.barna.com; it was entitled, "Survey Shows How Christians Share Their Faith."[26] According to this survey, "a slight majority of born again adults—55%—claimed to have shared their faith with a non-Christian during the prior 12 months." Now, that may sound impressive, but when you analyze the findings, the numbers aren't what they seem to be.[27]

First, *since when is sharing your faith once a year acceptable?* How do we justify this scripturally? What if we said that 55 percent of Christians prayed at least once in the last twelve months, or read their Bible once, or attended church once? Would this be acceptable? Then why do we think this is so great where promoting truth is concerned?

Second, *what does the respondent understand when we ask if he has "shared his faith"?* Does that mean mentioning Jesus in a conversation, saying, "I'll pray for you," or talking about something he did at church last Sunday? What does this mean to him? More importantly, what does this mean in biblical terms? From the perspective of the New Testament, sharing your faith is much more than the average Christian thinks it is. In fact, the survey even alludes to this.

According to Barna, the most common forms of "evangelism" were "to offer to pray with a non-Christian who was in need of encouragement or support" (78 percent) and "living in ways that would impress non-Christians and cause them to raise questions about that lifestyle" (74 percent). Now, these are definitely good things, but they fall far short of the pattern of Jesus and the apostles. Offering to pray with someone definitely can point them toward God and encourage them to pray when they are in trouble, but it doesn't teach them about the God of the Bible, the cross of Christ, or overcome the tough barriers formed in their hearts from years in the world.

Moreover, living righteously in front of people, while critical to successfully leading them into the kingdom (we'll devote an entire chapter to this later) is not the same as engaging them with the gospel. More than likely, this way of thinking comes from a misunderstanding of 1 Peter 3:15.

This passage is often used as both an evangelism and apologetics text, and it certainly can have limited application in these areas. Those who apply it as an evangelism text, however, often use it to justify waiting around for someone to ask about the believer's faith (hinted at in the Barna survey); this view of the text fails because it does not fit the overall tenor of the New Testament—Jesus and the apostles certainly didn't wait around—and the context of Peter's comments involves persecution, not outreach. The apostle is describing a situation where a believer is being questioned by those who are hostile to the faith and are in a position to make the Christian suffer. In this case, obviously, we should wait until we are asked and respond in a gentle and respectful manner with our courageous affirmation of faith. But this certainly is not our rule where promoting truth is concerned.

Finally, *the numbers could be skewed for a number of reasons*. Most Christians know they should be promoting truth to others, so, even if they aren't, they are very unlikely to say so in a survey. Also, this particular study says that 11 percent of Christians preached on the street or other public areas. To put it another way, according to this survey, one out of every ten Christians went to their local downtown area or mall and preached to strangers that came by. I find this highly unlikely. Something just doesn't add up here.

Sadly, what I've found as I've taught groups on both apologetics (defending the faith) and evangelism (promoting truth) is that less than 10 percent of Christians are actively and aggressively promoting truth to the lost. In my classes, I often ask about the types of questions my students get from lost people, or how many of them know an atheist, or who they are talking to about the gospel, and the vast majority of the time I get blank stares. Is there any wonder 80 to 85 percent of our churches are dying?

HOW DID WE GET HERE?

So, in truth, most of us do not promote truth as Jesus and the apostles did. But why? We all know we should be doing this, but what keeps us from stepping out? Let me offer five core reasons and their biblical answers.

1. we are afraid

Although we're going to highlight five reasons we don't spread the good message in America, the greatest reason undoubtedly is the fear of man.

The New Testament word for fear is *phobeo*; it comes from the word *phobos* and means "to be put in fear, to frighten, or to be terrified."[28] Scripture promises us that, as God's people, fearing human beings will always cause us problems. Proverbs 29:25 says it explicitly, "The fear of man brings a snare" (NKJV). The Hebrew for *fear* in this verse has a similar meaning to *phobos* in the New

Testament: "anxiety, quaking, trembling, or anxious care."[29] The word *snare* comes from a word that means "to lure, entice, or set a trap."[30] In other words, when we fear people, we are setting a trap for ourselves. But a trap for what? *Disobedience to God.* Consider a couple of key biblical figures for confirmation, Aaron and Saul.

Aaron was Moses's brother and the first priest of Israel. Furthermore, he, unlike Moses, was an eloquent man, what you and I might call a "good speaker." But Aaron feared man, and it brought shame—perpetual shame—upon him (Exodus 32:1–24). When Moses went up to receive God's law, Aaron was put in charge of the Israelites. The people, angry because Moses didn't come down fast enough, demanded that Aaron make them idols like they had in Egypt. Without so much as one word of opposition, Aaron gave in. When Moses came down, the scene was a madhouse of partying and idol worship. What happened to Aaron? Did they promise him a few extra gold bars or the best camel in Israel? No. They didn't have to. He feared the people, so he gave in to their desires, even though he knew those desires were contrary to the will of God.

Then there was the first king of Israel, Saul. In the beginning, it seemed he might actually make a good king, but quickly his promise dwindled. The last straw came when he was commanded through Samuel to destroy the entire Amalekite community for their past sins against Israel. Saul was not to leave even an animal alive (1 Samuel 15:1–24). But he only did half of what he was supposed to do. After the victory was won, he saved the best sheep and cattle to "sacrifice to the Lord" (15). God was not pleased; he condemned Saul for his half-baked obedience and ripped the scepter from his hands. And what did Saul offer as an excuse? "I was afraid of the people and so I gave in to them" (24).

What's the bottom line? The bottom line is that in each case the fear of man caused these great men (notice *great* men) not to do the will of God, either partly, as in Saul's case, or completely, as in Aaron's. They feared man more than God and therefore disobeyed his clear commands.

Today, the fear of man keeps us from obeying clear commandments as well, including the commandment to promote truth to others. Their actions, their anger, their questions, these terrors choke us, conquer us, master us as we try to speak. Doubts and questions clog our minds. How will they look at me? Will I lose my job? Will they think I'm weird? What if I don't have the answer? Then the trap closes. And when we break free, only shame and frustration hobble away with us.

how do we overcome the fear of man?

How, then, do we overcome this fear and avoid its trap? Before we get into the biblical answer, keep one thing in mind: No matter how great you think the greatest preacher is, or how powerful you think the most powerful evangelist is, or how witty you think the wittiest apologist is, they *all* suffer from fear—no exceptions. You may think someone like me (who is writing a book on promoting truth to others) would not be subject to fear any longer. I've been doing this for a long time and, presumably, am close to God, so I should be like Superman when it comes to this. But I'm not. I get scared all the time. I give in to my fear and let opportunities pass me by because of it. So, don't think you have to have *no fear* before you can talk to someone about Christ. If you wait until then, you'll never talk to anyone.

To be bold in the face of the lost, we must learn to *master our fear by trusting God.* This is the biblical answer. The wise man of Proverbs finishes his thought, "The fear of man brings a snare; *but he who trusts in the Lord is safe*" (Proverbs 29:25). The psalmist repeats this admonition: "When I am afraid, I will trust in you. In God, whose word I praise, in God I trust; I will not be afraid. What can mortal man do to me?" (Psalm 56:3–4).

There are several ways we can trust God when struggling with fear. I'll list them as bullets:

- *Trust that God is much more terrifying than they are.* Don't underestimate the reality of facing God when you die. He will make you account for your service to him, and it won't be a pleasant experience for many who have hidden in a corner. Jesus recognized the fearful power of God when he warned us, "Fear him who, after the killing of the body, has power to throw you into hell. Yes, I tell you, fear him" (Luke 12:5).

- *Trust that God will cause your efforts to bear fruit.* There's nothing more encouraging than success. Virtually every time I've put myself at risk, I've seen God bring fruit from it, and that success has encouraged me to keep pushing beyond my fear. Jesus guaranteed this in the Great Commission itself (Matthew 28:18).

- *Trust that God can protect you and that no one can hurt you unless he wills it.* When I start to get afraid of man, one of the verses the Holy Spirit often brings to my mind is Isaiah 51:13, "You forget the Lord your Maker, who stretched out the heavens and laid the foundations of the earth, that you live in constant terror every day because of the wrath of the oppressor, who is bent on destruction? *For where is the wrath of the oppressor?*" We fear things that never come to pass, while we forget God. Oh, how this describes our weak faith! So let's remember who has the real power and, by that power, choke, conquer, and master our fears.

- *Trust that God will give you a bold, fear-no-one-but-God mentality when you ask for it.* Prayer is the lifeblood of courage, so ask Christ to make you fearless. Paul did. "Pray also for me, that whenever I open my mouth, words may be given me so that I will *fearlessly* make known the mystery of the gospel...Pray that I may declare it *fearlessly*, as I should" (Ephesians 6:19–20).

Table 4

Overcoming Fear Through Trust	
Step	*Passage*
Trust that God is more terrifying that man	Luke 12:5
Trust that God will cause your efforts to bear fruit	Matthew 28:18
Trust that God can protect you	Isaiah 51:13
Trust that God will give you courage	Ephesians 6:19-20

2. we believe if we aren't evangelists or preachers, we aren't responsible to promote truth to others

Just a few days ago, while at the gym, I asked a fellow Christian if he thought he had a personal responsibility to promote truth to the lost in his life. He looked at me and said, "Pastors, like you, or maybe priests, yes—but me, no."

Then this morning an article appeared on the Internet about Jack Kemp's funeral service, the former congressman from New York. The article discussed the overtly Christian nature of the memorial service and the strong Christian witness of Kemp's life. But then a revealing statement is made, revealing not only for Jack, but also for most of us: "You see, Jack gave his life to Christ two decades ago. *But he didn't feel comfortable sharing his faith.* He would talk about being a Christian, and he left no doubt about his faith. *But he wasn't an evangelist*—or so he thought"[31] [emphasis mine].

Now this man may have done many good things for our country, he may have raised wonderful children and grandchildren, he may have had a powerful funeral service where the gospel was clearly set forth—and for all this I applaud him and thank God—but let's be clear on this point: Inasmuch as he did not actively promote truth to others, he failed Christ, he failed the church, and he failed the lost.

While it is true that some are specifically gifted by the Spirit to be evangelists and pastors (Ephesians 4:11), it is also true that the New Testament pattern is that everybody shared the good news regardless of whether they thought themselves specially gifted or not.

You may remember the woman at the well from John 4. She met Messiah and proceeded straight into town to tell others about him (John 4:39). And then there's the demon-possessed man, who, after being healed, wanted to stay with Jesus. But Jesus thought otherwise, "Go home to your family and tell them how much the Lord has done for you, and how he has had mercy on you." Then the Scripture witnesses to his obedience. "So," comments Mark, "the man went away and began to tell..." (Mark 4:20). And finally, who could forget the blind man and his declaration, "I am the man," and his testimony concerning what Christ had done for him in the verses that follow (John 9:8–12, 25)?

But the one that seals the deal (if these aren't enough) comes from the time immediately following Jesus' ascension into heaven. In Acts 8:1 the Scripture says that "*all except the apostles* were scattered throughout Judea and Samaria" because of the persecution in Jerusalem. Make sure you notice that the apostles, the pastors and evangelists, were still in Jerusalem. Then the actions and obedient character of the early disciples is made evident. "Those who had been scattered," recorded Luke, "preached the word everywhere they went" (8:4). The leaders of the church were in Jerusalem (the pastors and evangelists) and all those scattered (the regular people) spread the word.

Now, let me run a rabbit for a moment. You're familiar, I'm sure, with Jesus' words in Luke 19:17, "Well done, my good servant!" In fact, you're not only familiar with them, you take for granted that you will hear them when you close your eyes in death. You think you're doing a really great job at being a Christian; everybody at church thinks you're so spiritual and mature.

But what if you don't hear it? What if you have deceived yourself?

In this passage, the reward comes from bringing maximum fruit to God based on the skills and opportunities given, a reward that one of the three servants doesn't get. Each of us has been given the "talent," or opportunity, to reach those around us (not to mention the direct commandment), but so many of us—like my gym buddy and Mr. Kemp—are hiding that talent in the ground. Given this dereliction of duty, I would not be surprised if instead of, "Well done, my good servant," many in the church hear, "You have failed me, you wicked servant" (Luke 19:22). How about you?

But back to the point: the early disciples took the Great Commission *as their personal commission,* and we could learn a great lesson from them. You don't have to be a super-Christian to promote truth to those around you. You have more ability than you know, and, as we get into the how-to chapters of this book, you'll begin to see why.

3. we don't know how

Many believers recognize their responsibility to promote truth—they just don't know how. How do I get the conversation started? How do I deal with objections? How do I share the gospel? Their questions and uncertainties paralyze them, but they don't have to. You can learn how starting today, and this book is a great first step. In "Part 3: The Strategy," I'll give you the meat-and-potatoes of how to do this in your world. So be encouraged. You're on the right path, and God is going to use you in spectacular ways.

4. we don't understand its benefits to us as disciples

You and I are disciples, or learners, of Jesus. We are called to pattern his life in our own. To this end, everything he did (not just what he said) can teach us something about him and help complete our discipleship.

Jesus promoted truth to others. Not just a project for him, it was his way of life. And so, we cannot be disciples—complete disciples—unless we make promoting truth a way of life for us as well.

This Christ-like work brings many benefits. Here are a few:

- *It finishes our obedience.* God calls us to do things we don't like, but don't feel bad; he called his own Son to suffer crucifixion. A powerful lesson there is in learning to submit to God so fully that you will do whatever he asks, even if it is uncomfortable, distressing, or deadly. When we learn this kind of obedience, there is nothing we cannot accomplish because there is nothing Satan can put in our way. What leverage can you use on a dead man?

- *It challenges us to think through why we believe what we believe.* How do you know Christianity is true and all other belief systems false? Is your faith foundation strong? Or could someone come along with a few cleverly worded questions and throw you for a loop? By talking to others in detail about issues of faith, and God, and Jesus, you'll be challenged to learn about your faith, why it can be trusted, and why it is superior.

- *It gives us a chance to suffer for Christ's sake.* The world will love you as long as you're quiet. Just keep your mouth shut and don't push truth into any dark corners, and everybody will applaud you as a "good" Christian. But when you start promoting truth like Jesus did, you'll quickly find out what it's like to suffer as he suffered, and there's something beautiful and sweet about that. Paul made this the aim of his life. "I want to know Christ," he declared, "and the power of his resurrection and the *fellowship of sharing in his sufferings…*" (Philippians 3:10). The Christian experience is but a hollow shell until it is filled with the mysterious substance of suffering; promoting truth will help fill your empty shell.

- *It teaches us about evil spiritual realities taught in Scripture.* As God has sent me to people trapped by Satan and the lies of our world system, I've learned how devious they really are. Its teaching about the hostility of the sinful mind toward God (Romans 8:7) and the delusion that overtakes the minds of the lost (2 Thessalonians 2:11)—no longer just intellectual concepts—have become flesh and blood reality for me. I don't need anyone to prove to me how these things can be true. I have experienced them myself, and it has blessed me to do so. In this way, Scripture has come alive for me, and my walk with Christ has been greatly enriched. Yours will too.

Table 5

Personal Benefits of Promoting Truth
1. It finishes our obedience
2. It challenges us to think through why we believe what we believe
3. It gives us a chance to suffer for Christ's sake
4. It teaches us about evil spiritual realities

5. we misunderstand what it is

When you hear the word *evangelism,* what image pops into your mind? Maybe you see Billy Graham? Maybe you see people handing out tracks at the train station, or maybe you see two guys walking through a neighborhood knocking on doors. Maybe the words *fighting* and *arguing* pop into your head, or *stranger* and *anxiety.* Without question, there are many ways to spread the Word, and there are some fabulous Christians doing God's work in ways we just enumerated.[32] However, that doesn't mean you and I *have to do it that way,* or that these are the *only ways to do it.*

Table 6

Why We Don't Promote Truth	
Reason	*Answer*
1. We are afraid	Trust God
2. We are not evangelists or preachers	All are called, even if not evangelist or pastor
3. We don't know how	Get training
4. We don't understand its benefits to us	Complete discipleship must include promoting truth
5. We misunderstand what it is	Expand your definition to include friendship, non-confrontational

Evangelism is the process of promoting truth to others. That's it. It doesn't come with a built-in method that everyone must follow. In fact, some models we've pushed for many years have actually hampered our efforts to get average Joe Christian involved in this way of life.

Now, when you hear the word *friendship,* what image pops into your mind? You likely see people smiling; maybe you see a cookout or a dinner table. Words like *trust* and *loyalty* probably flash in your mind, and *love* and *fun.* Your anxiety levels are lowered and comfort eases its way into your soul.

Well, what if I told you there is a way for you to be involved in the Great Commission in the context of friendship? Would you prefer that over what you consider typical evangelism? If so, there's good news for you: that's exactly what you'll learn in this book. I won't promise all fear will be removed, but I will promise a natural way to share your faith. I won't promise all effort will be eliminated, but I will promise an understandable process to follow. I won't promise all will be saved, but I will promise you all will be challenged. If this sounds good to you, please read on. A pleasant surprise awaits.

RESPONDING PROPERLY TO SIN

I have but one hope for this chapter, one passionate prayer: that it has convicted you. If you have abandoned your personal responsibility to the Great Commission, either knowingly or unknowingly, I hope now you see clearly your sin before God. I pray a great sense of remorse is pouring over your heart right now and that you will do away with any excuses you may have used in the past and accept full responsibility for your failure in this area.

I desire all of this, not because of some malice I have for you, but because this is necessary for your forgiveness and restoration. Only after you see your sin for what it is can you be restored and used in significant kingdom work going forward. So, I ask you to take a moment right now and confess your sins specifically to God; acknowledge your failures, identify your excuses, and ask him to release you from this debt. When you do this, you will receive his forgiveness.

Once confession is complete, ask him to use you to grow his church and change the culture. And ask him to teach you how to engage others and give you the power to overcome your fear. He will most certainly do both.

GROUP DISCUSSION QUESTIONS

1. Have you ever experienced anything like Taylor—going through life with Christians around you but no interaction with them—or do you know anyone like him? Elaborate.

2. Do you agree that the lack of evangelism is one of our greatest sins? Why or why not?

3. Of the five reasons listed, which one most often keeps you from promoting truth to others? Why?
   - I'm afraid.
   - I'm not responsible if I'm not an evangelist or preacher.
   - I don't know how.
   - I don't understand its benefits.
   - I misunderstand what it is.

4. Can you think of other ways to overcome the fear of man? List and explain each.

5. Would you like to take a moment and pray a prayer of repentance?

PART TWO

The Necessary Foundation

CHAPTER 5

NO MORE HYPOCRITES: HOW IMMORALITY UNDERMINES OUR MESSAGE

Julie worked for a technology contractor in Lynchburg. In her early fifties, she was part receptionist, part purchasing agent, and part scheduler for a thriving small business in the hills of central Virginia. Julie's ever-happy face and booming voice gave the office a certain life and energy. One day, while waiting in the reception area for my meeting with the owner, Vance, Julie and I started talking.

A Christian for three or four years at that point, I was just beginning to engage others about spiritual things. I don't remember how we got on the subject, but before long we were discussing her spiritual upbringing. Although she had not followed her faith as an adult, she was raised as a Catholic. About the time serious matters came up, like Jesus and heaven and hell, Vance poked his head out of his office. "Come on in," he said.

Seeing my time running out, I said to Julie, "I'd love to continue our discussion. Why don't we get together for lunch sometime and talk?" She agreed, and I stepped into Vance's office for my meeting.

Several weeks later, the day of our lunch meeting came. I was very excited—not to mention nervous—and had been praying about what to say and how to say it. I was pretty new at this type of thing and was a bit unsure of myself; I didn't really know where to start. But, as it turned out, that was the least of my worries.

After we placed our drink orders, Julie surprised me by jumping right in. "Wes," she said, with a serious look, "I'm glad we got to meet today. I've been thinking. I know you're a spiritual guy, and there's something I'd like to ask you." *Wow! All my prayers have paid off. Let's go,* I thought. *She probably wants to talk about salvation, or discuss some Catholic tradition she never liked, or ask me how I know God is real.*

She went on. "I have Christians at my office. They gossip and they don't turn in their time cards on time. Why would I want to be one of those?" I sat there for a moment, stunned, speechless. *What do I say to that?* I wondered.

A COMMON DILEMMA

If you've tried to share your faith with any regularity, or if you've spent much time around people who claim to be Christians, you've undoubtedly heard this objection—or harbored it yourself. The world is full, it seems, of hypocrites: super-Christians who fall quickly to the ground, legalists with their dos and don'ts, and people who go to church on Sunday and act like Lucifer himself the other six days of the week. This reality is, well, a big turn off. As my friend Julie put it, "Why would I want to be one of those?" Good question.

The way we live—it's one of our greatest weaknesses when it comes to promoting truth to others. If I've talked to one Julie over the years, I've talked to a thousand. From the pastor who has an affair with his secretary, to the jerk at the office who happens to be a deacon, to the overbearing boss who can't miss his Monday night Bible study, Christians today cause more problems for the gospel than all the devil's demons put together. And it isn't just the anecdotes that confirm this reality; it's the hard data too.

An article appeared on The Barna Group Web site not too long ago. Entitled "A New Generation Expresses its Skepticism and Frustration with Christianity,"[33] the article summarized the results of a survey of sixteen to twenty-nine year olds regarding their impressions of Christianity. The study sites the increasingly negative perceptions of Christianity in America, especially among young people. Interestingly, the top two negative perceptions—87 percent said that Christianity was "judgmental," and 85 percent said it was "hypocritical"—are both related to Julie's objection.[34, 35] So, according to the data, almost nine out of every ten lost people think Christians are judgmental hypocrites. Any wonder they don't respond to the gospel?

Now, before we move on, let me make an important point. This objection, though many times based in reality, is not always valid and does not always require a change on our part. Sometimes the hypocrite objection is only an excuse to justify the unrighteous lifestyle of someone else, usually the person or group making the charge. If I can point out imperfection *in you,* the logic goes, then I can justify imperfection *in me.* Since nobody is perfect, I can do whatever I want. Obviously, this logic doesn't hold up. *My* imperfection does not change God's will for *your* life. I will be judged for my sins, as will you, no matter how others act.

Furthermore, the hypocrisy objection is sometimes only the natural response of fallen man to the law of God. When a Christian promotes biblical truth, people naturally will get angry about it; they hate God and don't want him to rule over them. Your words convict their consciences, and they respond in anger and bitterness. "You Christians are all just hypocrites, anyway!" they challenge, not because you have shown any real hypocrisy, but simply because you spoke the truth, revealing their immorality and bringing them under conviction of sin.

I point this out because I've seen pastors, church leaders, and pew-sitters act on surveys like this without really thinking them through biblically. They hear these statistics and automatically conclude we need to take out all "judgmental" language from our preaching, teaching, and outreach so we don't appear hypocritical. This is simply not the case. In fact, this is a dangerous adjustment to make, because it often requires we muzzle the Word of God in the process.

WHAT IS HYPOCRISY, ANYWAY?

First, let's start with a definition of the word *hypocrite*. The word literally means "one who wears a mask."[36] A fake, a phony, a pretender—all are apt descriptions of this word. And when applied to religious people, a hypocrite is someone who pretends to be religious but really isn't; they have other motives behind their religiosity. It could be popularity or business, or power or prestige, but whatever the case, their religion is not real.

Jesus dealt with these spiritual phonies in his day. In fact, he was quite harsh toward them, finding their actions deplorable.[37] Saint Paul chided the religious hypocrites of his time as well, observing how they, by their actions, caused people to speak poorly of God (Romans 2:21–24). Sadly, as I learned from Julie, the legacy of hypocrites is no different today.

The point? If you've seen a poor image of Christianity, you may just have been viewing a fake.

But do real Christians offend people, fall into sin, and give the church—and Jesus—a black eye? Do real Christians act hypocritically? Yes, absolutely they do. In fact, all real Christians sin on a regular basis. They all are imperfect, fighting each day to be more like their founder, Jesus Christ. According to God's teaching, a real Christian struggles internally with two natures: the old man trying to do evil, offend, destroy; and the new man, given by God, fighting to do right, live at peace with others, and bring about good in the world (Romans 7:13–25).

Unfortunately, the old man wins out more than we'd like to acknowledge. King David is the classic case. David was called a man after God's own heart—how can you get a stronger testimony than this?—yet we read in black and white the great sins of this man of God: adultery, deception, and ultimately murder (2 Samuel 11–12). All real Christians have this same polarized (and paradoxical) potential to be people after God's own heart, or ax murderers.

OUR HABITUAL FAILURES

In my experience, our failures fall into four broad categories. Let's take a minute to review these and God's teaching regarding each.

key areas of failure

1. *Language:* Many Christians lose their witness because of the way they talk. Instead of demonstrating a changed life, they act (and sound) like everybody else. Common curse words, harsh criticism, sexually suggestive talk—these are the besetting sins of many of our people. But it should not be so. Let me remind you that God requires his people to have clean, pure language. In his letter to the Ephesian believers, Paul addressed this subject not once but twice.

First, he writes, "Do not let any unwholesome talk come out of your mouths, but only what is helpful for building others up according to their needs, that it may benefit those who listen" (Ephesians 4:29). The strength of the words doesn't come through in translation. The word *unwholesome* means "rotten, worthless, or corrupt."[38] Visualize banana peels, eggs, and raw chicken in the bottom of a hot, dirty garbage can in mid-July; breathe in the smell as you open the can and bat away the flies. When your gag reflex kicks in, then you're starting to understand this word. Spoiled, rotten, putrid language is in mind here.

None of this language—did I say none?—is to come out of a Christian's mouth. This applies to all blasphemies (taking the name of God or Jesus as an expletive), common curse words (and we all know what they are), and harsh words of condemnation and reviling. On the contrary, our speech should be "helpful" or beneficial to those to whom we speak, "building others up" by encouraging them and complimenting them and turning them to God. Coming as a gift to them, bringing joy and pleasure to their lives, this speech offers many "benefits" to those who listen.

A couple of paragraphs later, Paul takes up the subject again, but this time his target is sexual speech. "Nor should there be obscenity," he warns, "foolish talk or coarse joking, which are out of place, but rather thanksgiving" (5:4). The previous verse gives a sexual context to these words: "But among you there must not be even a hint of sexual immorality," the apostle charges.

The word *obscenity* means filthy or dirty talk that brings shame upon the speaker and hearer; *foolish talk* refers to silly talk or joking about sexually related things; *coarse joking* is what you and I would call a dirty joke and can mean speech that is "irreverent" or "coarsely mocking" in a sexual context.[39] Peter O'Brien notes, "All three terms refer to a dirty mind expressing itself in vulgar conversation. This kind of language must be avoided as utterly inappropriate among those whom God has set apart as holy."[40] Amen.

One final note in this area. We should be reminded that God is recording every word we speak and—much to our shame—will parade those words before us on Judgment Day. Christ himself made this known to us. "But I tell you," the living Christ said, "that men will have to give account on the day of judgment for every careless [useless, lazy, barren[41]] word they have spoken" (Matthew 12:36). D.A. Carson says these are "words that might be thought 'insignificant'… except for their revealing what is in the heart. Jesus is saying that every word spoken reflects the heart's overflow and is *known to God*"[42] [emphasis mine].

2. *Personal character:* Character, as someone said, is what a person is in the dark. It's who you are on the inside; something no one can hide forever. And you can't fool an unbeliever; if your actions are not consistent with your profession, your witness will be ignored. Here are three common areas of failure for Christians in the realm of personal character.

Work ethic: A strong work ethic is a powerful witness to the lost. A hard worker, not one who cuts every corner; a faithful worker, not one who does only what's required; a diligent worker, not one who's just plain lazy—these will gain the respect of those outside our faith and earn the opportunity to be heard.

Again, to St. Paul's teaching. Some believers in Thessalonica didn't like to work hard, or work at all, for that matter. At the end of his second letter, he addresses these lazy Christians in very strong terms (2 Thessalonians 3:6–15). They were being disorderly, not working for their food and sustenance, and they ignored Paul's example of a day's work for a day's wages. We "worked night and day, laboring and toiling so that we would not be a burden to any of you," he commented (8).

By the words *laboring* and *toiling* we see Christians who were working to the point of exhaustion, hurting and wearied from their constant and difficult labor. Some believers in this church—far from this—were lazy busybodies, not working at all, but spending their time meddling in other people's affairs. Not only did the apostle condemn their behavior, but he also commanded the church to refuse them fellowship until they changed their ways.

In describing his work ethic, Paul set the standard for Christians of all generations. We should be the hardest working people at the office, striving for excellence in our work and putting in a full day, every day. Far from being one who everybody knows is a "slacker," we should be the standard-bearers in our workplaces.[43] Does this describe you?

Honesty: When you claim the name of Christ, others will pick your life apart. Whether at work or on your taxes, they'll watch to see if you are honest in your dealings. Again, in this culture, someone who is truly, consistently, and sacrificially honest will gain a hearing with others.

As I have observed people over the years in business, whether on the sales side or buying side of a transaction, or in the administrative and support functions of an organization, what I have concluded is that there are very few—and I mean *very* few—honest, tell-the-truth-always kind of people in this world. The ones who are I could count on one hand. Consequently, they stand out like a single white pearl in a bin of black coal.

It is utterly horrifying how often we lie. We are lying machines, popping out one lie after another all day long. When we are born into Christ's kingdom, however, we are to set aside that old pattern and become the sparkling, white pearl of God's glory. In Ephesians 4:25, Paul exhorts, "Therefore each of you must put off falsehood and speak truthfully to his neighbor." The phrase *put off* means "to cast off or lay aside," sort of like taking off a garment.[44] Why? Because "you were taught, with regard to your former way of life, to put off your old self … and to put on the new self, created to be like God in true righteousness and holiness" (Ephesians 4:22–24). To quote O'Brien again, "The readers have been instructed that to become believers signifies a *fundamental break with the past*"[45] [emphasis mine].

How about you, fellow Christian? Have you put off your old ways, or is lying still a part of your daily witness?

Convictions: Invariably, your convictions will be made known to those around you; and, at some point, they will be put to the test. Will you stand firm when your conviction not to lie is challenged? Will you refuse to sin even when it costs you the order? Pass the test and watch the door open with the unbeliever.

I remember a situation a number of years ago when God put my convictions to the test. My company had season tickets to the Washington Redskins, and I was asked to take some customers to a game. Wanting to be a good sales guy, I made arrangements with a couple of important clients and was preparing to go. Of course, the game was on a Sunday. At that time I'd been speaking at my church for about a year and had become, by definition, a role model to the young people in the church, a charge I took very seriously.

Although I was excited about going to the game—pro football is a blast live—as the time for the game grew closer, I became more bothered by what I was doing. It wasn't that I didn't have the freedom to miss church and go to a game, but it was the example I was setting for the young people. I knew they would ask where I was and possibly conclude from my actions that it was no big deal to miss church if you had something "fun" to do (a plague in the church these days, I might add). I tried to dump the tickets on some of my coworkers, but no one would take them.

I faced a tough decision. Would I follow my conviction or give in to avoid the embarrassment and trouble that might follow if I cancelled? With no little distress, I decided to cancel. And then—as is the way of providence—my non-Christian boss, Tom, e-mailed me asking why. I laid out my convictions and why I had given up the tickets. As you can imagine, I was expecting an aggressive response; however, to my great surprise, he wrote back and said something like this: "Wes, I wish you would have told me. I didn't know you were preaching. I understand and respect your decision. We'll find someone to take the tickets. No big deal."

Tom is no longer my boss, but to this day I still witness to him, and he always listens to me because he knows I'm a man of conviction. Now, I'm not setting myself up as something I am not. I struggle just like everybody else to stand true to my principles. But what I'm saying is that if, by God's grace, you stand tall when your heart demands it, you may be surprised at the result; instead of turning the lost away, you may just open a door with them, a door otherwise closed to you.

3. *Transparency/Being Genuine:* To what extent do people get what they see with you? Are you trustworthy, open, and real? Here are a few areas to evaluate yourself.

Gossip: The temptation to gossip is overwhelming sometimes. However, once we engage in it, we lose trust with others. Scripture teaches this plainly. Solomon said, "A gossip *betrays a confidence,* but a trustworthy man keeps a secret" (Proverbs 11:13). Why don't you give this a test? The next time someone is sharing some inside information or juicy piece of gossip with you, ask yourself, "What will keep them from doing the same to me when I'm the topic of conversation at the office?" To draw from my business experience again, when someone calls me and says, "I'll tell you what I heard about your competitor, but you didn't hear it from me," I know I can't trust them. Why? Because what they are doing now to *help me* is what they will do later to *hurt me*.

When you get close to someone and really start talking about their beliefs about God, their experiences in the past, their pain, and their worries, you must keep their trust. When it comes to disclosing their secrets to others, you must carry on as if you never heard them. This is an absolute rule. Once I asked a customer if there was anything I could pray about for him. He paused and said, "You can pray about my drinking." So I did. Later that night, about 10 p.m., he called me crying because that night he'd tried not to drink but lost the battle. Since then, I've had many meetings with him, and, frankly, some struggles with him as a customer. But I've never told anyone about what he confided in me. Even if he takes a million dollar order from me, I will not use this personal information against him, nor will I tell anyone about it.

Grace: Christians believe in moral standards, and this is good. However, we must be careful not to make issues out of every quasi-sinful thing an unbeliever does. Majoring on the majors is the rule here.

Jesus chided the religious leaders of his time for their attentiveness to minutia while they missed the more important teachings of God's law. They tithed of the most minor spices but forgot to be merciful and just and faithful (Matthew 23:23). In the same way, Christians sometimes pick nits with the lost; we want to make sure they keep this little commandment and that little commandment, but we overlook the deeper causes and more important principles we should be stressing with them.

Here in North Carolina there is a law that you can't sell alcohol before noon on Sunday. I find this especially ironic since we probably think we've won some kind of great battle by having this law on the books, but in all the bars I've ever been in—both as a drunk and an evangelist—I've never seen a believer in any of them sharing Christ.

Openness: Real people with real problems with real struggles—this is what we need to be when interacting with those outside our faith. Some Christians, however, come across as having perfect little lives, with perfect little families and perfect little marriages (even though none really do). We don't always do this because we believe we're perfect, but because we're afraid to let the unbeliever see our imperfection, as if, when they do, that will somehow shame Christ or sacrifice our witness. However, the opposite is true many times. If you are genuinely trying to follow Christ and seeing him work in your life, then you shouldn't be afraid to admit your weaknesses or share your struggles with the lost. They'll know you're one of them and will learn that becoming a Christian doesn't mean becoming perfect.

It's fascinating how honest Paul was about his struggles. Sometimes I find myself, as a writer and ministry leader, afraid to tell others about the sins I struggle with or the deficiencies I see in my own skills. I suppose I'm afraid others will see me as weak and write off what God has given me to say and do; but Paul the apostle was not like that, and, ironically, it makes me respect him all the more. I find I'm just as encouraged by his honest admission of his difficulty and weakness as I am by his powerful theology. Here are a couple of examples:

> For when we came to Macedonia, this body of ours had no rest, but we were harassed at every turn—conflicts on the outside, *fears within*.
>
> 2 Corinthians 7:5

> I have labored and toiled and have often gone without sleep; I have known hunger and thirst and have often gone without food; I have been cold and naked. Besides everything else, I face daily pressure of my concern for all the churches. *Who is weak, and I do not feel weak? Who is led to sin, and I do not inwardly burn?*
>
> 2 Corinthians 11:27–29

Do you know why these words mean so much to me? *Because I have experienced some of them myself.* I feel like Paul and I have something in common, and that makes me trust and appreciate him more. The lost should feel the same about us.

4. *Pornography.* I'm going to guess with the mere mention of this word, virtually every Christian man reading just felt a sting of guilt and shame in his chest. Well, don't feel bad; so do I. When I was a kid, my dad hid dirty magazines in a cabinet in the kitchen. I remember flipping through them in my bedroom with my door closed tight. Later, when I was in the service, I picked up the habit again. I didn't have the nerve to get a real subscription, so I just sent off for the "trial" issues. And today, it's all-out war in my mind to keep from clicking on those links. Sometimes I think I can actually feel a physical pull inside me to do it. I don't always win the battle, but I do fight. I know it's wrong.

The word *pornography,* like many words in our language, comes from Greek. The root word is *porne,* which means "to sell"; derivatives have similar meanings: *porneuo* means "to prostitute" and *porneia* means "prostitution."[46] According to one source, the word *pornography* dates to the mid-1800s and literally means "writing about harlots."[47]

So, pornography is when a woman sells herself for your pleasure. She strips down for the camera so you can buy a copy. No, you don't actually *touch her,* but nevertheless, you are participating in a form of prostitution every time you take a peek. Is that the kind of man you want to be?

The Lord Jesus Christ strictly forbids this type of lustful looking. "But I tell you," he declared sharply, "that anyone who looks at a woman lustfully has already committed adultery with her in his heart" (Matthew 5:28). The Greek group from which the word *lustfully* comes "denotes desire, especially for food or sex."[48] It can also mean "passion, as if breathing hard."[49] Sounds a lot like what we do when we catch a glimpse, doesn't it?

Peter could have been talking to our generation when he wrote, "With eyes full of adultery, they never stop sinning" (2 Peter 2:14).

So what's the big deal, you say? Nobody knows about it, especially the friends I'm trying to convert. While an entire book could be written to answer that question (and many have), let me just mention a few where promoting truth is concerned.

First, *it distances you from God.* Sin—and that's what this is—separates you from your Maker. Therefore, it distances you from the power and wisdom you need to promote truth aggressively in your circle of influence.

Second, *it distances you from your wife.* Your marriage is the foundation of your ministry; when it is damaged, your ministry suffers. Jesus called lust mental adultery. So how can you be right with your wife when you've been intimate with ten different women on the Internet today? Even if she doesn't know (and don't be surprised if she does), you know, and that's enough.

Finally, *your boldness is limited.* Pornography corrupts your conscience and makes you timid when speaking for God. Paul knew this, so he always fought to keep his conscience clear. Though he faced many overwhelming situations, he always responded with fearlessness because of the confidence he gained from a clear conscience.

In two situations in the book of Acts, one before the Sanhedrin and one before Felix, Paul's courage was breathtaking. And what was his source? A clear conscience. "My brothers," he said before the Jewish council, "I have fulfilled my duty to God *in all good conscience* to this day" (23:1). And then again, "So I strive always to *keep my conscience clear* before God and man" (24:16). How's your conscience, brother?

Therefore, we must battle these urges and squeeze this immorality out of our lives permanently. Otherwise, our ability to forcefully advance the kingdom will be impaired. Here are a few simple ideas to assist you in this task:

1. *Confess your sin to God and your wife.* Confession has a cleansing effect and is the only place to start when fighting sin. Be blunt, be truthful, and be transparent to the two you have offended.

2. *Get an accountability partner.* With God's help, find a man you respect who will meet with you on a reg-

ular basis and ask you the tough questions.

3. *Seek counseling from your pastor.* Don't think your pastor is immune to it, and don't think you're the only guy who has come to him about it. You need the wisdom of others to win this battle.

4. *Buy Internet accountability/blocking software.* I just purchased Covenant Eyes (www.covenanteyes.com) for my three computers at home. The great thing about Covenant Eyes is that in addition to blocking Web sites, it also sends your accountability partners a list of the sites you've visited and searches you've done. Get it now.

5. *Grow closer to God.* Seek him in his word; increase your prayer time and frequency; give more of yourself to his service.

Table 7

Summary of Our Habitual Failures		
Area of Failure	*Aspects to Consider*	*Texts*
Language	Curse words Perversities Sexual talk	Ephesians 4:29 Ephesians 5:4-8 Matthew 12:36
Personal Integrity	Work ethic Honesty Convictions	2 Thessalonians 3:6-15 Ephesians 4:25 Daniel 3:16-18
Transparency	Gossip Grace Openness	Proverbs 11:13 Matthew 23:23 2 Corinthians 7:5 and 11:27-29
Pornography	Forbidden by Christ Damages relationships Limits boldness	Matthew 5:28; 2 Peter 2:14; Acts 23:1, 24:16

CHALLENGES TO CHRISTIANS IN THIS AREA

As we close this chapter, let me challenge you to overcome this problem of hypocrisy for our people. Here are three simple steps each of you, as Christians, can put in place in your life to keep our enemies from making this charge against us in the future:

1. *You are a Christian—act like one.* Be sure you are not a fake. Watch your language, the dirty jokes, the gossip, the sex talk. Do your business with integrity, work hard, tell the truth, and be real with those around you. You can do a lot for the faith if you'll just do this.

2. *Respond like a Christian when you wrong someone.* We all make mistakes. Sometimes we can be a greater witness for Jesus after we make a mistake than if we never made one. Therefore, always follow biblical principles in your relationships and when dealing with conflict with others.[50]

3. *Confront other Christians who are not living up to their calling.* "Once you name the name, you're open game"; that's my motto. If someone claims to be a Christian, you and I, as fellow believers, have the right, and, in fact, the duty, to make them aware of ways their witness is being hindered. It doesn't matter if you've known them for ten years or ten minutes. Don't do this in a non-Christian manner, however; take them off to the side, alone, and lovingly rebuke them for their sin. They'll love you for it in the long run.

Our witness is killing us. In order to see the Julies of the world come to God, we must do better. We don't have to be perfect, but we must strive for excellence in our witness to the world. Prayerfully and honestly evaluate yourself against the criteria mentioned, repent of your mistakes, and strive to do better tomorrow. If you do, your words will carry the weight they should, and those around you may just find God through them.

GROUP DISCUSSION QUESTIONS

1. Have you ever heard anyone object to Christianity like Julie did? Is so, explain. How did you respond?

2. What other areas of moral failure have you noticed in the church that are not mentioned in this chapter? How can we overcome those?

3. What is your greatest weakness in terms of your witness to the world? What might Julie call you out on if she worked in your office?

4. Do you think it's necessary for Christians to hold other Christians accountable for weaknesses in their witness? Why or why not? Is this recommendation biblical?

CHAPTER 6

THE PRICE OF BLOOD: SACRIFICE AS A FOUNDATIONAL PRINCIPLE OF THE KINGDOM

I was a loser in high school. At the start of my junior year, I had this big breakup with my girlfriend that devastated me. I failed four classes in the eleventh grade and missed over thirty days of school that year alone; in my senior year, I missed another thirty and got stuck with the underclassmen taking junior-level English again just to graduate. Humiliating for a senior, to say the least. Now, I *did* graduate, but it was only by the grace of a very nice chemistry teacher named Mr. Wright (yeah, I had trouble with chemistry too ... and French, but let's not go there). I was completely lost in his class all year but stayed after school a couple of times for some tutoring. He gave me a D for the effort. I don't know where he is today, but I still owe him one. Thanks, Mr. Wright!

Not too long after graduation, I joined the Air Force and started to turn my life around. Fueled by the failures of my past, I strove for excellence in the service and worked hard to earn a college degree. The service valued education, so they were not only helpful financially (through the GI Bill) but also in terms of working hours. Again, God blessed me with good people around me (though I didn't know him at the time). Throughout my stint in the military, my supervisors were more than supportive of my efforts to finish college. Demorah, Marty, and Terry—my bosses through three plus years in the military—let me off early if I needed to attend a class and let me work on my homework while at the office. Like Mr. Wright, I owe them a debt of gratitude as well.

During this time, I began to learn one of the most important concepts of my life, a concept that Christ would teach me the real meaning of some years later. That difficult yet revolutionizing concept was this: *sacrifice*. I wanted my degree so badly; I was willing to do anything to get it. In only three years, I earned ninety credit hours *while working full time*. I went to school four nights a week, sometimes all day Saturday and Sunday, throughout the entire year; while other guys were playing softball or throwing darts, I was driving to night school. By God's grace, the day I left for home was the day I graduated from college.

Of the things God has blessed me to do in my life, I am probably most proud of that degree (proud in the right way). That time of sacrifice—intense sacrifice—has set the standard for my life since then and separated me from the path of defeat I had taken in my last years of high school. I praise the name of God for his kind providence to me during those days.

Today he is still teaching me about sacrifice. While I've asked him again and again to free me from my secular job to devote myself to his ministry, he has time and again refused my request. Yet the passion and energy for his work remains. So I find myself constantly challenged to give up what I would rather be doing or what would be "fun" for me in order to build something that makes his kingdom stronger and blesses the people of my nation. Today, as I juggle full-time employment, a wife and four children, and launching a ministry, I chuckle at what I thought was sacrifice in my days in the Air Force. But that's fine with me; his work is my pleasure anyway.

SACRIFICE AS A FOUNDATIONAL PRINCIPLE OF THE KINGDOM

Why do I tell you all this? To point out that great accomplishments are always accompanied by sacrifice. Survey humanity's greatest acts, humanity's greatest projects, humanities greatest achievements, and you will undoubtedly find intertwined in their narratives loss, hardship, and, occasionally, tragedy for those who dared attempt them. It is a universal truth.

The kingdom of God is the greatest project ever undertaken—by God or man. The one organization that will last until the end of time and crush all nations and systems posed against it has more blood at its feet, literally and figuratively, than any entity in human history. Even its founder was not spared this absolute requirement but set the standard by giving his own, innocent life.

Like a wide stream, the theme of sacrifice for kingdom advancement flows freely through the marrow of the New Testament. Jesus first forges its path when speaking of his impending death. "The hour has come for the Son of man to be glorified," he announces. "I tell you the truth, unless a kernel of wheat falls to the ground and dies, it remains only a single seed. But if it dies, it produces many seeds" (John 12:23–24). To Jesus, death must precede life; self-sacrifice, the good of others; pain, growth in the kingdom.

This principle applies not only to Jesus but to every person who truly becomes his disciple. It is, in effect, a rite of initiation into his service. Jesus goes on in John, "The man who loves his life will lose it, while the man who hates his life in this world will keep it for eternal life. *Whoever serves me must follow me ...*" (John 12:25–26a). Follow you where, Jesus? To the cross, of course. Each believer must have his own crucifixion event.

For years I missed the obvious and sobering meaning of Jesus' well-known words from Matthew 16:24, "If anyone would come after me, he must deny himself and take up *his cross* and follow me." What is a cross? It is a place where human beings are put to death. And this cross is not just any cross; it is *the disciple's* cross, or, to put it another way, it is *my* cross. It is the place where I died to myself to live for God. I must pick it up each day and take it with me wherever I go. Why? To remind me that I am still dead to me.

Knowing Jesus' teaching full well, Paul reinforces it strongly in his own writings. "For Christ's love compels us," he penned, "because we are convinced that one died for all, and therefore all died. And he died for all, that those who live should no longer live for themselves but for him who died for them and was raised again" (2 Corinthians 5:14–15).

Sacrifice, it seems, is the fuel in the engine of God. The Great Commission—the activity of promoting truth to others and forcefully advancing the kingdom of God—has, from its inception, exacted a heavy price from those who were willing to obey it. And as you and I consider a genuine return to Great Commission activities in modern America, we must face the sober realities of our contemplation, the personal sacrifices it may require of us.

Let's talk about some of those for a moment.

the sacrifice of your time

We are too busy. As modern Americans, we constantly delve out more time vouchers than we have. *Hurried, stressed, overburdened.* These words describe most of us daily. So it should be no surprise that we have no time for promoting truth to others, and time it will take to break the chains of bondage Satan has on our fellow Americans.

The culprits are many and, in some cases, surprising. I'd start the list with *church stuff.* Now, understand me clearly. The day-to-day work of the church is very important, and I applaud the faithful who bear these burdens. Our churches need workers, so don't go out after reading this and resign every volunteer position you hold. However, we must ask ourselves if the things we do at the church and for the church are really that important and necessary when compared to our personal responsibility to the Great Commission.

In America, if you are a "faithful" member of a church, there is an invisible pressure on you to volunteer for every event the pastor and church committees dream up. "They're there every time the church doors are open," is the highest accolade you can receive in many of our churches today. But is that really a great compliment from the perspective of the crucified Jesus?

As I have noted already, American Christianity has become an introverted subculture. We become Christians and then get lost in a powerful activity machine, all the while thinking we are being *really bountiful* disciples, when actually we are only *really busy* disciples. Are all of these fellowship and discipleship activities really required by Jesus? Do these events, classes, and group meetings supersede the importance of Jesus' last command to us, especially with the state of things in our nation? I would argue that they do not.[51]

So, if you are to create the time to invest in the pagans around you, one of the things you must work through is how much time you can give to the formal, organized events of your church. What are you doing at your church that you can sacrifice in order to make the time to engage the lost around you?

And I would ask pastors, bishops, and church leaders: Are you burdening your people with activities that are getting in the way of their keeping the Great Commission? Take a hard look at your calendar and schedule. Can you eliminate or consolidate activities in order to free your people to invest in promoting truth to others?

Another culprit is *kid stuff*. Again, I'll start this with a qualifier. I believe in family and family time, and I believe fathers and mothers should spend time with their children and spouses first. Growing up without a father, I know how it feels to be neglected by a parent and the great pain and difficulty parental absence fosters. Whatever time you set aside for God, invest it first in your family.

Having said this, I ask you the same question as before: Is it really necessary for your children to be involved in all the activities in which you have them involved? Do they need to be in sports year round and every weekend? Do they really need to do dance, and piano, and art, and band, and soccer—and all of that around the calendar, nonstop? I met a guy a few weeks ago whose kids play soccer *five nights a week* and travel to tournaments *every weekend*, virtually year round. I know Christian parents who run shuttle services as a part-time job with no pay. It's getting out of hand.

And let me ask you: When do you *raise* your children? No, I didn't ask when you are physically in the same vicinity as your children. I asked when do you *raise* them—teach them about God, interact with them in a one-on-one, alone-time way? When do you really get to know them as people, discuss their difficulties, and simply be with them with no scheduled activity and with no strangers around? When was the last time you had the entire family at the table for dinner or did a family devotional together? When do you disciple them—no, not your youth pastor or Sunday school teacher, but you?

Here's the sad truth. The vast majority of Christian parents in America don't raise their children—the world does. We get them up and throw some breakfast in them and cart them off to the bus stop or school parking lot where the world raises them for six to eight hours a day, five days a week, nine months out of the year; then we pick them up and drive them around to activities for the remainder of the day, grabbing a quick bite at McDonald's sometime before bed; then we take them home, get them bathed up, and the next day do it all over again.

On Sunday morning we drive them to church (actually rush them to church is more accurate), where they go their way and we go ours. And then when they're thirteen or fourteen, they don't want to be around us anymore, and when they go off to college, they can finally shed the silly faith of their parents, the faith the public schools took from them one day at a time since they were five.

And we wonder what happened?

What happened is the world raised your children, and you, without realizing it, worked and struggled and paid your hard-earned money so they could do it. So, I ask you again, for their own spiritual well-being, do they really need to be involved in all that stuff?

Outside the personal impact of busyness on your children, with all of these activities, how can you possibly find time to have your neighbor over for dinner, or have a cookout for your lost friends, or study to respond to a coworker's question, or any other truth-promoting venture? If you're serious about keeping the Great Commission, you must refocus your family time and sacrifice some of the activities to which you and your children have become so accustomed.

Then there's *me stuff* and *work stuff*. I put these together because they both relate back to the same core problem: selfishness. In reality, pure selfishness may get in the way of promoting truth more than anything else. Whether it's our drive to climb the corporate ladder or our "need" to play golf every Saturday or watch football all day Sunday, what little discretionary time we have is quickly chewed up by putting self first.

Now, I'm certainly not against relaxing time or downtime; we need them to keep healthy. Nor am I against hard work and excellence in the workplace. But many of our people place far more emphasis on these things than God requires while passing over their spiritual responsibility—not to mention the great joy—of stepping into the footsteps of Jesus and bringing the lost into the kingdom.

Table 8

Sacrifices Necessary to Forcefully Advance the Kingdom	
Area	Description
Church Stuff	Church activities that get in the way of the Great Commission
Kids Stuff	Events for your children that take up your discretionary time
Work Stuff/Me Stuff	Selfish desires that consume time we could be using for the lost

putting yourself at risk

Sacrificing time is a key component of making promoting truth to others possible. But there is a deeper concept we must take up in order to make an impact: the concept of personal risk. The twin sister of sacrifice, risk is so important that the work of God cannot go forward without it.

Imagine terrorists hold hostage some key city in a foreign war zone. As a commander, you know the value of that city to the overall mission; if you don't capture it, you could lose the war. But to take it you must risk not only the lives of your men, but also your own. You have a choice to make: either take the risk and go after the city—even though it could cost you greatly—or play it safe and accept the potentially greater loss. Which will you choose?

In a spiritual sense, our situation is not unlike this one. We are in a war where the stakes are high and the risks are tremendous. If we don't take the risks necessary, however, we cannot win. To many, the idea of taking on Satan's kingdom—aggressively promoting truth to the lost—may seem like an exciting idea. As exciting as it is, however, it is also very sobering because it can't be done without taking a tremendous amount of personal risk.

The book of Psalms may be the last place you would look for an example of taking risks for God; you would first turn to the gospels or the book of Acts for clear-cut illustrations of this principle. However, even in the poetic language of the psalms we find convicting examples of risk. In Psalm 119:109, the writer exclaims, "Though *I constantly take my life in my hands,* I will not forget your law."

In the context of the surrounding verses, it appears the author was being mistreated because of his love for and obedience to God's Word. In verse 106, he proclaims his faithfulness to the ways of Yahweh, saying, "I have taken an oath and confirmed it, that I will follow your righteous laws." Then he tells of the consequences. "I have suffered much," he laments, because "the wicked have set a snare for me" (107a and 110a).

Now the psalmist doesn't say exactly what commandment

brought him this persecution, and he really doesn't have to. What's important is that he was committed to keeping God's commandments even at risk to his own safety. "Go and make disciples," as we have already noted, is not a request; it is a command. Therefore, we too, like the psalmist, should be willing daily to put ourselves at risk to obey it.

Have you ever thought about the risk Jesus took with every word he spoke and the heroic courage he showed time and again in the face of such risk? We've read the accounts of his life so often we've lost the reality of the moment in the process. On one occasion, he was teaching in a synagogue and his enemies were there. They—the liars, villains, and cowards of Israel—had come to critique his every word, hoping, even praying, to catch him breaking one of their laws. Of course, he knew they were there and that they wanted to kill him.

Now, don't let that last statement slip by without understanding the weight of it. Put yourself in his shoes. You're getting ready to give a presentation at work and you know some of your coworkers in the meeting want to murder you. They'll be listening to your words, filtering every comment through their wicked minds, trying to catch you saying something "wrong" just so they can justify running you over in the parking lot, smiling as your body is forced under their wheels. How would you feel? How would you respond? I would probably cancel the meeting and go home—and call the cops!

But Jesus didn't flinch. He stepped up and took the risk. A hurting human being needed healing, and he wasn't going to let the possibility—the real possibility—of personal harm stop him. "*He looked around at them in anger* and, deeply distressed at their stubborn hearts, said to the man [whose hand was shriveled], 'Stretch out your hand.' He stretched it out, and his hand was completely restored" (Mark 3:5). Nevertheless, the Pharisees stayed true to their evil intentions: "Then the Pharisees went out and began to plot wit the Herodians how they might kill Jesus" (3:6).

What Must I Risk?

In America today, the most common risks can be placed into one of the following three categories:

1. *Relationships you hold dear and enjoy as they are.* As you allow God to identify the lost in your circle of influence, he may, for the sake of redemption, burden you to risk a relationship you love and enjoy as it is. A close family member, a relative, a friend at work—all could be put on the altar for the sake of the kingdom. And in the end you may lose that relationship. Furthermore, as you transfer your investment of time from some of your Christian friends to the lost, you can see detrimental consequences in those relationships as well.

2. *Financial welfare in terms of promotions and employment.* The work place is a ripe field for promoting truth; through work we can come into contact with many unsaved people and have access to them on a regular basis. In our society as it stands today, however, promoting truth at work can bring serious consequences. We can lose a promotion or even our job—and today that's a scary thing. But how else can we win them if we stay silent and comfortable? What would Jesus do, or Paul or Peter?

3. *Reputation and standing in your circle—the risk of abandonment and loneliness.* We all want to be held in high regard by the people we know. No one wants to be thought a fool or a weirdo. But make no mistake; when you begin to promote Jesus, people will never think of you in the same way. Don't forget, a crucified Messiah is "foolishness to the Gentiles" (1 Corinthians 1:23) and, today, a true Bible-believing Christian is even worse. You may find it a lonely place when you promote truth like Jesus.

The principle the Bible gives us is this: when faced with potential loss due to God's work, put the kingdom of God first and our well-being second. I've put myself at risk many times in my job, and I've often had to have a talk with myself and be reminded that he comes first, not me. We must not allow ourselves to focus on the consequences for us, but on the good that God can and will do through our faithful risk-taking.

Table 9

Risks Necessary to Advance the Kingdom
1. Relationships you hold dear
2. Financial welfare
3. Reputation and standing

Not too long ago I had an opportunity to speak with a lady at our corporate office on the telephone. During our conversation, she expressed how frustrated she was and how difficult things had been for her lately. I asked if she was a spiritual person, and she said she wasn't. I encouraged her to think about God and why he may be bringing this difficulty into her life.

After I got off the phone with her, I got the idea of sending her *The Purpose Driven Life* by Rick Warren. (This is a good book to send someone who is seeking spiritual insight.) But I had to pause because she, being at our headquarters, could easily have taken that book over to one of the higher-ups and made a big deal about it. It was not out of the question that I could get written up or even fired for what I had done.

But God whispered to me, *You'll never make any real difference if you don't take any real risk.* So I sent the book with a nice note. A few weeks later, I got this e-mail from her:

> Finished the book, Wes. Thank you for thinking of me and the kind words. My favorite chapter, 16—What Matters Most. May not always feel it, but that is one thing I have always believed in. Maybe one day I will find God; thank you for wanting me to. I am bringing the book home today so my

husband can read it; we can then discuss. As we have gotten older, we are always asking each other a million questions about life ... so thank you.

My friend, indeed there are risks and we may have to pay a great price to save others, but let's not forget the great rewards waiting for us, not the least of which is being used to impact a life. That's worth all the risk.

One final thought for pastors and church leaders. As our people start to step out and risk themselves in the workplace, wouldn't it be great if they could count on the church to back them up if they lose their jobs? Many don't take the risks necessary because they can't afford to—if they were fired, they would be homeless in only a few weeks. With this in mind, I'd like to recommend churches who implement the Forcefully Advancing strategy start a reserve fund to help Christians who lose their jobs because of the gospel. This would embolden many of our people to promote truth much more aggressively because they would know if they were persecuted, their brothers and sisters would be there.

Another way to support our people as they risk themselves for the gospel is to develop a network of Christian business people across the country who could help place persecuted Christians in new jobs. Not for just any purpose, this network would be specifically set up for those who lose their jobs because of promoting the gospel in the workplace. Maybe someone reading this book would step out and start such a network.

WHAT TO DO WHEN THE TIMES GET TOUGH

These injunctions—to sacrifice and take risks—as much as they may stir the soul, will nevertheless bring difficulty, discouragement, and loneliness from time to time. But we must persevere. So how do we do that? How do we endure when the work is just too heavy to bear? The answer is *stay close to God.*

Our lives are rooted in Christ, as John teaches us (John 15:1–

8), and when we actively seek his strength, we can do anything he requires of us (Philippians 4:13), even endure persecution and difficulty. So how do I, practically speaking, stay close to Jesus? Let me mention three key activities, or spiritual disciplines, that will foster the nearness you need.

First, *the discipline of praying.* As you walk longer with God, you begin to take prayer more seriously. Prayer is not doing nothing; it is foundational and, in some sense, the purpose of our existence. Of course, Jesus prayed. John adds an interesting word to his description of Jesus' prayer life in John 6:15. He says, "[Jesus] withdrew *again* to a mountain by himself." Time does not allow for a detailed study of the Messiah's prayer closet, but it doesn't take much time to see that Jesus prayed a lot, especially in times of intense stress like Gethsemane (Matthew 26:36–42). So, you and I, to last in our work, must follow his lead. Here are a few adjectives that describe a biblical prayer life:

- *Constant:* A strong prayer life is not on again, off again; it is consistent throughout time. We learn to pray as a way of life, not as a distinct act.

- *Intense:* Christ-like praying is passionate discourse with God. It takes on the serious topics of our lives and the kingdom, growing beyond clichés and trite expressions.

- *Solitary:* Alone with God, this is where prayer takes us. While we can and do pray everywhere and at all times, there is special power and intimacy in slipping away to be with God alone.

- *Protracted:* There is so much to pray about, but so little time. A growing prayer life leads to lengthened time in prayer. There is no magic number, no measurement of time that makes us more holy. However, the more time with God, the more strength and peace for us.

Here are few things to pray for on a regular basis where promoting truth is concerned:

- *Faith:* That you will trust God no matter where his providence leads.

- *Endurance:* That you will receive the mental, emotional, physical, and spiritual strength to make it through your time of testing.

- *Love:* That he will give you his love for the lost, even when they reject you and treat you poorly.

- *Integrity:* That your witness will not be compromised by hidden sin or by hateful reactions to others.

- *Boldness:* That God will grant you boldness and moral courage to speak the truth—all parts of it—to everyone he sends your way.

- *Success:* According to God's will, that men, women, and children would transfer their trust to him alone through your efforts.

- *Glory:* That God's name and character will be elevated in the hearts of the lost through your ministry.

Then, there is *the discipline of the Word.* God sustains his people through his Word. I can't explain it to you, but I know it's true. The Word of God is integral for a man's redemption and a disciple's condition. The biblical writers, the disciples of old, often expressed their love and need for Scripture. The writer of Psalm 119 spoke in detail about his unbreakable connection with God's Word. He called it "sweeter than honey" in Psalm 119:103, his source of strength (28), life (50), hope (81), direction (105), and joy (162).

Given this reality, a regular part of our lives must be reading and meditating upon God's Word. There are several ideas out there about how to do it, but one I find helpful is to read one Old Testament and one New Testament chapter each day. This provides a good balance. Also, don't be afraid to underline verses or words and write comments in the margins of your Bible. Sometimes I'm really encouraged when I read back over my notes. Finally, in times of difficulty, I find special help in the

Psalms (some good ones are Psalm 7, 10, 11, 18, 37, 43, and 119, among others) and the Old Testament miracle and war stories found in Joshua, Kings and Chronicles, Esther, and Nehemiah. Perhaps they will help you as well.

Table 10

Spiritual Disciplines for Persevering Strength	
Discipline	*Text(s)*
The discipline of praying	John 6:15; Matthew 26:36-42
The discipline of the Word	Psalm 119:28, 50, 81, 103, 105, 162
The discipline of fellowship	Hebrews 10:25-31

Finally, there is *the discipline of fellowship*. It's helpful during a season of difficulty to spend time with those who have experienced what you are experiencing. Yet when we are under great pressure, we are often tempted to withdraw ourselves from others. Please don't let this happen to you. Remember, God has always called his people together in groups, and for good reason.

Hebrews 10:25 gives us a direct command in this area: "Let us not give up meeting together, as some are in the habit of doing, but let us encourage one another—all the more as you see the Day approaching." There are some very interesting lessons here. We can see that some people were abandoning (that's what the word means in Greek) the gatherings of the people. Many do this today. But the writer exhorts them not to because they need to be "encouraged" by the other believers. Later in the chapter we see that this encouragement is a way to preserve the believer's faith and ensure their salvation (26–31).

So when the times get hard for you, be even more committed to gathering with fellow believers. It is one of the methods of preservation—your preservation—God has built into his community.

The possibility of success is always before us. But, as in the day of Jesus and Paul, only those who are willing to pay the price and maintain key spiritual disciplines will experience it. I know you are willing; translate that willingness into sacrifice and risk today. Kingdom success awaits you.

GROUP DISCUSSION QUESTIONS

1. Have you ever done anything that required an extended period of personal sacrifice? If so, what was it? Looking back on it now, how do you feel about it?

2. What ways have you not died to yourself to serve Christ? Explain.

3. Of the types of sacrifices listed in the chapter (church stuff, kid stuff, me/work stuff), which one will be the most important for you to make in order to reach others? Why?

4. In your particular context, what kind of personal risk will you need to take in order to promote truth (relationships, financial, reputation)? Elaborate.

5. Where do you lack in the spiritual disciplines listed? What can you do to strengthen these?

CHAPTER 7

A JOURNEY, NOT A LIGHTNING BOLT: UNDERSTANDING STAGES OF FAITH

T he rifle barrel was curled on the end and smoking. The young Tennessee farm boy was lucky to be alive after a single bolt of lightning took his gun from his hand and his drenched body from his horse. A millisecond before, he was an angry drunk on his way to carry out vengeance; someone had taken something valuable from him, and he was determined the naughty deed would not go unpunished. But the powerful sign from heaven had not only sobered him instantly, but also revealed God to him. Instead of completing his work of revenge, he led his startled horse to a nearby church and surrendered his life to Jesus Christ. From that day forward he was a transformed man, the bright mirror image of the dark character he had become.

So is the story of Sergeant Alvin York as portrayed by Gary Cooper in the classic film, *Sergeant York*. The image of Alvin's movie conversion, like that of the Bible's apostle Paul, incarnates how we have come to view conversion in America—sudden, instant, and miraculous. This mental picture, as moving as it is, has given us a false and unduly narrow view of biblical, real-life conversion, a view that is damaging our work of forcefully advancing the kingdom.

You may not realize it, but our efforts to promote truth are in large part shaped by the way we think people are saved, whether gradually in steps or quickly in a sudden event. If you believe the latter, you'll do those things that focus on bringing that magic event to fruition, standing in an open field with a lightning rod, if necessary. However, if you see it as more of a progression—a journey, if you will—then you will not focus so exclusively on the point of decision, but, like a patient farmer, on working your crop through its stages until the time of harvest has come.

HOW DO WE COME TO CHRIST?

Contrary to popular opinion, most people don't come to faith in Christ in a flash like a lightning bolt. Even those who appear to have been converted quickly (like York or Paul) have gone through some progression before making a commitment to Christ. To demonstrate this, let's take a closer look at Saint Paul's experience.

Yes, Paul was converted in a fantastic event, but if you think about it for a minute, you'll realize he was very far along in his faith journey when he started down the Damascus road. In fact, when the light from heaven appeared, Paul was already primed to be converted. He knew the one God, the Old Testament Scriptures, and was looking for a Messiah; he just didn't believe Jesus was the one. He knew what sin was, what atonement was all about, and understood the concept of divine judgment. If only our fellow Americans—including many in our churches—had such a clear understanding of truth, then maybe our "revivals" would actually live up to their name.

Given this reality, it is vital for us to understand the progression to faith people experience so we can be used more effectively by God in his work of redemption.

BIBLICAL BASIS FOR THE STAGES OF FAITH MODEL

The concept of stages of faith can be seen in the teaching of Jesus in John 4:35–38. This familiar passage reads as follows:

> Do you not say, "Four months more and then the harvest"? I tell you, open your eyes and look at the fields! They are ripe for harvest. Even now the reaper draws his wages, even now he harvests the crop for eternal life, so that the sower and the reaper may be glad together. Thus the saying "One sows and another reaps" is true. *I sent you to reap what you have not worked for. Others have done the hard work, and you have reaped the benefits of their labor.*

We've all heard verse 35 a million times. Every time a preacher wants us to go out and save souls, he uses this passage. Not sure about you, but, ironically, when I would go out and share the gospel after this type of message, I would invariably meet with tremendous resistance and find most people not ready for harvest. Perhaps this is because we have neglected the teaching of the next three verses, especially the last one.

Jesus gives the principle in verses 36–37: one person sows and another reaps; in other words, converting someone to him is a team effort. Then, in verse 38, he applies this principle to the harvest the disciples were getting ready to take in. The great harvests of the early Christians were not due to their efforts alone—their eloquent preaching, their powerful altar call, their undeniable logic—but the natural end result of the hard work of other people. "I sent you," he said, "to reap what *you have not worked for.*" Who did the work then, Jesus? Someone else. He goes on, "*Others* have done the hard work, and you have reaped the benefits of *their* labor."

Those who converted to Christ in New Testament times didn't start their faith journey when the evangelist came to town, but when some unnamed person began working with them, tilling the soil, ripping out the rocks, and tearing down the briars cluttering their hearts. Someone did the "hard work," as Jesus calls it, so someone else could reap them for the kingdom.

We don't see a tremendous harvest today because we have not done the hard work of cultivating people and preparing them to be harvested. We always want to harvest—which is the easiest part of farming—sharing the gospel message over and over, hoping eventually our friend, our coworker, our neighbor will accept it. But it just doesn't work like that. Just like you can't go out and pick the apples off the tree you haven't planted, cultivated, or watered, so you can't save a soul who has not been farmed and readied to receive the kingdom.

So, to be more effective in building God's kingdom, we need to adopt a broader view of conversion to reflect the process, or journey, people experience when entering it. To affect this, I have developed a three-part model I call *Stages of Faith*.

the stages of faith model

There are many ways to outline the progression we take in coming to faith in Christ. We'll use the three-stage method outlined below. For each stage, I'll describe the type of person you will encounter and give you an example from real life to solidify the concept.

Stage 1: Gospel-hardened: This type of person is, in terms of their progression, a long way from faith in Jesus. They may be able to traverse the process in a relatively short period of time—or maybe not—but no matter the timeframe, there is a lot of work to do.

Skeptical, apathetic, antagonistic—these are the critics who don't trust what you say, and, though they may listen to you pleasantly enough, won't believe because they have already made up their minds. They may be atheists, agnostics, or idolaters. In any case, they're the tough nuts of outreach, the fields overgrown with small trees, thick grass, and filled with rocks.

Right now I'm working with someone just like this. His name is Sam. Sam was raised in a Christian environment but was never taught how to think (an unfortunate plague in Christendom these days). He's not sure if there is a God or not, although he allows for the possibility; he says he is very open-minded but is also very sure that Christianity is wrong; he's not convinced there is such as thing as absolute truth, though he holds to many of his own truths absolutely; he thinks the Bible is a good book, but also believes it is full of errors and allegories. Needless to say, Sam is gospel-hardened—a long way from faith in Christ. I'll tell you how I'm dealing with him in the next section.

Stage 2: Gospel-open: This person is closer to Jesus than the gospel-hardened. Willing to talk about Christianity and faith, they'll listen with an open mind to your case. They have a lot of questions and are willing to express them to you. Although they are not ready to make a decision, their hearts are thawing to God and the Bible. They may even go to church with you or attend a small group.

An example of a gospel-open person would be Charles, a guy from work I've been talking to. Charles was raised in a Catholic environment and even attended Catholic school when he was growing up. He's living with a girl now who is not his wife. He believes in God and Jesus and says he has a holy fear of them both (probably instilled into him in Catholic school). He's not sure about how to get to heaven, but he wants to live a life that pleases God. He and his girlfriend are talking about finding a church soon.

Stage 3: Gospel-ready: Decision time—that's what you need to remember with the gospel-ready. They have learned about Christianity, may already understand much of the gospel, and are considering making a commitment to Christ. Having satisfied most of their questions, their hearts are open to the true message of the Bible and its ramifications upon their lives.

Table 11

Stages of Faith Overview		
Stage	*Proximity to Salvation*	*Description*
Gospel-hardened	Far	<ul><li>Skeptical or apathetic</li><li>Possibly antagonistic and/or critical</li><li>Mind is made up</li><li>Atheists, agnostics, or idolaters</li></ul>
Gospel-open	Closer	<ul><li>Willing to talk and listen</li><li>Have lots of questions</li><li>Hearts are thawing to God, Bible, and Jesus</li></ul>
Gospel-ready	Near	<ul><li>Ready to make a decision</li><li>May understand Christianity and basics of the gospel</li><li>Most questions satisfied</li><li>Hearts are open to true message of Jesus</li></ul>

A few years ago, one of my coworkers from Pennsylvania, Dallas, came down to travel with me for a few days. I had never met Dallas, but, as I usually did, I asked God to show me if he wanted me to talk to him about Christ. As providence would have it, after our morning meeting, Dallas said, "Wes, I understand you're a spiritual guy and I'd like to talk to you about a few things." He was on the verge, believed the Bible was God's Word, and wanted to know how to be right with God. He was gospel-ready.

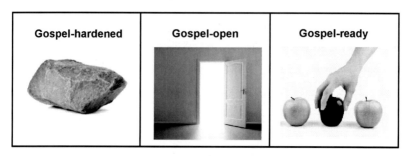

Stages of Faith Pictured

Before we move on and talk about how to deal with people at each stage, let me make a few important points about this model.

1. *As you talk to new people, learn to recognize where they are along this progression.* When you become their friend and understand their spiritual background and present beliefs (we'll talk about this in the following chapters), you'll be able to get a sense of where they are. Ask yourself which of the three descriptions listed above fits your new friend best.

2. *Because everybody is not at the same place in their faith process, you're not going to reap every time you engage someone.* So take the pressure off yourself. Labor with each person with the goal of moving them to the next stage; if you do this, you will always be successful and, in the process, will prepare many for future harvest.

3. *Finally, let this concept give you a longer-term view of promoting truth to others.* We need to be in it for the long haul with people today because in many cases that's what it will take to bring them to Jesus as real disciples (not ones who just sign a card and disappear). Relax and remind yourself you are stepping into a process—sometimes a very long one—and the important thing is not that you do *everything*, but that you do *your part* and do it well.

an effective farming process

As you can imagine, the way you deal with people at each level is different. Not that your ultimate goal is not the same—true salvation and radical discipleship—but what you need to emphasize during your interactions will vary based on where they are in the process.

Below are some general rules for each stage. To help you visualize what needs to be emphasized at each of these stages, we'll use the terms *cultivate, sow,* and *reap,* farming terminology that mirrors a farmer's process for preparing, planting, and receiving his crop (picking up on Jesus' metaphor from John 4).

Cultivate

As a farmer must first *cultivate* his field—knocking down trees, pulling up rocks and weeds, and tilling the soil—before he can plant seed, so we must cultivate a person's soul and mind by working to remove spiritual impediments to belief. Goals at this stage can include showing a strong witness through a holy lifestyle, developing and strengthening a friendship, identifying and addressing barriers to faith in a nonthreatening way, and sharing the basics of Christianity and the gospel without pressure to accept it. Also, in many cases, you'll need to teach the person how to think biblically, which is the right way to think anyway. While most of your work at this stage will be done on a one-on-one basis, you may find a content-relevant apologetics event as a helpful tool here.

Sow

Then, after the land has been cultivated, the farmer can *sow* the seed, attending to it so it will grow while simultaneously removing weeds and impediments that can stunt development and reduce the crop. In the same way, we must, after the soil is cultivated, sow seeds of truth and the good message into the softening heart of the lost. Here you'll focus on more aggressively overcoming barriers to faith, teaching the key concepts of the Christian faith, and sharing the gospel with more personal application. In terms of events, content-relevant apologetics events and events that cover the basics of the Christian faith or the gospel (without a lot of pressure) are ideal.

Different Work at Different Stages

Reap

Finally, a farmer will *reap* his harvest when the time has come; he will pick the fruit and rejoice in a successful season. So, we too must harvest a soul whose heart and mind have been cultivated, sown, and is now ready to enter the kingdom of God and receive eternal life. This we do by sharing with clarity, passion, and persuasiveness the good message of Jesus and inviting our fellow man to receive our Creator's kind offer. Your standard evangelistic events can really hit home in this situation.

Here is a chart that overviews the points discussed so far.

Table 12

Cultivate, Sow, and Reap Activity Overview		
Work	*Description*	*Activity*
Cultivate	Action whereby we work to remove spiritual debris, rocks, and weeds that prevent the sowing of gospel seed	▪ Witness through holy lifestyle ▪ Develop and strengthen friendship ▪ Overcome barriers in a non-threatening way ▪ Teach to think biblically ▪ Share basics of Christianity and the gospel ▪ Events: Apologetics
Sow	Action, following cultivation, where we sow seeds of truth and the good message into the softening heart	▪ Aggressively overcome barriers to faith ▪ Teach basics of Christianity ▪ Share gospel with more personal application ▪ Events: Apologetics, basics of Christianity, or gospel overview
Reap	Action, following cultivation and sowing, where we take in the harvest of a soul whose heart and mind now are ready to enter the kingdom of God and receive eternal life	▪ Share the gospel message in detail, clarity, and passion, and ask for a personal commitment ▪ Events: Typical evangelistic events

what to do at each stage

Now, let's apply these three terms to our stages of faith model.

Gospel-hardened—Major: Cultivation, Minor: Sowing

For those who are gospel-hardened, your major emphasis should be on cultivation, with a minor emphasis on sowing. With this person, it is critical that you focus on living righteously before them first; many people who are hardened have had a bad experience with Christianity and need a good witness before they will hear the message (see chapter five). Then, make sure you develop a friendship with them outside of spiritual things. When you've accomplished these two steps, the rest of your work will be much easier. Finally, get them to talk openly about their issues or questions. Start to work on them one-by-one over time, teaching them how to think along the way. Be patient, but don't let up. It is important here that you share the basics of the gospel as information only, *no pressure*, and that you don't push them to come to church with you or attend a small group.

Let's apply this to my friend Sam. Where Sam is in his journey, I really don't need to shove the gospel down his throat—it wouldn't work anyway. So, what I'm doing is slowly picking away at his objections and teaching him to think biblically. One of the best ways to do this is to communicate over e-mail. It gives each of us time to think about the points the other person is making and research our answers. Sam and I have agreed to discuss matters of faith without feeling offended. We put our comments in a Microsoft Word file and save them each time we respond. Based on where he is presently, I started our discussion with the concept of truth and am getting ready to move to the Bible difficulties he has mentioned. Eventually, of course, I want to get to Jesus and salvation. But I'm not starting there. Even if I don't get to "finish," as I would define it, I've started the farming process, which God can finish with someone else down the road.

That's a real key to get out of this process. You don't have to take the ball all the way to the goal line. Like the apostles in John 4 who were entering into someone else's work, we too can work hard now while we are in their lives and allow someone to take over for us later. Either way, as Jesus said, we all rejoice because it was our collective efforts that will win the heart of that lost person.

Gospel-open—Major: Sowing, Minor: Reaping

More trusting and approachable, the gospel-open don't require as much time in friendship development. The emphasis for this type of person is on sowing, getting them to lay out their questions and issues regarding Christianity. Why are they not Christians? Because of this person's attitude of openness, you can engage them aggressively, though respectfully, at this stage. Don't be afraid to tell them you don't agree with them and share the gospel with more personal application. Invite them to an apologetics event or an event that reviews the basics of the Christian faith and the gospel.

So what am I doing with Charles? Well, Charles is further along than Sam, so I don't need to work on as many apologetic-type questions, like truth and the existence of God and Bible difficulties. He already accepts the Bible as true. Therefore, with Charles, I'm starting by teaching him about Scripture—its role in revealing God's will to us and what is true about ourselves, our Maker, and the life that is coming. To start this effort, I ordered Charles a study Bible and a book about the basic teachings of Christianity (R.C. Sproul's, *Essential Truths of the Christian Faith*). My plan is to give them to him as a gift and then pick up our discussion where it left off.

As you can see, it's like rolling a bowling ball down a lane. First, you find out where it is; next you get behind it and push it until your turn is up; then, you trust someone else will come along and finish the task.

Table 13

Emphases at Each Stage	
Stage	*Work*
Gospel-hardened	Major: Cultivation Minor: Sowing
Gospel-open	Major: Sowing Minor: Reaping
Gospel-ready	Major: Reaping

With the gospel-ready, reaping is the order of the day. Therefore, you can quickly move to share the gospel message in detail and clarity. Spend your time making sure they understand the message and its implications. Ask them if they would like to trust in Jesus. Invite them to an evangelistic-type event.[52]

Now, this is the fun part of farming and promoting truth. Dallas started asking me questions about all sorts of things. I could tell he didn't need to be "convinced" about Christianity or the Bible. Based on the questions he was asking, I knew I didn't need to start in the middle like I did with Charles. So I steered the questions and answers directly to salvation. I talked to him specifically about the role of Christ in redemption, how to apply his work on the cross to us individually, and about what forgiveness really means. When I felt like he understood what I was saying, I popped the question, "Would you like to trust Christ and be saved?" Without blinking, he said, "Absolutely." We prayed together in my Trail Blazer, and to this day, Dallas is an on-fire disciple of Jesus. Whenever I see him, we embrace.

Interestingly—and in direct support of the model I'm presenting here—Dallas had someone in his life that was working on him like I am working on Sam and Charles (I believe his name was Marty). Marty was a Christian and a close friend of Dallas's and had been working on Dallas for some time, preparing the way for him to be saved. And, just like Jesus said, someone else (me, in this case) entered into his labor and reaped the crop. Beautiful!

WHAT IS SUCCESS ANYWAY?

As we close this chapter, let's pause to answer this question: What is real success anyway? This is an important question because how we answer it will impact our own self-perception (are we accomplishing our mission?) and our long-term endurance in this effort (if we think we're failing, we won't last long in the work).

The impression we get from most pulpits in America is that successful outreach is measured only by the number of decisions made for Christ. One great evidence of this is how important it is to most preachers and most churches that those who receive the gospel during a church service communicate this to them in some way. This desire is manifested in various ways. It could be the call to come forward because "Jesus died for you so the least you could do is walk an aisle for him," or an urging for the person to raise their hand while "all heads are bowed," or even the directive to "be sure to fill out your commitment card," or, "make sure you see me [preacher] in the vestibule after the service."

While making a decision to trust Christ is an essential part of being a disciple—and certainly the end goal for which we all strive—is it the only sign of success? I would definitely say no. A disciple, after all, is not simply a *decider;* he is a *learner.* A disciple is someone who has been taught the gospel message, understands its stringent demands, accepts it as authentic and coming from God, and then makes a conscious decision to surrender himself to follow and serve the Jesus of the Scriptures. This necessarily implies a longer process than a five-minute altar call.

When you view disciple-making as a process that starts before the decision point (and in some cases many years before)—as Jesus taught in John 4 and as we have described in this chapter— you can begin to understand that *every interaction* in the spirit of the Great Commission and with the intent of moving someone further along their path to genuine faith is a *major victory.*

So, let us change the way we view and measure successful truth promotion. Perhaps we should think of "interactions with the lost" as a success measure or "questions answered" or "new friendships established" because these are steps along the road of genuine faith, steps that, if not taken, can prevent many from finding faith in Christ at all.

THE PROCESS MOVING FORWARD

The next section, "Part 3: The Strategy," will outline a process for moving from cultivation to sowing to reaping, giving you concrete steps and real-life examples of how to deal with people in whatever stage of faith you find them. To help you remember this process, I have developed the acronym REAP, which is, of course, our ultimate goal. Below I'll outline the REAP process and the associated chapter that details each step.

Table 14

The Reap Process				
Letter	Term	Memory Statement	Description	Chapter
R	Relate	Become a Friend	Develop a genuine friendship	8
E	Educate	Become an Expert	Understand their spiritual background and barriers	9
A	Answer	Give Answers	Overcome barriers with answers	10
P	Present	Present the Message	Share the message of Jesus	11

As you read the chapters that follow and start your own work with those around you, keep the REAP acronym in mind. It will be a helpful tool as you are used of God to move people along in their journey to genuine faith.

Now, let's move on and talk about how to develop genuine friendships with others, the "R" in our acronym.

GROUP DISCUSSION QUESTIONS

1. What has been your impression of how someone comes to faith in Christ: a journey or a miraculous event? How has that impression shaped your thoughts about promoting truth?

2. Had you ever thought about John 4:35–38 in this way before (as showing a staged approach to conversion)? How should this teaching impact our efforts to promote truth?

3. Do you agree with the stages of faith model? Why or why not? What are its benefits?

4. Do you believe we should change the way we evaluate our outreach success, not just counting decisions but other activities as well, such as friendships, questions answered, and so on? Elaborate.

PART THREE

The Forcefully Advancing Strategy

CHAPTER 8

GETTING INSIDE THE GATE: BECOMING A TRUE FRIEND TO THE LOST

You can say virtually anything to a real friend. They will allow you into the secret places of their hearts, seeing their fears, sharing their joys. Even their deepest disappointments and greatest sorrows are open to you if you are one of these. But if you are an outsider, you can forget it. You are kept at a different distance. You haven't earned their trust so you can approach the compound but not get inside the gate.

To build a real disciple in today's environment, it helps to be the former.[53] God and faith are sacred, emotional, personal things to most people. Some have been so hurt by religious people, some have terrible sins to hide, and others are just hard-headed and stubborn (and need to be told). But whatever the case, to go where you need to go and deal with the issues you need to deal with, you have to gain the trust that is only given to a genuine friend.

I've heard it over and over through the years. People often say to me, "I've never told anyone this before." I suppose it is because I have tried to be a real friend to the people I've met over the years. God has helped me to care about them as people, not just names on a commitment card; and, as they have discovered that, they have shared with me their most sensitive issues.

Therefore, in this chapter, we will lay out the first point of our strategy, the "R" in our REAP acronym, Relate, developing genuine friendships with the lost. Before we discuss the practical steps to do this, however, let's peek into the life of Jesus to identify two important foundational principles of friendship building.

THE MESSIAH AS OUR BENCHMARK

Jesus was a different kind of Christian. Promoting truth and rescuing others was an integral part of who he was, activities that flowed naturally from his very nature. By observing him we can learn a great deal about the kind of people we need to be to continue his work. Two things in particular are very instructive about Jesus: the *friends he had* and the *way he loved.*

Jesus' friends were not like ours. Think about it. Most of our friends are Christian. No cursing, no drinking. No pornography, no dirty movies. No heavy metal, no hip-hop. Our friends are the "clean" people of society, with no dirt on their hands or in their lives (at least, that's what we tell ourselves). They never make us uncomfortable and wouldn't dare violate our sensitive consciences. But Jesus' friends weren't like that.

Remember, he was known as the guy who hung around with the ugly, out-crowd. It was so widespread an infamy that *he even knew about it.* In a discussion with the Pharisees at one point, he brought it up himself. "The Son of Man," he pointed out in Luke 7:34, "came eating and drinking, and you say, 'Here is a glutton and a drunkard, a friend of tax collectors and "sinners."'" He didn't hang with the church crowd; this was his common reputation. He befriended people who didn't walk the white line of morality, ones who had obvious sin in their lives.

It's fascinating to notice who Jesus befriended. He went to weddings where alcohol was served, and, apparently, where much was consumed (John 2:1–11). He spent time with floozies and prostitutes (Luke 7:36–38). And he was especially fond of tax collectors, a group particularly despised among the people.

Tax collectors not only mustered taxes for the occupying empire, but were also widely known for extortion. Though they were the mob of their time, Jesus wouldn't leave them alone. He stayed in the home of Zaccheus, a wealthy tax collector from Jericho (Luke 19:1–9), he used them as examples of true repentance (Luke 18:9–14), and he even called one as his apostle, Matthew (Matthew 9:9–13).

What's the lesson for us? We cannot set parameters on who we will call our friends and with whom we will share Christ's message. We must "go and learn what this means: '[God] desire[s] mercy, not sacrifice,' for [Jesus did] not come to call the righteous, but sinners" (Matthew 9:13). We don't necessarily have to find a prostitute or mobster to befriend—although if God leads you, go for it—but we cannot limit our friends to those who are pearly white and clean.

Jesus' friendships serve as a great example to us, but so does the way he loved those friends. He loved people just because they were people; his love had no prerequisites or contingencies. As we've already observed, he loved people of all social classes, races, sexes, and sexual persuasions.

However, what I especially want you to see is that he loved people *even when they rejected him and his message.* You may recall the rich young man who turned away from Jesus because of his wealth. Right in the middle of their conversation, the Scripture says, "Jesus loved him" (Mark 10:21). Then on the cross, while his murderers looked on and mocked, he asked the Father to forgive them (Luke 23:34).

One of the most moving demonstrations of his love for those who had rejected him is seen when he entered Jerusalem for the last time, as recorded in Luke 19:41. The NIV translates this verse, "As he approached Jerusalem and saw the city, he wept over it." This translation, however, doesn't relate the full emotion of his reaction. "To sob or wail aloud"—this is what the word *wept* actually means.[54] Kenneth Wuest translates this verse more expressively: "And as he came near, having caught sight of the city, he burst into tears, weeping audibly over it."[55] Jesus saw God's city and all of its people and just lost it. His powerful emotions simply overcame him.

If you've shared the gospel more than once, you know how hard it is to love someone when they reject you. It would be easier if the rejection was couched in kind language and an affirmation of you as a person, but so often it isn't. People can be cruel in their replies to us. They don't just say no; they reject everything we stand for and believe. Loving them is so difficult. Yet we must seek from God a love that overcomes our natural reactions. We need supernatural love regularly apportioned to us not only to serve as our motive to reach those who are contrary to us, but also to preserve our witness when we are rejected. May this be our continuing prayer.

BECOMING A FRIEND

Now, let's turn our attention to the practical side of developing friendships. We have the spiritual underpinning, so let's move on and detail the real-life process.

reach out to whom?

So who should I reach out to? The key is to select anyone with whom you have ongoing contact. Places to look first are neighbors, friends, coworkers, customers, dorm mates, or family (immediate or extended). Bingo partners, bridge club members, the waitress at your favorite restaurant, your son's little league coach, an old friend from high school—all of these are examples of opportunities we so often overlook. You don't have to go far to find more than you can handle.

Most importantly, do not spend your time developing friendships with new Christians with whom you come into contact. Remember, it's the lost we're after. You and I only have so much time to devote to promoting truth, and we need to have a laser focus on non-Christians. Most of us have all the Christian friends we can handle anyway. It may sound harsh, but if you find out your neighbor is a devoted Christian, be a good neighbor but move on to the next house on the block.

how long will it take?

You may be thinking that making a friend will take a long time, but it doesn't have to. The process of earning trust and becoming a friend doesn't have to take years. Keep in mind, when I say friend, I don't mean that limited number of people you might consider your lifelong, true, dyed-in-the-wool, do-anything-for-you friends. These are truly rare. What I mean is someone who trusts you, likes you, and is more than a mere acquaintance. What you might call a "buddy" or "girlfriend."

Although some are slower to open up and give trust than others, many are willing to take a chance on you in only a few interactions if they see that you value them as a person and show genuine interest in them. If I had to put a number on it, I would say it takes between five and ten separate interactions with someone before you earn trust and become a friend. The point is not how long it takes—God will show you when you've made it—but that you eventually become someone they consider to be genuine, trustworthy, and deserving of insider status.

THE BUDDI SYSTEM

It isn't always obvious how to initiate and develop a friendship with those around us. It can be intimidating, especially in the beginning. The BUDDI System[56], outlined below, lays out five helpful steps to developing friendships with the non-Christians around you. Begin putting these ideas into practice, and you'll be a professional friend-maker in no time.

1. *Be*friend: Make an initial acquaintance. This is sometimes the hardest part. However, it doesn't have to be difficult or complicated. Here are some ideas of how you can do this.

   - When you check the mail, walk over and say hello to your neighbor when he pulls in the driveway.
   - Stop that new guy from work in the hall and introduce yourself.
   - When you see your neighbor cutting grass, walk over and say, "Hi."
   - Introduce yourself to a stranger in your college dorm.
   - Sit down beside someone new during lunch in the office break room.
   - Take a walk down your street in the summer and see who is outside. Make eye contact and say, "Hello."

   Remember, you're just trying to introduce yourself. There's no religious discussion involved, no commitments of any type. You just want to chat, get to know them a little, and remember their name for later (and start praying for them).

   I know you may be a little scared, but trust me. You're a friendly person. All you have to do is be yourself. Once you take the first step, you'll see how easy it really is.

2. *Un*cover: Learn more about them over time. Once you've introduced yourself, you can start to uncover more about them as time goes by. This is important for two reasons: First, you want to be their friend; in order to do this, you need to become more acquainted with their lives. Second, later, when you are trying to engage them spiritually, you'll need this information to approach them in the right manner.

   Here are three categories of information that will be helpful to you in your endeavor.

- *Personal:* You want to know about them personally. Here are a few things you can ask to help you get to know them. I'll phrase them as questions you can ask to help you see how to use them.

  Where do you work?
  Where were you born? Were you raised there as well?
  What do you like to do in your spare time?
  What is your favorite movie? TV show?
  Are you a sports fan? Who do you like?

- *Family:* You want to learn about their family. Here are a few specifics to talk about:

  Are you married? How long?
  Do you have children? Ages? Locations?
  Where do their parents live?
  Do you have brothers and sisters?

- *Spiritual background and barriers:* Eventually, you'll want to learn about their past experiences with religion, spirituality, and Christianity, as well as any barriers they have to faith in Jesus. We cover this topic in detail in chapter nine. For right now, just keep in mind that spiritual questions flow nicely right after family questions.

asking good questions

Before we move on to the next step in the BUDDI System, let's discuss a critical part of becoming a friend: learning to ask good questions.

Much of our anxiety related to getting to know new people comes from the fact that we don't always know what to say to a stranger. We make an introduction and then the conversation goes cold; nobody knows what to say next. The easiest way to avoid this is to learn to ask questions that will get your new friend talking. Use the questions listed above when you first meet someone, and you'll find you're well on your way. In addition, you can use the following question-asking tools to keep the conversation moving.

- *Follow-the-answer* principle. After you ask a question, ask another question related to the answer to the previous question. Here's an example.

  Q: Where are you from? A: Buffalo, New York.

  Q: Did you grow up there? A: We lived there for a few years, and then we moved to Arlington, Virginia.

  Q: What took you to Arlington? A: My dad was in the military.

  Q: Oh, yeah? I was in the military too. What branch was your dad in?

- *Tell-me-about-that* principle. Here you ask an open-ended question related to the answer to a closed-ended question. An open-ended question is one whose answer is more than one or two words. A closed-ended question is the opposite. Open-ended questions get people talking in a free flowing manner. Your question is a few words; their answer, many.

  In this approach, you follow any answer with the statement, "Tell me about that" (or something similar). Here's an example.

  Q: Where are you from? A: Buffalo, New York.

  Q: Tell me about Buffalo.

  Q: What took you to Arlington? A: My dad was in the military.

  Q: Tell me about growing up in a military family.

- *How'd-you-like-that* principle. Although technically this isn't an open-ended question, it often has the effect of getting people to talk because it invites them to share their feelings. Here you follow any answer with the question, "How'd you like that?" (or something similar). Here's how it would work:

  Q: Where are you from? A: Buffalo, New York.

Q: How did you like Buffalo?

Q: What took you to Arlington? A: My dad was in the military.

Q: How did you like being in a military family?

Table 15

Question-asking Techniques	
Technique	Description
Follow-the-answer principle	Ask a question about the answer to a previous question
Tell-me-about-that principle	Following an answer, say, "Tell me about that"
How'd-you-like-that principle	Following an answer, ask, "How'd you like that?"

3. Dine: There is no better way to open the doors of the heart than to have someone into your home for a meal. The barriers and resistance we get when we go door-to-door to share the good news instantly melt away when we, as neighbors, coworkers, or friends, invite a fellow human being into our homes for dinner. In my experience, there is no better path to friendship—and ultimately meaningful spiritual interaction—than this.

If you go this route, here are some things to keep in mind. First, don't invite someone over for dinner until you have had a few chances to interact with them and learn a little something about them. If you are too quick with the invite, you can appear a little weird. On the flip side, don't wait too long; once you have a cordial relationship going, invite them over. You'll know when it's the right time.

When you do put out the invitation, it can sometimes be good to hint at it before you actually make the formal invitation. In other words, you may want to mention it at one encounter and then make the invite at another. Let's say you see your neighbor walking his dog and you walk out to say hello. This is the second or third time you've talked to him and you're now on a first name basis. You can go ahead and invite him then, or you could just say something like, "Hey, we should get our families together and cook some hotdogs or something." More than likely, he'll say, "Sure, that's a great idea." Then, you can say, "Let me talk to my wife [husband], and I'll get back to you." This is sort of an in-between invitation that comes off pretty natural.

Also, don't go overboard on dinner. You don't need to pull out the fine China and serve the roast beast. Keep it simple, and they will feel a lot more comfortable, and, it will be easier to pull off.

Finally, spiritual conversation is not required. In fact, the first couple of occasions you want to be very careful here. Your first goal is to become their friend (their *real* friend). Spiritual things will come later. Relax, have fun, laugh a lot. No pressure for you or your guests.

4. *Do*: Other than dinner, this is the best. When you find out what your friend likes to do, do it with them. Fishing, golfing, scrap booking, Wii-ing (is that a word?); the field is wide open. Take the time and initiative to engage them in activities that are fun and interesting *to them*. (Of course, don't go to the strip club with them if that's what they're into.) Again, spiritual things don't have to come up, especially in the beginning. After your friendship is solid, these events will be little mission trips for you.

Table 16

BUDDI System Summary		
Letter	Name	Description
B	Befriend	Make an acquaintance
U	Uncover	Learn about your friend
D	Dine	Have them over for dinner
D	Do	Do things they like
I	Improve	Help them when they need it

5. *Improve:* As you get to know more and more people and call more of them friends, trials inevitably will come up in their lives. These are your golden doors of opportunity to put into practice what you preach: love. Be available to help when they need you or when they are hurting. Call them to check on their sick mother-in-law; take them a dish after their baby is born; host the baby shower; cut their grass when their mower is down; go to their brother's funeral; clean their side of the dorm when they're sick. If you're paying attention, the opportunities will be limitless.

One pointer here: When you help, don't preach. In other words, don't shove the gospel down their throats every time they're down. You'll have your opportunity, but be sensitive as to the timing.

TALKING TO GOD ALONG THE WAY

I would be remiss in my duty to you if I didn't point you back to God as you begin and continue this process. As I noted previously, nearness to God is essential, not only in times of difficulty, as we discussed in chapter six, but also during the entire process of promoting truth. Once you take the first step, the game is on, and you had better believe the adversary will bring his best game. The fight is bigger than you, so never forget to pray. Here are a few things to pray about not only at the beginning, but throughout the REAP process.

- *Leading:* That God will show you exactly who to talk to, the ones he has chosen for you.

- *Courage:* That God will grant you the grace to do what is uncomfortable, like starting conversations, asking questions, and transitioning to spiritual topics.

- *Wisdom:* That you will be led to places where you can find solid answers to questions and that God will enlighten your mind as to how to deal with difficult subjects.

- *Time:* That he will grant you the discipline to make time in your schedule for this work.

- *Love:* That love will overflow from your heart for people regardless of their openness or reaction.

- *Success:* That God will save all those he desires to save and his purposes will not be blocked.

WRAPPING UP

Sometimes the hardest part about sharing your faith is getting to know new people who don't know Jesus. If you'll put into practice the simple things listed in this chapter, you'll quickly have a host of new friends that God will use you to influence.

Now let's move on to the *E* of our process, Educate, understanding the spiritual background and barriers of those we engage.

GROUP DISCUSSION QUESTIONS

1. How can we imitate Jesus in terms of the friends we chose? Elaborate.

2. Do you think it is hard to love a) non-Christians and b) non-Christians who reject your message? Why or why not?

3. Make a list of three people in your life that you could promote truth to now. How would you start the process?

4. What point in the BUDDI system seems most natural for you? Which is the most *un*natural? Why?

CHAPTER 9

UNDERSTANDING THE TERRAIN AHEAD: DISCOVERING OBJECTIONS TO FAITH

W e were sitting across the table from each other sharing a plate of meatloaf and gravy. Nat and I were traveling through my territory doing training for clients and showing our new technology. He was my "brains" guy, a super-guru engineer who helped customers with technical issues and explained the latest happenings in the industry.

I had met Nat some years before. In fact, he was one of the first people I met when I came on with the company. He took me under his wing and showed me the ropes. Although he was super smart, he was also fun to be around; he laughed a lot and didn't take things too seriously. But he had a deep side too, a philosophical tendency I liked. Like two peas in a pod, whenever we got together, we always seemed to gravitate toward spiritual topics. Today was no different.

On and off over the last few years, we had talked about God and Jesus and Christianity. Nat was not a believer, but he was nice about it. I was just starting to learn how to talk to non-Christians. Nat was my guinea pig, so to speak. I really didn't know where to go with him; his objections were way over my head, but I was starting to understand the real problem. A question formed in my mind, one I've used many times since to ferret out core issues. "What is the Bible to you, Nat?" I asked, my fork still in my hand. He paused for a moment and glanced off to the side, thinking it through, trying to find the right words. His eyes returned to mine. With a slight nod of the head, he said, "Mythology."

THE IMPORTANCE OF BACKGROUND AND BARRIERS

The devil is an expert marketer. Fifth Avenue's best are no match for him when it comes to promoting his product: lies. From cable television programs to the university and high school classroom, his message is everywhere. And what is it? Simple: the Bible isn't true. Whether it's "The Universe" on the History Channel promoting a false history of the world, or Dan Brown's novels questioning the trustworthiness of the gospels and integrity of the church, or Oprah Winfrey's New Age "god is in everyone" heresy, Christians and non-Christians alike are immersed in doubt-inspiring propaganda from every side.

In this environment, to assume the average non-Christian (like my friend Nat) has no issues that will keep him from being a sold-out, Bible-believing Jesus freak is absurd. Think about it like this: Why would you believe in the Jesus of the Bible if you have rejected the Bible of Jesus? Yet this is in practice what we do every Sunday. We preach and teach and talk like everybody accepts our faith as the foundation of all truth in the world. All we need to do is just proclaim our message a little longer, a little louder, and we'll win the day. Not only this, but our people get virtually no training in how to discover and diffuse the faith-destroying arguments of the culture. And we wonder why our outreach efforts fall flat.

So, after we have entered their lives as real friends, we must uncover anything hindering their full acceptance of our message. This is the *E* in our acronym for Educate, where we seek to understand the spiritual background and barriers of those we engage. Uncovering this information has two important benefits.

First, we can't get someone on the right road until we know which road they're on. Each person will have different issues based on their religious experiences and training, present theories about spiritual things, and hang-ups where Christianity is concerned. To ignore this is to handicap our efforts and risk not only failing to lead them to God, but making it harder for them to find him in the future. Secondly, when we engage people in these areas, it makes transitioning to the gospel easier later. Talking about God, the Bible, and Jesus become only a natural extension of the conversation when we're talking about spiritual things already.

Before we begin, it is important to note that these two issues are connected in most people; their religious background will shape not only their present beliefs but also their objections to Christianity. If a person is a second-generation agnostic, for example, they will likely view Christianity much differently than a person who was raised as a Mormon. But the views of both are driven by their religious background—and that's the point.

Although there is a definite connection, we'll deal with them separately in this chapter. So, let's begin with spiritual background.

SPIRITUAL BACKGROUND DEFINED

Spiritual background is defined as a person's past religious experiences and present religious beliefs. Everyone has a belief system they've formed over their lifetime to make sense of reality. This system contains convictions about spiritual matters, even if they don't believe in a supreme being or go to church. Everybody in America has an opinion about God, heaven and hell, morality, Jesus, and the Bible. Count on it. What we need to do first, in order to lead them into the kingdom, is understand that history and uncover those beliefs.

Here are some categories of information you'll want to uncover during this stage:

What is their spiritual history?

- Was their family Christian, atheist, agnostic, Muslim, Hindu, or something else?

- Did they go to church growing up? If so, where and what kind?

- Were their parents spiritual or church-going?

- Was their parents' faith real? Did it flow through and change their lives so that they practiced what they preached?

- What kind of experience did they have in church?

- Have they attended church as an adult?

What are their present beliefs?

- About truth?

- About God?

- About Jesus?

- About the Bible?

- About heaven and hell?

- About life after death?

This information will be critical later when you attempt to get them past their issues to the cross of Christ. If you don't really understand where they are coming from, you'll struggle to give them an answer that connects with them. Once I was talking to a man about the Bible. He said he didn't think all that it said was absolute. I, not knowing his background, proceeded to talk about why we should receive Scripture as our authority. Only later did I realize that he came from a heavy Catholic background where the church spoke for Scripture. His issue wasn't with the Bible necessarily—it was with the Catholic Church's interpretation of and additions to Scripture. I could have done a better job of leading him if I had not jumped to conclusions, assuming I knew where he was coming from when I really didn't.

You can gather this information by using some of the questions listed later in the chapter.

SPIRITUAL BARRIERS DEFINED

A spiritual barrier, in this context, is any objection that must be overcome before a person will commit fully to being a disciple of Jesus. From evolution to hypocrisy to Bible errors—barriers to faith are rampant today; from copies to truth to false religion—reasons to disbelieve, a plentiful commodity.

Here are some of the things you will want to know:

- Of what are they skeptical? Religion, hypocrites, truth, the Bible, Jesus, God, or other?

- Why are they skeptical? What are their specific issues?

- What are their questions about Christianity and its teachings?

- What are their misunderstandings about true Christianity and its teachings?

- What is keeping them from trusting the Bible and believing the gospel?

Barriers are revealed when you start to ask about their spiritual background and present beliefs (previous section). In other words, when your friend starts talking about his background (religious or non-religious) and his present beliefs at the same time, he will be revealing his barriers to trusting Christ. All you have to do is listen carefully and compare his answers to the biblical truth you already know. That comparison will highlight for you key areas of concern and the objections or barriers you must overcome. Let me give you an example.

Let's say I'm talking to a person for the first time and I transition our conversation to spiritual things. As we move through the discussion (I'll walk you through how to do this in just a moment), I ask him about his background and present beliefs. Based on my simple questions, I learn the following:

- He was raised in a Methodist church.
- His parents were not really religious people; they just went to church on Sunday.
- He left the church after he entered college.
- He now attends a Universalist church (everybody is saved).
- He believes in the Great Entity (this is "god" to him).
- He doesn't believe in hell.
- He believes all religions are equally valid.
- He thinks the Bible is full of errors and contradictions.

You see, just by letting him talk about his religious past and present beliefs I have all I need to move on to the next step. I don't have to ask him directly why he doesn't believe in Jesus or the Bible, though I certainly can. He'll tell me on his own. Of course, this information may stir me to ask other questions, but the point is, I get both things I'm looking for with one set of questions.

So what kinds of questions can I ask?

COMMON QUESTIONS TO IDENTIFY SPIRITUAL BACKGROUND AND BARRIERS

Here are some questions you can use to uncover this information.

General Questions: These are questions you ask to get your friend talking about their past and beliefs. They make for good questions at the beginning of a spiritual discussion.

- Was your family a spiritual family?
- Is your family a spiritual family?
- Are you a spiritual person?
- What are your beliefs about God?
- Are you a "church-going" person?
- Tell me what you believe about heaven and hell.

- What are your views on religion?
- Tell what you believe about Jesus.

Specific Questions: These are follow-up questions you can use to get more detailed information on important spiritual subjects. Use them to drill down in areas of concern or to clarify statements made to a general question (above).

God
- Do you believe in God?
- What is God to you?
- What kind of a person is God?
- Can we know God?
- Do all religions lead to the same God?

Bible
- What do you think of the Bible?
- What is the Bible to you?
- Have you ever studied the Bible?
- Do you think the Bible is "God's Word"?
- Is the Bible true?

Jesus
- Who is Jesus to you?
- Why did Jesus die?
- Do you think Jesus was a real man?
- Do you think Jesus was God?

Salvation
- Do you believe in heaven and hell?
- How does a person get to heaven?
- What is "sin" to you?

- How does a person remove his/her sin?

Truth
- Can we know truth?
- How can we know truth?
- Is there absolute truth?
- Is truth relative?

Church
- Did you go to church when you were younger?
- What was your parents' faith like?
- What do you think of church?
- What kind of experiences have you had in the church?
- Why have you given up on church?

How do you know when you've got a problem? I can't give you an exact rule here. However, in general, when a person's beliefs reject a major biblical teaching, a red flag should go up. Major teachings include the existence of God, the nature of God (Triune, personal, knowable, creator, judge), the existence of truth, the reliability of Scripture, the deity of Jesus, the exclusivity of Jesus, the existence of heaven and hell, the reality of miracles, and salvation by faith in Christ alone. I'm sure you can think of others, but this is a broad-brush list to get you started.

Also, you can tell by the types of answers you get. If you get one or more of the following types of responses, you have some work to do before you can get them to the cross.

God
- I don't believe in God.
- I have my own view of God.
- God is the Great Entity.
- God is in all of us.

- God would not send anyone to hell.
- No one can understand the infinite.
- I don't know if there is a God or not.

Bible

- The Bible is a good book, but was written by men.
- The Bible was good until it was distorted so badly.
- The Bible has been copied so many times; how can you trust it?
- I believe in evolution, not the Bible.
- I don't believe in talking serpents.
- I believe in science.
- The Bible is full of mythology.
- The Bible is full of contractions and errors.

Jesus

- Jesus was a good person, but he wasn't God's Son.
- Jesus died to show us an example of sacrifice.
- We don't even know if Jesus ever lived.
- The church made Jesus divine, not Jesus.
- Jesus never claimed to be God.

Salvation

- I'm basically a good person, so I know I'll go to heaven.
- Sin is something we imagine, but it isn't real.
- If it's wrong to you, it's sin.
- There is no afterlife.
- God would not send anyone to hell.

Truth

- I don't think anyone can really know truth absolutely.
- That may be true for you, but not for me.

- Truth is relative.
- No one can know truth for sure.
- How do you know you're right and I'm wrong?
- It doesn't matter what you believe as long as you love others.

Church
- I don't believe in organized religion.
- I think all religions are the same.
- All Christians are hypocrites.
- All religions lead to the same God.
- I am a Muslim (or any religion other than biblical Christianity).

You may be asking yourself where to start. People in our culture are so twisted in their thinking, they may reject virtually every major biblical teaching. How do I know where to go first? What should my priorities be? Good questions. But for right now, we just want to get the information out of them. We'll discuss what to do with it in the next chapter.

POINTERS AND A CASE STUDY

Let me give you a few pointers where gathering this information is concerned. These are practical suggestions I've picked up over the years that may help you as you begin.

1. *Move through a progression in your questions.* In other words, don't just blurt out something like, "So, you a spiritual guy, Bob?" as soon as you meet the guy. It is much more natural—and less in-your-face—to lead up to that question. Start with personal questions and then to family questions (from chapter eight). From family questions transition to spiritual questions.

Question Progression Funnel

2. *Pick a transition question and use it as often as you can.*
   You want to develop a pattern in your questions so
   you can get comfortable and come off as natural
   as possible. I like to use one of the first two from
   the General Questions listed above, like, "Was your
   family a spiritual family?" or, "Is your family a spiritual family?" The former if we are talking about my
   friend's family growing up (mom and dad, brothers and sisters); the latter if we are talking about his
   immediate family now (spouse and kids). It flows
   very well when I do it like that.

Question Progression

Tell me about your family.

Is your family a spiritual family?

Are you a spiritual person?

Question Progression Example

3. *Get the big picture before you think about answering.* Find out what your friend believes in at least the first four areas listed in the Specific Questions section (God, Bible, Jesus, Salvation) before you try to respond in any way. Don't jump to conclusions with partial information.

4. *Ask clarifying questions.* You'll be tempted from the outset to start answering their questions or arguing against their beliefs. Resist that temptation. Relax and make sure you really understand what they are saying. Their will be a time for responding, but

this isn't it. You are not in a fight. You are trying to understand so you can enlighten. Also, when you do answer, answer only specifics—you can't answer a generality.

5. *Gather this information in a conversation, not an interrogation.* You must practice having a conversation with your friend. You are not a highly paid attorney on a capital murder case. Ask questions and listen. Be interested. Smile. Ask more questions. Listen some more. Remember, you're just talking with a buddy or girlfriend.

6. *This conversation may happen in installments.* You may start your discussion at lunch break one day and then get cut off, finishing it three weeks later. Be patient. God will arrange for another meeting. You're in this for the long run anyway, right?

So, how might this conversation take place in real life? Picking up with the spiritual transition, here's a quick dialogue between me and a friend.

Wes: "Did you grow up around here, Mark?" [This is a question intended to get him to talk about his family growing up.]

Mark: "Actually, I didn't. I grew up in Omaha."

Wes: "Is that right? Tell me about Omaha." [This is one of the question techniques from chapter eight.]

Mark: [He tells me all about it.]

Wes: "So did you have a big family in Omaha?"

Mark: "I have two younger brothers."

Wes: "Was your family a spiritual family?" [Spiritual transition question.]

Mark: "Well, we went to church here and there, mostly around the holidays. But my parents weren't really religious people."

Wes: "How about you? Are you a spiritual guy?" [More specific spiritual question to get him to tell me what he believes.]

Mark: "Not really. I've always been the analytic type. There's just not enough proof for me."

Wes: "Proof for what? God?" [God is always a good place to start. It is a foundation point.]

Mark: "Yeah, I guess. I'm a man of science, and it's just hard to believe in things you can't see or prove."

Wes: "I know what you mean. So what do you believe about God?"

Of course, the conversation could go on and on, but you get the point. All I'm trying to do is lead him to tell me what is already there inside of him. Then, later I can determine how best to handle his issues.

STOP HERE, THIS IS AS FAR AS I CAN GO

You may be reading this, thinking, *Okay, I'm with you thus far. But I just can't go any further. I can be a friend, ask better questions, entertain, and maybe figure out why my friend won't believe. But I just can't take the next step of getting into a deep discussion about their issues or presenting the gospel. Should I just give up, or are there other options for me?*

Well, I have some good news for you: You are not alone. Many Christians have this same struggle. Sometimes we feel like we don't have the right gifts or skills to engage the person at the next level. Other times, frankly, we're just too scared. Yet we feel a responsibility and a desire to be a part of God's redemptive plan for those around us. We want to do more.

So, first, let me tell you *it's all right to feel this way.* You are not a disobedient disciple because you have this struggle. Don't feel inferior or be down on yourself; our Father knows the intent of your heart, and he is overjoyed with your desire to please him through obedience. Secondly, be encouraged because *there is a lot you can still do.* You are and can continue to be a critical player in God's purpose for those around you. Let me share a few things you can do from this point forward.

WHAT TO DO WHEN YOU CAN'T DO ANYMORE

1. *Don't underestimate yourself.* You may think your sense of fear or inadequacy is a sign that you've reached the limits of your abilities or calling. While possible, this may not be the case. Feeling fear or inadequacy coupled with a desire to do something more anyway can be a sign to step out of your comfort zone and grow. Your gifts may be hidden or simply need further development through experience. In my own case, early on when I thought about or tried to promote truth to others, I experienced a tremendous amount of trepidation and found myself ill equipped to deal with the questions and objections of others. But there was something inside me pushing me to engage others anyway. Over the years, I have learned how to do it better (which is what you are reading in this book) and have acquired, through a lot of hard work, many of the answers I need.

2. *Accomplish the plan up until this point.* Develop friendships with the lost around you, understand their spiritual background, and identify their barriers to faith—those things we have outlined thus far. You may wonder what you can or cannot do after these steps, but if you are to be used in any way, you must be engaged at this level. Remember, do these naturally; don't put pressure on yourself. Ask questions and listen to the answers. Make the friendship strong.

3. *Share resources to help address barriers and make the gospel presentation.* So, in this situation—where you don't think you can continue alone—the key to fulfilling the next two steps, the *A* and *P* of our acronym, is to use the gifts of others to finish the process. You don't have to know all the answers, just *know the people who do;* you don't have to give an eloquent gospel presentation, just *put them in front of someone who can.* Here are a few different ways to do this:

a. *Get input from your Christian leaders.* Have a conversation with a wise Christian you trust about your friend, their background, and their issues. Get some ideas as to what to do next or how you should respond to a question or objection. Wise Christian leaders can recommend strategy, share stories of similar experiences with others, and send you to resources you never knew existed.

b. *Give them a book, article, CD, or DVD that addresses their issue.* This is a low-pressure way to start overcoming their objection. A couple of pointers here. One, make sure you ask them what media they prefer (do they read a lot, or do they prefer to watch something on video or listen on their iPod?). You want to get them the resource they are most likely to use. Two, review the resource yourself. You don't have to know it all; just be familiar with it in case you get a question or it leads to further conversation. Three, follow up on the resource. Don't call them the next day or anything, but make a note to follow up after a few weeks to see if they got anything out of it.

c. *Schedule an introduction to someone else.* When your relationship is strong enough, you can ask your friend to have lunch with you and another Christian who can help you deal with their concerns. Make sure the Christian you invite is good with people, aware of the sensitivities of the lost, and knowledgeable in the subject matter at hand. An enhancement to your relationship, a credit to Christ—this is what you want this person to be.

d. *Invite them to an appropriate event.* Group events can be a real plus here. At any one time, there may be several events in your area that would address your friend's issues. Whether they are answers about evolution, the basics of Christianity, or the gospel itself, you are likely to find helpful gatherings in close driving distance to which you can take your friend. A couple of recommendations here as well. Make sure the event fits the need. Don't take them to just any gathering; ensure it focuses on their interests. Also, don't take them to some high-powered evangelist unless that is the need at the time.

5. *Pray earnestly.* Nothing—no event, no resource, no other person—can do what prayer can do. No matter where you are in the process, never stop praying for real spiritual change in your friend, the success of your efforts to reach him, and wisdom to know what to do next.

6. *Keep the friendship alive and growing.* You may reach a stage where you are not sure what to do next. Or, your efforts to move the spiritual conversation along may meet some resistance or delay. Regardless of these things, keep the friendship alive. Continue to reach out in a non-spiritual way, strengthening the bonds for when God brings about the next step.

Table 17

Steps When You Can't Go Further
1. Don't underestimate yourself
2. Accomplish the plan until this point
3. Share resources to address issues or share gospel
4. Pray earnestly
5. Keep the friendship alive and growing

You may think you can't do much, but if you will step a bit out of your comfort zone, you can still make a big impact by following these simple guidelines. It isn't important who does the work, only that it gets done. Using your friendship as the foundation and your Christian brothers and sisters as your resources, you can complete your task and see your friend become a genuine, radical disciple.

THE NEXT STEP

Now that you understand some of their potential roadblocks, you can begin to address them. That's what the next chapter is all about. What is the most important issue to address? Where do I go for resources? What process should I follow? These questions and more will be covered next.

GROUP DISCUSSION QUESTIONS

1. Have you ever met or talked to someone who was like Nat, with a tough objection to Christianity or the Bible? Elaborate.

2. In your own words, how will understanding your friend's spiritual background and barriers help you lead them closer to faith in Christ?

3. Of the General Questions listed to get your friend talking about spiritual things, which did you like best? Why?

4. Are you encouraged that there are things you can do even if you don't feel comfortable getting into a detailed discussion of your friend's objections or presenting the gospel yourself? Why or why not?

CHAPTER 10

ROADSIDE ASSISTANCE: OVERCOMING BARRIERS WITH ANSWERS

I can still remember the '84 starting lineup of the Atlanta Braves, my favorite baseball team growing up. There was Chris Chambliss at first, Glenn Hubbard (he was a short guy with a beard) at second, and Rafael Ramirez at short. Bob Horner played the hot corner, and Bruce Benedict caught. In the outfield you had Claudell Washington (a lefty with a smooth swing) and Gerald Perry in right (actually, I forgot about Gerald, so I had to look him up). And then there was *the man, my man,* Dale Murphy. Boy, how I loved that guy.

Born to be a baseball player, Murph—that's what they called him back then—played center, ran like the wind, and hit homers like rockets. I remember one in particular, a zinger over the right field wall. From the instant it left his bat, it couldn't have gone higher than twenty feet all the way out. That thing was a missile!

Murph was my baseball hero. Yet there is one big disappointment for me where he is concerned: he's not in the Hall of Fame. And I don't like that … at all. Let me tell you why.

First, his stats for that time period were absolutely stellar. He led the National League twice in homeruns and RBIs (that's runs-batted-in for those of you who live on Mars); he was only the sixth player ever to have thirty homeruns and thirty stolen bases in the same season. Moreover, he was the only player ever to have a .300 batting average, hit thirty homeruns, drive in 120 runners, score 130 runs himself, and steal thirty bases in the same season (1983). And, don't forget, this was way before steroids.

Dale Murphy should be in the Hall of Fame. That's my position. But, obviously, not everybody agrees with me. While acknowledging the facts I just presented, some will say his weaknesses are too great to merit Hall admittance. They will point out, for example, his high career strikeouts—1,748—his not-so-impressive lifetime batting average of .265, and his decline in productivity at a relatively early age.

In response, I say he has more than made up for these weaknesses by his positive influence on the game and sports in general since his retirement, like founding iWontCheat.com, a nonprofit organization that encourages kids, parents, and coaches not to cheat by using performance enhancing drugs.

I think he should be in the Hall of Fame, and I believe you should too.

What does this have to do with promoting truth? Why am I telling you this? This isn't a book about baseball players who should have been elected to the Hall of Fame, after all. Why, then, take the time to debate the issue here? Because this is apologetics (what I call *giving answers*). What I just did on behalf of my hero, Dale Murphy, is, in effect, apologetics, the subject of this chapter.

Apologetics is a big word, but don't let it intimidate you. It comes from the Greek word *apologia,* which means "to defend." Any time you take a position on something—from politics, to movies, to Dale Murphy—someone will disagree with you. They will challenge your position, and you will have to defend it. I have a position about Dale Murphy (and I just happen to be right), but others disagree, so I must defend what I believe. When I do this, I'm engaging in apologetics.

I also take a position on Jesus Christ, the Christian Bible, and the Christian faith. I believe—as do you and millions of others on planet earth—that Jesus is the unique Son of God; that the Bible is God's singular, complete, and credible communication to man; and that Christianity is the world's only true, God-given faith system. Not everybody agrees with me, so I must defend what I believe. Furthermore, as someone called to convert others, I must also use apologetics to help others overcome their objections to Christianity and put their faith in the Jesus of the Scriptures also.

People attack our belief system every day. Through instruments like evolution, questions about God's existence, the possibility of miracles, and the lies of false faith systems, the arrows fly from every corner. And the adversary's tactics, as J.R. showed Carter in the opening chapter, are taking a heavy toll on the kingdom now and will be only more devastating in the future if we don't overcome them.

THE ROLES OF GIVING ANSWERS (APOLOGETICS)

Giving answers accomplishes two important objectives. First, it strengthens the faith of the believer. All of us have questions about our faith, nagging issues that exist in the back of our minds that make us wonder. Each of these is like a time bomb in our faith foundation. If we aren't careful, these time bombs can explode and destroy our faith. Over time, the doubts mount up, but the answers never come. So eventually we give up and walk away from Jesus altogether. Sadly, you and I both know people who were raised as Christians only to turn away from the faith because of questions that were never answered.

A Believer's Faith Foundation

Questions Destroy Our Faith Foundation

We can't afford to ignore the questions our members, fellow Christians, children, or new disciples have about Christianity. Far from this, we must proactively identify and remove these doubts, solidifying their faith in God, the Bible, and Jesus. This is what giving answers can do.

The second critical use of giving answers is as an aid to conversion. Today, when someone glances at the cross, they see a stone wall. That wall represents the doubts they have about our faith. If we want them to take the cross seriously, we must tear down that wall and rebuild it on the other side, showing the lost that the truth always leads to the cross. Giving answers is our way of doing this.

Questions Create a Stone Wall for the Lost

Giving Answers Moves the Wall

One final note before we move on. It is important to under-stand that *giving answers is not the gospel*. In other words, it is not in itself God's good news of the way of salvation. Giving answers is only a tool to get people to take the good news seriously, to receive it as more than mythology or fairy tales. I've heard people say, "Nobody ever got saved through apologetics." While this may be true, I know many who have been lost without it.

GIVING ANSWERS IN THE BIBLE

The concept of giving answers is a biblical one. God, the Creator of our minds, has made us thinking, reasoning creatures. And while there is always a requirement for faith, *it is not a blind faith.* We believe in things we cannot see, but not in things of which we have no proof. Let me illustrate it for you.

You remember the movie *The Wizard of Oz,* I'm sure. Dorothy follows the Yellow Brick Road to see the Wizard. She takes the road in the first place because Glenda, the Good Witch of the

North, and the Munchkins tell her to. As she walks, she sees signs that say, "Emerald City—This way," and she follows. The people who live along the road confirm the signs—Emerald City up ahead. Then, as she gets closer, she sees the city in the distance with the road heading off in that direction. But she still can't actually *see the road entering the city;* her view is blocked by the rolling hills.

All of sudden, the Scarecrow stops her and says, "What if the road doesn't lead us to the city after all, Dorothy? We can't actually *see it* going into the city, you know." Dorothy replies, "Yes, you're right, Scarecrow. But we have plenty of evidence to support believing it does. Remember the Witch of the North told me it would take us there, and the signs along the way said it would, and even the people who lived along the road said it would. And now you can see for yourself that it heads off in that direction. No, we *can't see it actually entering the gates,* but we *have faith it will* because the evidence confirms that conclusion." Convinced, they continue, reach Emerald City, and meet the Wizard of Oz.

That's how the Christian faith works. We finish our journey with faith, but the evidence overwhelmingly confirms our conclusion.

So, does anyone in the Bible give answers? The short answer is yes. First, there are the explicit instructions. Many would point to 1 Peter 3:15, which reads, "But in your hearts set apart Christ as Lord. *Always be prepared to give an answer* to everyone who asks you to give the reason for the hope that you have." As I've argued previously, I'm not sure this is a command to do what we would traditionally call apologetics, or giving answers. It uses the Greek word, *apologia,* but Peter uses it when referring to claiming Christ in the context of persecution. Furthermore, if we only defended the faith when someone asked us, as the text clearly states, we wouldn't be doing a lot of giving answers. The fact is, most people don't ask.

Perhaps a better direct text is 2 Corinthians 10:5 where Paul writes, "We demolish arguments and every pretension that sets itself up against the knowledge of God, and we take captive every thought to make it obedient to Christ."[57] While the word *apologia* does not occur in this verse, the word *arguments* does. This word literally means "reasonings," and the word *demolish* means "to wage war against."[58] So we are waging war against reasonings that set themselves up, or exalt themselves, against the knowledge of God. While Paul is probably talking about any argument that leads to unrighteousness or sin, the principle is very much applicable to giving answers in the traditional sense.

While the actual direct commandments to give answers may not be numerous, the examples of it taking place in Scripture are plentiful. Let me give you just three, starting with two lesser-known examples and concluding with a famous one.

There's an intriguing example in the book of Joshua (4:1–9). Just after the people crossed the Jordan in a breathtaking miracle, God sent twelve men back into the riverbed. They were to find twelve stones and bring them back to the camp where Joshua would stack them. The Scripture tells us the reason God did this—to serve as a sign. These stones are to "serve as a sign among you. [So that] in the future, when your children ask you, 'What do these stones mean?' tell them that the flow of the Jordan was cut off before the ark of the covenant of the Lord" (6–7).

Now, why didn't God just have the eyewitnesses tell their children about this miraculous event years later? Certainly, people are expected to believe without *any proof*, right? Wrong. God knew these stones would serve as *evidence* that what the children were told was true, and if they didn't believe it, they could go back and check it out themselves. The writer even says, "And they are there *to this day*" (verse 9).

Table 18

Giving Answers in the Bible	
Commands	*Passage*
Peter	1 Peter 3:15
Paul	2 Corinthians 10:5
Examples	*Passage*
Joshua	Joshua 4:1-9
Jesus	John 10:38
Paul	1 Corinthians 15:3-8

A second example comes from the words of Jesus in John 10:38. Jesus was having another confrontation with the Pharisees; they were objecting to his claims to deity (John 10:30). In his response to their unbelief, he says this, "Even though you don't believe me, *believe the miracles...*" Did you read that? *Believe the miracles.* In other words, he knew what he was claiming—that he was God in person—challenged their minds to the maximum. So he gave them *proof,* evidence, that his word was true, the miracles.

If Jesus gives answers, shouldn't we?

Then, of course, there's St. Paul's famous passage in 1 Corinthians:

> For what I received I passed on to you as of first importance: that Christ died for our sins according to the Scriptures, that he was buried, that he was raised on the third day according to the Scriptures, and that he appeared to Peter, and then to the Twelve. After that, he appeared to more than five hundred of the brothers at the same time, *most of whom are still living,* though some have fallen asleep. Then he appeared to James, then to all the apostles, and last of all he appeared to me also, as to one abnormally born.
>
> 1 Corinthians 15:3–8

So, again, why did Paul even say this? Apparently, some people were claiming that Jesus was not resurrected at all (15:12). Paul was defending this truth not by simply declaring it to be so louder than others were claiming it wasn't. *He offered proof.* He listed those who had actually seen him alive. Then, he went even further, claiming that many of them were *still* alive. Why? So if you were one who doubted, you could go check it out for yourself. Just like Joshua's twelve stones, Paul pointed skeptics to the evidence, in this case, the hundreds of eyewitnesses.

BARRIER CATEGORIES

Barriers to faith are about as wide ranging as people. However, in our culture there are several categories we can identify that contain most of what you will face on a day-to-day basis. Here is a short list of categories and a brief explanation of each. (A more detailed discussion of these, along with important strategy tips, is included in Appendix 2.)

Science and evolution: Our culture is bombarded with scientific information that supposedly makes the Bible obsolete and foolish. Whether it's the Bible's creation account, Adam and Eve, Cain's wife, the global flood, or Noah's Ark, science takes aim at Scripture and rarely lets up. Children are trained from their earliest years in evolutionary theory; they learn it in school, watch it on the Discovery Channel, and read about it in their history books. It undermines the authority and reliability of the Bible and causes many to reject the biblical Jesus.

Document Issues: There are a host of false ideas floating around in the culture about the documents of the Bible. Many of these issues surfaced in a novel a few years ago entitled *The Da Vinci Code.* Many believe the gospels were chosen as part of a conspiracy; still others don't trust the Bible's documents because man had a part in their writing, while others believe the Bible has so many errors that it—in its modern iterations—hardly represents what was originally written.

Truth Questions: Some doubt there is any truth at all, while others simply say we can't know; still others claim that it's relative, changing with every situation. This objection gets in the way of biblical faith because the Bible not only assumes there is truth, but that there is someone who incarnates that truth, Jesus of Nazareth (John 14:6).

God Questions: These are questions about the existence of God, his nature and attributes, and whether he is knowable or just an impersonal force. This category also includes questions about suffering—how he could allow suffering if he is good?—and skepticism about miracles.

Bible Questions: Supposed contradictions or mistakes in the Bible, questions about peculiar biblical sayings, misunderstandings about the teachings of Scripture, different "interpretations" held by different Christian groups—these are the concerns of this category.

Jesus Questions: Who was the real Jesus? Was he only a man, a teacher, a wise man? Does he still exist today? Is he an impersonal force or a real person? Was he divine, or did others make up this claim about him? Was he really resurrected? Why did he die?

Christianity vs. Other Faith Systems: How can Christianity be the only true religion with all the other religions in the world? What makes Christianity unique? Are Islam and Christianity the same? Can you prove you are right and others are wrong?

Table 19

Barrier Categories Summary
Science and Evolution
Document Issues
Truth Questions
God Questions
Bible Questions
Jesus Questions
Christianity vs. Other Faith Systems

THE PROCESS OF GIVING ANSWERS

So, at this point in our process we have asked a lot of questions and should have a good idea what our friend's issues really are. What next? Well, first of all you need to decide which particular question or group of questions (sometimes you can distill them down into an underlying theme) to address. Prioritize them in your mind, either by importance theologically or importance to them. Obviously, whether or not the Bible has been corrupted by man is a more important issue than whether or not Moses actually wrote the book of Genesis.

Furthermore, if the person brings up hypocrisy five times and Cain's wife only once, you may want to attack the hypocrisy issue first. Another good rule is never get caught up with trivial matters; you want to major on the majors. Things like the trustworthiness and validity of Scripture, key gospel concepts like sin, judgment, and forgiveness; the deity, resurrection, and death of Jesus; and key elements of God's nature and character are where you should spend most of your time. On a related note, don't feel like you have to answer every question. We'll talk about this more in just a moment, but what you really want to do is pick a few foundational issues, address them, and move to biblical truth.

You can also start by undermining their belief system first. You know what they believe based on your questioning; now take what you know and shoot it down. For example, let's say your friend believes that evolution is true and, therefore, Christianity cannot be. Most of us would start by defending our faith—because we're offended by their unbelief—but our arguments will hit harder if we show some discipline and put our friend on his heels first. So you start by revealing the weaknesses of evolutionary theory—mutations and natural selection don't add information, dating methods are based on unproveable assumptions, the fossil record is incomplete—knocking him off his intellectual high horse and giving your arguments for the faith more impact.

Once you've settled on the question you want to overcome, here's a simple process to work through to bring a solid answer.

1. *Understand the issue.* Don't jump to conclusions. Make sure you understand exactly what the person is saying before you start answering. I've wasted a lot of energy giving an answer only to find out I didn't really understand the subtle nuance of the person's issue.

2. *Research the issue.* If you don't know the answer when the question comes up, be honest. Promise to bring back a good answer in the future (even if you think you know, it may be wise to take some time and get it exactly right). Then go research the answer. If you get stuck, reach out to a Christian friend or pastor for advice. Also, be sure to bathe the entire process in prayer. Places to research answers are listed in Appendix 1.

3. *Share the information.* When you have the answer, organize it in your mind or write it down on paper so you can clearly communicate it. Think through any objections you may get and how you could respond. When you give the answer, if an issue comes up you can't answer, again, be honest; go get the answer and come back. Don't just start babbling. In the long-term, you'll have more credibility and you'll learn more yourself. Finally, be sure to leave them something to read so they can investigate it in more detail later.

   You have several options when it comes time to give the answer to your friend. You can schedule another meeting with them and share it in person, or you could send them something (like an e-mail response, article, book, CD, or DVD) and then set a follow-up meeting to discuss what you sent. Another option, if you think the discussion could be a lengthy one (this happens in the cultivate and sow stages in particular), agree with your friend to have an ongoing dialogue about the subject over e-mail. Also, as I mentioned in the last chapter, you can invite them to an event that addresses their issue, if one is available.

4. *Drive to the Bible at a minimum, the cross if at all possible.* Remember: our goal is not to win an argument but to remove barriers so this person can believe. Therefore, I recommend you think through how you can transition from the question at hand to the authority and reliability of the Bible or to Jesus Christ directly and salvation. We don't want to get bogged down trying to answer every question and never getting to the core issues. Spend the time needed, obviously, but at some point drive them to the truth.

   Here's an example. Let's say my friend has an issue with the errors in the copies of the New Testament. First, I need to give him the answer to his question. In short, although the New Testament documents aren't perfect, they are the most well-preserved documents in the world. (See Appendix 1 for specific resources for this question.) Then, I'd say something like this, "So, you can see, though many people doubt the Bible because they think it isn't reliable, the reality is just the opposite. And this is what we'd expect if the Bible is what it claims to be—inspired and preserved by God. Maybe there's something to this Bible thing after all."

5. *Plan the next step.* After the meeting, spend some time thinking through how you can engage the person again in the future to lead them even further down the road to genuine faith. Ask yourself, "Now that we've dealt with that issue, what is the logical next step in our discussion?"

THE IMPORTANCE OF STARTING ASSUMPTIONS

Giving answers, overall, is about facts, evidence, and arguments—sharing information that isn't commonly reported about our faith or about false belief systems. But there is one thing we must keep in mind when considering facts and evidence: they don't speak for themselves.[59]

Everyone comes to the facts with a set of starting assumptions that color their view of facts. Some call this their "worldview" or "bias." Whether it's the facts about the preservation of the New Testament copies, the dinosaurs, dating methods, or God himself, we are all biased in some way. Peter Galling of Answers in Genesis discusses this idea in relation to the creation/evolution issue, but it applies across the board. He writes the following:

> Much of the problem stems from the different *starting points* of creationists and Darwinists. Everyone, scientist or not, must start their quests for knowledge with some unproveable axiom—some *a priori* belief on which they sort through experience and deduce other truths. This starting point, whatever it is, can only be accepted by faith; eventually, in each belief system, there must be some unproveable, presupposed foundation for reasoning (since an infinite regression is impossible).
>
> For Bible-believing Christians, God's Word is our starting point: our presupposed foundation through which we interpret and balance fallen man's ideas, including those derived scientifically. Although some may consider this a foolish faith, *everyone* has such faith in *something*. But which is foolish: faith in the unmovable Word of the omniscient creator God or faith in man's fallible, changing ideas?[60]

The truth about starting assumptions will impact how those outside the faith accept the answers you give them. People in our culture are raised skeptical of Christianity and biased against its major teachings. Consequently, as you share answers with people, you may notice that many resist your ideas and always come up with another objection. Talking to them becomes a little like a verbal tennis match; no matter what you say, they have a comeback. If this happens, you may need to regroup and address the issue of starting assumptions before you can make any real headway with your answers. In fact, in some cases you may even want to begin here as well.

Also, keep in mind that bias toward Christianity is not always based on what one has been taught through the years. Sometimes questions or intellectual objections are only a smoke screen for the real issues. Some cling to objections because they have sin to hide; they have some lifestyle that they know is wrong but don't want to change. Perhaps they're living with their girlfriend, love porn, or are entangled in some immorality they don't want to give up. They don't want God telling them what to do, so they find a way to write off Scripture based on what they saw on television or read in high school biology. These are the sons and daughters of Psalm 2.

Then there's the person who rejects Christianity intellectually but is actually just defending themselves from pain in their past. The faith is off the table because some Christian years ago hurt them. They don't want to say this directly, so instead they use a false intellectual concern to justify their heart-born rejection.

Whatever the case, our job is the same: deal with the objection as if it were real. Once you deal with the intellectual issue, you'll be free to explore other possible causes. But if you don't deal with the question, you'll never know.

When you feel it's necessary, here's a simple way to take on the starting assumptions issue:

1. *Pray that God will open their eyes,* allowing them to consider evidence with a different set of starting assumptions (namely that the Bible is true) and recognize the bias they already have.

2. *Challenge them with the truth about starting assumptions and bias* when you discuss spiritual truth with them. Politely call them out on their bias and explain the role of starting assumptions to them. Ask them to consider the possibility that your answers are right in order to objectively consider them.

3. *Give them information to challenge their starting assumptions.* Make sure your answers are sound, reasonable, and well thought out. Be ready for counter arguments and always be kind and respectful in your

discussions. Eventually, with the Spirit's help, you'll win the battle.

CONCLUSION

Giving answers is an essential part of expanding the kingdom of God and bringing genuine cultural change to our nation. This critical action is taught in principle in the Bible, and characters throughout its pages—from Joshua, to Jesus, to Paul—have used its power to illicit faith. While a limitless number of objections exist, there are fact-based, reasonable answers to every question. By understanding the issues of our friends, researching answers, and presenting truth in a compelling and loving way, we can overcome any barrier and see true transformation in those around us.

Now for the final leg of our strategy, the *P* of our acronym, Present, sharing the gospel in a relevant and impactful way.

GROUP DISCUSSION QUESTIONS

1. What are the two roles of giving answers (apologetics)? Do you see these as important functions? Why or why not?

2. Were you surprised at the prevalence of giving answers in the Bible (Joshua, Jesus, and Paul)? Can you think of any other examples in Scripture? What are they?

3. Can you name any barrier categories other than those listed? What would they be?

4. Have you ever debated back and forth with a non-Christian without getting anywhere? After the discussion of starting assumptions, would you change any of your tactics? If so, what would you change?

CHAPTER 11

HITTING THE BULL'S-EYE: COMMUNICATING THE GOSPEL WITH IMPACT

Oh, how my feet hurt, she thought as she slipped her toes into the steamy, hot water. Ginger was sitting in her living room chair, soaking her feet after a long day of waiting tables. She ran a small restaurant in the corner of a strip mall department store. They sold hamburgers and BLTs and French fries. She didn't make much, but it's the only skill she had and the only job she could find since Ted left several months ago.

I'm glad he's gone, she admitted to herself bitterly. He had hopped from job to job, bar to bar, and woman to woman for most of their sixteen-year marriage—if that's what you wanted to call it. With him, it was always an excuse, always somebody else's fault. Oh, the opportunities he had over the years to change and make the family's life better! But he blew every one, and with each failure drained a little more hope from her life. *This was not what I pictured my family would be like,* she lamented. *How did I get here?*

It wouldn't have been so bad except for their four young children. Though Ted was never much of a father, the kids missed him, as they always did in these situations. It was especially hard on their oldest son, Hugh, who was only ten the night his daddy walked out the front door for the last time. *He so needs his father*, she thought.

As the hot water peeled away layers of pressure from her feet, the weighty concerns of a lone breadwinner invaded her mind. *How am I going to pay for the heating oil next month? We're almost out … and the kids need new shoes. What about bread? I think we're out of bread. Maybe my tips will be enough.* "Help Mommy count the change, kids," she said. As they fingered through the quarters and nickels and dimes, Ginger looked at their precious faces, sensing a sudden fear ripple through her body. *How am I going to make it?* she wondered. *I'm just not sure I can make it.*

WHAT'S THE GOOD NEWS FOR GINGER?

So, what's the good news for Ginger? If she was your neighbor, coworker, or old friend from high school, how would you present the gospel to her? Would you take her down the Roman Road or use the Four Spiritual Laws? Would you draw the chasm diagram or use a gospel cube? How would she respond if you knocked on her door and asked her, "If you died today, would you know for certain you would go to heaven?" Maybe she would welcome you in, or maybe she would just close the door as you continued, wondering how you—the voice box of God—could be so out of touch with what was really troubling her.

Moreover, what do you think Jesus would say to this struggling woman? What words would he choose as she wrestled with loss and disappointment, financial crisis and worry? Would he present his gospel in the way we've always heard it from our pulpits or the way we've been taught to do it in our outreach classes? Probably not.

As we look at how the Savior promoted truth with others, we find he expressed the benefits of his coming not in one repetitive way, but in different ways to different people in different situations. He wasn't *changing* the gospel, only *rightly applying* its benefits to make it most relevant to the hearer. This is a critical element often overlooked as we study, teach, and carry out the work of promoting truth; as we have attempted to distill the gospel to make it easier to present (and this is not a bad thing), we have at the same time stripped it of its flexibility in speaking to diverse people in distinct life situations. We are chained to one way of expressing the gospel to Ginger, in spite of what real good news the gospel may have for her.

WHAT IS THE GOSPEL ANYWAY?

The word *gospel* means "good news" or "good message." Something new that is good or something new that brings good—this is what the gospel is. Jesus, of course, is at the center of the good news of the Bible.

The Gospel Funnel

You can look at the biblical good news as having three parts. First, there are *the benefits*. These are the good things that come our way through Jesus. The New Testament gives us many benefits that result from his coming into our world. The promise of deliverance from struggle, spiritual light and wisdom, and entry into the paradise of God are but a few examples of the positive impact of his life.

Then there is *the root cause*. The root cause is that which Jesus did that brought about the good results mentioned above. Whereas the benefits are many and varied, the root cause is more concise and focused and ultimately can be summarized in just two words: *the cross*.

Finally, there is *the activating action*. This is the action a person must take when they hear the gospel in order to make its benefits personally applicable. It's what I must do to be saved and have all of the gospel's benefits applied to me. Like the root cause, this aspect of the gospel is succinct and can be boiled down to just one word: *believe*.

When we share the gospel, we should be sharing all three elements: the benefits, the root cause, and the activating action. The first part makes the gospel relevant to my life, the second tells me how it was accomplished, and the third tells me how to make it mine.

Equipping you to do this is what this chapter is all about. With this in mind, let me give you four goals for the pages that follow:

1. Give an overview of four benefits of the gospel.

2. Articulate the root cause of these benefits.

3. Explain the action a person must take for the gospel to apply.

4. Share how to ask a friend to believe and what to do if they do not.

GOSPEL BENEFITS

In the following paragraphs, I'll list and explain four benefits of the gospel. You should use these options as a tool bag as you promote truth to others. When the time is right to present the gospel message, pick one that applies to your friend's specific circumstances and share it with them. You know your friend well by now, after all, and—with the Spirit's help—you can laser in on the portion of the gospel that will impact them most.

The first two benefits are specific and will apply only in certain situations. The last two, however, are universal as they apply to everyone at all times. Familiarize yourself with these and refer back to them later as you interact with different people.

jesus, deliverer from trial and struggle

The down, the struggling, the hurting—these types of people were the Savior's favorite target. It seems those who were most open to his message were those who were most impacted by the cruel turns of life; and it is no different today. Trials have a way of breaking our arrogance and revealing our frailty and need. If you become a genuine friend to the lost around you, you will absolutely, positively see them go through a trial. And when you do, this may be the best benefit to share.

a god who cares

There are two ways to approach sharing the good news when your friend is in a trial. First, you can *introduce God as someone who cares*. You and I may have a hard time understanding this, but there are a growing number of people who don't think of God as a personal being who cares for them and desires to help. So, even though it may not seem like a lot, you can move someone along their path to salvation by simply pointing out that God is interested in their lives and cares for them.[61]

I have a friend in Moldova (near Ukraine in the former Soviet Union) named Eugene. A wonderful Christian man, Eugene organizes outreach efforts for Campus Crusade for Christ in that country. When he tells the story of his conversion, he doesn't begin with Jesus, but with God. He says he found himself in need in his life and for some reason prayed to God for help, and God answered his prayer; so, he prayed again, and again God answered. This happened over and over and eventually softened his heart to receive the gospel of Christ when he heard it.

jesus who delivers

So, you can introduce your friend to a God who cares, or you can be more specific and *introduce them to Jesus Christ, who promises ultimately to bring about a permanent change in their desperate circumstances.* In this case, you go one step further and set forth Jesus, God in human form, as the one who promises to deliver them completely from what troubles them.

Jesus often presented himself as the supreme answer to the ailments of this age. Setting forth this benefit to your friends simply means telling them what he promises to do for them in the future. Before we list specific examples, however, let me say a few things about Christ's promises where trials are concerned:

1. It is very important to remember that complete deliverance is promised *only* in the eternal state, not in the here-and-now. This is the promise we can make confidently and without reservation. The examples of immediate deliverance are meant to *point to* the reality of full healing in the eternal state.

2. Though miraculous deliverances are possible today, they are not promised in every case and are rare. Hence, do not promise someone a miracle as a solution to their situation.

3. Trials are God's instruments for good and are not always removed even when we trust in him. Therefore, do not promise that God will take the trial away, but that God will a) give strength to endure it, b) give wisdom to understand it, c) bring something good from it, and d) bring it to an end at the right time.

five troubles jesus has promised to end

Here are five examples of troubles from which Jesus has promised ultimate deliverance. The first four come from Jesus' proclamation in Luke 4:18, and the last is from his promise in John 11:25–26.

1. *Deliverance from earthly poverty to kingdom riches.* "The Spirit of the Lord...has anointed me...to preach good news to the poor." The good news for the poor is that God's riches will be theirs because of Christ. "Blessed are you who are poor, for yours is the kingdom of God," announced Jesus in Luke 6:20. In other words, Jesus came to act on behalf of the poor so they could call the kingdom of God their own, presently as a promised possession and at the end of the age as a physical reality. So, though stricken with poverty now, they could, by believing in him, call all that God has their own. When God leads you to someone struggling in this way, share this great benefit with them.

   You might say, "Sally, I know you and George are struggling financially, trying to make ends meet with so little. And I know it seems like there is no hope you'll ever get out of this hole. But there is a person who has promised one day to give you the greatest riches ever? Jesus said he would give God's riches to all who trust in him."

2. *Delivery from enslavement to freedom.* "He has sent me to proclaim freedom for the prisoners." Enslaved—it is a word that describes the human predicament perhaps better than any other. Although many endure the bonds of physical prisons, many more bear the shackles of spiritual ones. Christ here is promising eventual autonomy from all manner of enslavement, whether by people or spiritual powers or sin. This freedom, which begins at faith in him, will find its consummation in the eternal state. Make sure your friends with addictions (like pornography, alcohol, or drugs), those in abusive marriages, or those bound in prostitution—to name a few—encounter this liberating message.

   You could use these words, "Susan, there is someone who

has promised to bring an end to this abuse…forever. Not only will he help you now but also take you to a place where abusive relationships no longer exist. That person is Jesus Christ."

3. *Delivery from blindness to sight.* "He has sent me for recovery of sight for the blind." Of course Jesus did literally heal the blind on the spot on several occasions, but it is hard to overlook the larger spiritual significance of his words here. Physical blindness, as heartbreaking as it is, is no match for the tragedy of spiritual blindness; physical blindness, after all, cannot estrange one from the life of God, deny him authentic wisdom for living, or damn him to hell. With his coming, Jesus the Messiah advanced to all genuine spiritual sight and all of its rich benefits. Those who worship a false god, those who need wisdom for life (kids, marriage, work, and relationships), those who are bound by a cult, and those who are asking questions—don't withhold the blessing of light from these who need it most.

Try a statement like this, "Don, it looks like you need someone to show you which way to go. You've tried your ways, but they've only made things worse. You've tried the advice of friends, yet they haven't helped. But there is a man who promises to give us real wisdom if we ask? How would you like that? His name is Jesus Christ."

4. *Delivery from abuse to love.* "He has sent me to release the oppressed." To those so blessed to cross his path, Jesus offered love, tenderness, and empathy, while others, only cruelty, abuse, and exploitation. His appearance in time was intended to bring relief to those suffering such circumstances and apply the healing only the Father's love could convey. As you know, every day in our world children are abused, wives deserted, employees exploited; people are oppressed because of their color, age, sex, income, sexual orientation, and every other reason you can imagine. Consequently, countless souls for whom Christ died see no value in themselves and no love in their future. As you encounter those with such need, don't hesitate to bring them to the loving Jesus.

"Phil," you might say, "in your life, you haven't seen a lot of real love, not from your father, not from your mother, not even from your wife. I know how heartbroken you must feel. But there is someone who has always loved you and who wants to show you more love. His name is Jesus Christ."

5. *Delivery from the grave to the second life.* "He who believes in me will live, even though he dies; and whoever lives and believes in me will never die." In this situation as recounted by John, Jesus was faced with a family who had lost a loved one, Lazarus. In the exchange with Martha, Lazarus's sister, Jesus dispenses one of the most profound benefits of his gospel: resurrection from the dead. In so doing, he gave incredible comfort to all who will die—that's all of us—or have lost loved ones to the strong arms of death. There is another life, a second life, to follow; death is not the end of the story. Reach out with this message to those around you who are face-to-face with sickness and death.

You could approach your friend like this, "Bobby, I know you lost your brother a few weeks ago, and I know what an effect it's had on you. At our age, we aren't too far behind; you're probably thinking about your own mortality more these days too. But did you know there is a person who promises a second life to us, a life after death? Jesus Christ said, 'Whoever lives and believes in me will never die.'"

jesus, the giver of meaning and purpose

No Christ, no meaning. No Christ, no purpose. That's the hard truth about this life. Without Yeshua, there is no God to love our souls, no afterlife to revive our bodies, no forgiveness to ease our consciences, and no purpose to gather our passions—only loneliness, only darkness, only death. This life is it, like it or not.

People know this whether they can articulate it as such or not. I was talking with a man named Al once at a local home improvement center. He shared with me how at his age (he was in his late fifties) most of his relatives and family were dying off; the only one left was his father, who was eighty-five. When I asked him if he was a religious person, he told me this: "No, I'm not a religious person. I'm no better than a cockroach crawling across the floor. When I die, 'poof,' that will be it for me."

Yes, without Messiah, Al is dead on—we're all simply cockroaches doomed to a life of pointless labor, one day simply to vanish into the dust. But because Jesus has indeed come, because Jesus has indeed done his magnificent works, because Jesus has indeed made his tremendous promises, there is reason to live.

Try words like these, "Taylor, I can tell you're a person who wants their life to mean something. And lately it seems you're looking for something, a higher purpose and meaning to life. There is a person who can give you the type of meaning you're looking for. His name is Jesus Christ."

Table 20

Gospel Benefits	
Benefit	*Description*
Jesus, deliverer from trial and struggle	The Savior promises ultimately to bring all struggle and difficulty to an end in the eternal state
Jesus, the giver of meaning and purpose	Without Christ there is no lasting hope in life; Jesus promises to give meaning to our lies when we trust him
Jesus, the means to the paradise of God	God has described a world with no death, only brimming joy and perfect peace; Jesus is our access to this place
Jesus, the escape from the fires of hell	Eternal death awaits all human beings with no alternative payment for their sin; Jesus is our only substitute and only way of escape from this existence

jesus, the means to the paradise of god

This example is similar to a previous gospel benefit, Jesus as the deliverer "from the grave to the second life." However, I want to include this section because its truth—the paradise of heaven, biblical eternal life—provides a different and important motivation for the lost.

Perhaps the pinnacle of gospel benefits, and the one that

incorporates most others, is the promised blessing to all believers of a "paradise of God" (Revelation 2:7). In every way the photo negative of our present world, this is a paradise where no one will die again or ever feel sadness; even the threat of harm or fear will not exist. Human beings will be given new abilities to experience and enjoy life as never before; we will know and interact with God as we cannot now imagine; and the Creator will lavish his kindness on us without end. Those we love who have died believing we will meet again, even our infant children, and this experience, called eternal life, will continue into infinity.

Share this with those who are tired of this world and long for a better place after death. You can say it like this, "Ben, I know you're struggling with the harshness of this life. You've seen a lot of death and suffering in your time, and it's getting you down. You wish there was something more than this down the road. Well, what if I told you there was? What if I told you there was a 'paradise of God' out there? Would you like to know the way?"

jesus, the escape from the fires of hell

Hell. Don't be afraid to talk about it. Jesus did. In fact, he talked about it more than he talked about heaven. One writer comments, " ... the knowledge of hell comes almost exclusively from the teachings of Christ, who spoke emphatically on the subject on a number of occasions."[62] Some people cannot be persuaded by the positive benefits of Christ's gospel, many of which we have discussed in this chapter; so we must be willing to take them down a more difficult and dark path: the fearful reality of hell.

Hell is the place where God justly punishes those who have no covering for their sin. It is called "the fiery furnace" (Matthew 13:42), "the darkness" (Matthew 8:12), "the fire of hell" (Matthew 18:8–9), and is said to be far worse than death itself (Matthew 10:28).[63] According to the apostle Paul, it's a place where God's wrath is released without reservation, resulting in "trouble and distress for every human being who does evil" (Romans 2:8–9)—

all of us, unfortunately. Without question, it is both a very real place and a very awful place, and, according to the Bible, a place to which *all humanity is destined without Christ to rescue them.* To quote Paul again, Jesus is the one "who rescues us from the coming wrath" (1 Thessalonians 1:10).

Therefore, as God leads you in interactions with the lost, make use of this benefit of the gospel without fear or hesitation. It is a part of God's Word and Christ's teaching, and, therefore, an invaluable tool in fulfilling our commission to make new disciples.

"Shane," you could say, "I know you think you're young and invincible. You usually don't think about the future that much. But have you given any thought to what will happen to you after death? The Bible says there's a heaven and a hell, Shane. Hell is a real place [describe from above]. What if that's where you'll go when you die? Would you like to know how to escape that possibility?"

CUT-TO-THE-CHASE QUESTION

There may be occasions when you don't have the time to ferret out the specific benefits that apply to your friend. You might just want to cut to the chase and focus on the core gospel message. If so, there's a helpful question you can ask to focus in on a person's standing before God. It goes something like this: "If you died today and stood before God and he asked you, 'Why should I allow you into heaven?' what would you say?"

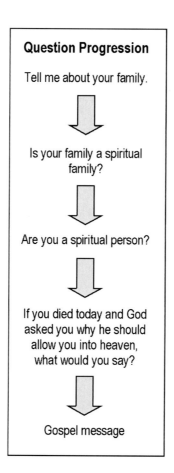

Cut-to-the-Chase Question Progression

How can I be right with God? This is the question your friend is forced to consider. You'll get a variety of answers to this query, but most of the time people will say something like this, "I'm a good person. I've tried to help others, and I haven't murdered or raped anybody." Most people think they're good enough to make it on their own. But, as we know, nobody is.

From here, you go directly to the root cause and activating action. You could say something like, "Yes, Jeff, it's good that you're trying to live a good life. But what if that isn't good enough? Did you know the Bible says that no one can be right with God by doing good?" [Then walk through the root cause and activating action.]

THE BENEFITS ARE COMPLETE

To this point I've outlined four good results of the gospel that you can share with your friends as applicable to them. If you have followed the Forcefully Advancing steps up to this point, the benefit you should apply will come fairly easily. But no matter which one you choose to share with your friend, you also need to tell them how this great benefit came about. What is the root cause of this wonderful promise or blessing? That's what we'll talk about next.

THE ROOT CAUSE

Imagine all of the benefits of the gospel as the upper portion of a funnel; these benefits flow into the spout, the narrow section of the funnel, which in our case consists of the root cause and activating action. Now, since we've discussed the benefits at length, let's discuss the items in the spout, starting with the root cause of gospel blessings.

As indicated earlier, the root cause of the innumerable benefits of the gospel is the cross of Jesus Christ. Ultimately, mankind suffers from a broken relationship with their Creator. Instead of having full access to his life, power, and blessings (which bring joy, peace, and hope), we have been banished from him, separated by an immense barrier—our immorality.

It is God's nature to hate and reject sin, anything that is contrary to his moral character. It is an irreversible, permanent part of who he is. Therefore, it is impossible for him to accept anything but complete and perfect morality in his creatures. This doesn't mean he's unfair or arbitrary, however; it means he's holy, pure, and separate in his perfections as a moral being. In order for us to come back into his favor and receive the great benefits of knowing him, the roadblock of our immorality must be overcome.

Another way to look at this roadblock is as a personal debt. Whenever we sin against someone, we incur a debt to them. If you've ever heard a criminal say, "I've paid my debt to society," you're familiar with this concept. What the criminal is acknowledging in this statement is that he has wronged society (by sinning against it) and, therefore, has incurred a debt to that society. In order for him to be "right" with society again, he must pay his debt. Prison is one way to do that. Some debts are so great, however, they're called "capital" crimes and require the person's life as payment.

In the same way, when we wrong God through sin, we too incur a debt; that debt becomes a barrier between us. Unlike crimes against people or society, however, *all crimes against God are capital crimes* and demand the life of the criminal as payment. The point? In God's system, *we're all on death row.*

For our roadblock to be removed and our debt erased, God must act on our behalf. We cannot do it ourselves—it is impossible for us. So God, who loves us unconditionally, has set a plan in motion to make things right again. This is where Jesus Christ and the cross come in.

In the end, what Jesus has done is healed the relationship between us and God, putting God back on our side; he has paid our enormous debt so we don't have to suffer our terrible punishment. God, then—who is all the blessing, power, and life we need—is again fully engaged on our behalf to bring life to completion in perfect happiness. God's lone instrument for this task? The cross.

To put it in personal terms, Jesus Christ lived the life I could not live—without immorality—to die the death I dared not die— the crucifixion—to pay the debt I shall myself never remove—my sin. On the cross, Jesus willingly gave up his life as a payment for me so God's justice could be satisfied and his love and kindness flow freely to me again. God accepted Jesus as my substitute and confirmed it by resurrecting him from the dead, something only God himself could do.

One of the best illustrations I've ever heard to describe what happens at the cross is that of a judge and a capital murder case. A man had been accused of a crime so horrific that, if found guilty, the punishment would be execution. The evidence was so overwhelming, the judge had no choice; after giving his verdict, he issued the sentence: death.

The irony of the story, and the real tie to the gospel, is that the man who committed this crime *was the judge's son*. You can imagine the pain and anguish of this judge as he sentenced his own child to death. Though he knew his son was guilty and though he was satisfied that justice had been served, he mourned beyond words what he had been forced to do. What could he do now?

His love only gave him one option. So, after the gavel fell, he stood up, took off his robe, and died in his son's place. "For God so loved the world that he gave his one and only son..." (John 3:16).

This is the picture painted for us in the Bible. God has been forced to judge all mankind guilty and sentence them to death for their crimes. But his love is so great, he takes off his robe and dies in their place in the person of Jesus of Nazareth. And now, far from standing over them, his finger wagging, he sends his word out to all, begging them to receive his forgiveness and deliverance.

Don't hesitate to share this powerful illustration with your friends.

Before we move on, let's summarize the elements of the root cause of gospel benefits:

- We have a broken relationship with God caused by our immorality.

- We owe a debt to God for our sin that we cannot repay.

- God has acted on our behalf through Jesus Christ.

- Jesus Christ has...

    - Lived the life we could not live, without immorality.

    - Died to remove the barrier between us and God and pay our debt.

THE ACTIVATING ACTION

Having shared the benefits of the life of Jesus and articulated the root cause of his benefits, it's now time to explain the *activating action,* the way in which we make the gospel benefits apply to us personally. The word that characterizes this action best is *believe.*

Regardless of the particular benefit you seek, the way you make the gospel message apply to you is to believe, or trust, the content of the message. More than simply accepting certain facts as true, believing in Christ is also putting trust in those facts, relying on them at risk to yourself. When we savingly believe the gospel, we trust that Jesus did as the Scriptures say—that he lived for us, that he died to remove the barrier between us and God, and that he rose again after three days to confirm his work.

Furthermore, by definition, we stop relying on what we had trusted in before. No longer believing we are good enough to earn God's favor or that our false gods can save us, we forgo any other means of being right with God or of entering into his paradise, transferring our trust completely to Christ. Further, as we now understand the horrible impact of our sin on our relationship with God, we repent, or mentally turn from our sin, and seek God's forgiveness. Believing also means I am willing to commit my life to God's service moving forward; inasmuch as Christ died for me, I now owe him my life. This is what it means to believe in him. And when we do, all the good God has accomplished through him courses our way irrevocably.

When we make this conscious choice, many things happen in a domino effect. We are instantly forgiven, and our debt is erased. We are adopted by God as his true child. Our names are written in God's book of salvation (called the Lamb's Book of Life), and we instantly become heirs of all his promises and future blessings. Moreover, God begins to work in us to change us into the pattern of his character. He gives us hope and confidence in the future, and he begins to use us to bring about good in the world.

Now, let me summarize the elements of the activating action:

- To be saved, we must believe, or trust, the content of the gospel.

- Trusting means we don't just accept certain facts, but trust in them at risk to ourselves.

- We trust that Jesus did as the Scriptures say.

- We must stop trusting that we are good enough or that any idol can save us.

- We repent of our sin.

- Since Christ died for us, we willingly commit to his service.

ASKING THEM TO BELIEVE

So you've shared the three parts of the good message. Now you need to ask them to believe. How do you do this? Let me lay out a brief process for you. But first, a few preliminary observations.

Remember that you are not responsible for their answer; God is. Ultimately it is God who brings men and women to faith, not me and you (Matthew 11:25–27, John 12:32, Ephesians 2:8–9). Furthermore, you don't need to apply pressure yourself; the message and the Spirit apply all the pressure needed (John 16:7–11). Also, before you do any asking, make sure your friend understands what you have told them. You can simply ask a question like, "Do you understand what I am saying?" If they don't understand completely, don't move to the next step until they do.

When you're sure they understand, ask them to believe. It is as simple as saying, "Do you believe Christ can do this for you?" or, "Do you want Christ to do this for you?" or, "Do you want to trust Christ?" When they have expressed a desire to believe in Jesus, tell them how to formally ask God to save them through prayer. You can pray with them or, if they seem uncomfortable, tell them what to pray in private. Here are the essential elements of the prayer: a) I want to be delivered, b) I believe Jesus died to deliver me, pay for my immorality, and to make me right with God, c) I repent of my sin, and d) I desire to give my life to Christ from this point forward.

example conversation

Here's an example of how a conversation might go. I'll pick up with Mark from chapter nine. First, I'll use one of the four benefits of the gospel, and then I'll use the cut-to-the-chase question, both from earlier in the chapter.

Gospel Benefit: Meaning and Purpose

Mark: "Well, I believe there's some kind of higher power out there, but I don't know that we can know anything about him."

[I continue to ask Mark questions about what he believes and over time give him answers (chapters nine and ten). During this time I discover that Mark is looking for some meaning in his life. He's become disenchanted with what he's been told in the world. All their promises are empty, and he wants more from life.]

Wes: "Mark, as we've talked over the past few months, I've sensed in you a desire for a greater meaning to your life. Am I on track?"

Mark: "I guess you are. You know I'm almost forty now, and I'm tired of the rat race. There's got to be more to life than this."

Wes: "I know what you mean. I had this same experience a number of years ago. Did you know there's someone who can give you the meaning you're looking for? His name is Jesus Christ." [From here I tell him about the meaning and purpose Jesus gives and what he has done in my own life. When I've explained it to him, I move on to the root cause and activating action.]

Cut-to-the-Chase Question

Mark: "Well, I believe there's some kind of higher power out there, but I don't know that we can know anything about him."

[In this example, I have a couple of options. First, I could ask him clarifying questions about what he believes, give him answers (chapter nine and ten), and then use the cut-to-the-chase question. In this case, I don't worry so much about which benefit I use, just go straight to the gospel. Or, I could leave off the additional belief questions and go straight to the cut-to-the-chase question. Either way, here's what I'd say when I got to the question.]

Wes: "Mark, let me ask you a spiritual question. If you died right now and stood before God, and he asked you, 'Why should I let you into heaven?' what would you say?"

Mark: "I guess I'd say that I'm a good person. I try to treat people as I would want to be treated. I try to do good. No, I'm not perfect, but I'm not as bad as some people."

Wes: "Yes, I know. Compared to other people, you haven't committed any great crimes. And it's good that you try to treat others right. But what if you're wrong? What if that isn't good enough? Did you know the Bible says that not even the best person on earth is good enough to be right with God? [From here I move on to the root cause and activating action.]

Now, after they trust Christ, your work is not yet done. You need to help them with some basic discipleship. Space does not allow a full treatment of this subject, so I've included a detailed discussion of this in Appendix 3.

WHAT IF THEY DON'T BELIEVE?

What if they don't want to believe? What do I do then? When they don't want to believe, first find out exactly what they don't believe. Ask a question like, "What exactly do you not believe?" or, "Why do you not believe?" Listen carefully to their response, and ask clarifying questions if necessary; make sure you understand their specific issues clearly. Then proceed to address their issues. You don't have to do it right then. You don't want to come off as too pushy, and the delay may give you time to think through and research their issue(s). At the right time (either then or later), give them answers to their questions. You may need to clear up misunderstandings, overcome existing or new barriers, or clarify your previous points. In any case, deal with the issues, summarize the gospel, and ask them again to believe.

What if they still won't believe? As before, don't get mad. End the conversation on a friendly note and leave the door open for future discussion. You never want to make it impossible for you to talk to them again later because of something you said in anger or frustration. Continue to develop your friendship outside of spiritual things, and keep praying for God's activity in their lives and guidance for you in terms of what to do next.

IT MAY BE TIME TO MOVE ON

In the end, if they don't want to believe, your relationship may change. You have laid it on the line with them, and they may react in a negative way. Don't forget, there is something inside all of us that hates God and resists Christ. You may be the object of this disdain after you've spoken so boldly for him.

Keep working on them. Be friendly, pray for them, and look for future open doors, but if you sense their attitude has changed toward you, this may be an indication that your work with this person has come to an end. Your love for them will not change (your friendship was not fake), but in terms of the time you have to focus on them for the sake of the gospel, you'll be forced to curtail it. Free your conscience to move on to a new friend and focus your energy there. With God, you must now trust their future.

But don't be discouraged. Your boldness, your courage, and your words have made an impact on their life. Have faith in God; he will bring fruit from your efforts in ways you cannot predict. Feel good about what you've done. You've just walked in the shoes of Jesus.

CONCLUSION

The gospel is a world-changing message. Its three-parts—benefits, root cause, and activating action—when presented at the right time and in the power of the Spirit can radically alter the life of our friends, neighbors, and coworkers. As the Spirit leads you, present the benefits of the gospel with rich variation, explain the power of the cross, and detail how your friend can make those alluring benefits their own.

In the final part of our time together, we'll talk about processes we can put in place in the church to ensure our aggressive, Forcefully Advancing strategy sustains itself into the future. And, finally, we'll visit again with Carter on his second vision of America.

GROUP DISCUSSION QUESTIONS

1. Had you ever thought about there being variation in Jesus' presentation of his gospel? What do you think about this idea?

2. Of the five troubles Jesus has promised to end, which means the most to you personally? Why?

3. Are you afraid to talk about hell? Why? Is this justified biblically?

4. Share your thoughts on this statement: "In the end, what Jesus has done is healed the relationship between us and God, putting God back on our side." Is it true? Why or why not?

5. Will it be hard for you to ask someone to believe? If so, why?

PART FOUR

Claiming the Future Now

CHAPTER 12

ORGANIZING FOR EXCELLENCE: IMPLEMENTING AN ACTION SYSTEM

I magine a new company is formed to make shingles for residential homes. We'll call them Acme Shingle Company. Acme's products can be used by roofing contractors anywhere in America. To promote their shingle line across the land, Acme's management hires a team of sales people in all fifty states. In no time, this powerful force will make Acme a top player in the market—or so they think.

About a year after startup, senior management notices that sales just aren't coming in. Upon investigating the matter further, they find three disturbing and, frankly, unbelievable practices within their sales force.

First, sales management has no type of accountability system for the sales people. Acme's reps don't report back to management on any measureable goal; they don't tell the company the firms they're talking to about potential business, and they aren't required to keep the company up to date on orders they have coming in the door. Once they're hired, they're just left to themselves.

Furthermore, the sales people receive no ongoing training in the company's products, nor are they kept abreast of changes with their competitors or the shingle market in general. A one-week orientation training—that's the extent of training for these critical employees. After that, they're on their own.

And, as if that wasn't enough, there's no ongoing communication within the sales department, either between individual sales people or between the sales force and sales management. Reps can't learn from or encourage each other, and sales management can't gain valuable insight into the market or give the team direction regarding critical business issues. Communication is nonexistent.

SO WHAT DO YOU THINK?

After reading how the sales team at Acme is handling their responsibilities, are you surprised the numbers aren't what they should be? More importantly, do you think this is a wise or competent way to carry on? I would guess you are probably thinking what I'm thinking: You don't have to have a PhD in marketing to know that running a business like this is doomed to failure. A five-year-old kid could probably do a better job.

So what does this have to do with the subject of promoting truth? Unfortunately, quite a bit. Many churches operate just like this when it comes to outreach. They hold training on promoting truth through small groups or a Sunday morning series, but have no ongoing accountability system to help their people focus, set goals, and overcome obstacles. They have no ongoing training, no way to reaffirm or add to their initial teaching; it's basically a once a year overview and then on to something else. And they have no way for their people to communicate with each other or church leadership where personal outreach is concerned. No infrastructure or system exists that allows them to share ideas, successes, and questions on a regular basis, or report to the pastoral team with needs, ideas, and difficulties. The net effect is an outreach effort that mirrors the sales efforts of Acme, disabled and ineffective.

Should we really expect anything else?

Moving forward, then, in addition to more relevant models for personal outreach (like the Forcefully Advancing [FA] strategy laid out in this book), we need to develop a means of providing positive accountability, ongoing training, and timely communication for those engaged in promoting truth to others. The overall infrastructure that provides these benefits I call a Forcefully Advancing *Action System* (FAAS).

A FAAS is a system designed to bring about truth promoting action—and success—on a regular and continual basis. In the pages that follow, I'll lay out a strategy for developing and implementing a FAAS within a group, such as a Sunday school class, life group, or entire church. The strategy has five parts and can best be remembered by the acronym REACT: *R*ecruit, *E*ducate, *A*rrange, *C*onverge, and *T*ell.

Before we get into the details, however, let me give a brief qualifier. Though we are now going to look at more of the organizational elements of effective outreach (as opposed to the relational elements discussed already), don't get the impression that those relational elements are somehow cheapened by this. In other words, we absolutely must genuinely love and care about those God puts in our path, and we must pray continually that God will give us an ongoing, unconditional love for others. However, we must also recognize the value of organizing ourselves to better minister to the lost we truly care about.

We are all busy people, and sometimes the most important things slip. We want to reach out to that friend again, but we forget to, or we get stuck figuring out what to do next, or we run out of time to pray for them, or we get a question we can't answer. The list goes on and on. As with every other part of our Christian lives, we need our brothers and sisters to help us do the important things and keep on track in our service to God and others. So, as you read through this chapter, think of it not as a hunting expedition, but as putting feet on our love and ensuring we can minister to our friends as effectively as possible.

Let's review the elements of the REACT strategy in detail now.

IMPLEMENTING AN ACTION SYSTEM

recruit

This is the initial stage of promoting the FA vision to the group. It involves generating interest and getting people to invest in the larger process. There are three key areas to address when recruiting:

1. *Explain the FA approach in detail.* First, people need to know what they are getting into so they can make an informed decision. Therefore, we must give them an overview of the FA strategy in the beginning. You can do this in a single discussion, perhaps at the start of a group gathering, or you can invest a series of meetings to explain the important concepts. If you do a series, you could develop a three- or four-part lesson or message series, or you can simply put the entire group through the book. Whatever you choose, you must give your people the detail needed to stimulate their interest and differentiate FA from other outreach models with which they are familiar.

2. *Overcome their fears.* Virtually everyone harbors fears about promoting truth. Therefore, as you explain and promote this new vision, you must address the fears of your group members by sharing how FA overcomes or minimizes many of them. Mention how FA is an outreach style based on genuine friendships with the lost—no knocking on doors or confrontational elements. Further, point out how they'll learn how to answer common questions about our faith and how they can use others to overcome objections and share the gospel if needed. And be sure to tell them how FA will teach them to talk to a lost person in a natural way.

3. *Present the benefits to them personally.* There are two things that most committed Christians in America really want: to be obedient to God by personally participating in the Great

Commission and to see our nation return to the God of the Bible. The problem—as I've noted already—is that we either don't know how to affect these things or we are going about them in the wrong way. FA provides a way for serious Christians to engage the lost world around them and, through that engagement, bring about lasting change in our nation. Drive this point home at every opportunity.

Let me make one final recommendation on the subject of recruiting. As you are promoting this to the group as a whole, don't forget to specifically target those who may have gifts in this area or in whom you see great potential where promoting truth is concerned. You may want to sit down with other leaders of your group and brainstorm about who may be good to have in the program. Take that list, split it between leaders, and personally reach out to each person on the list, explaining and promoting the FA vision to them and inviting them to be a part.

educate

Here you give your new FA team their initial training. Whatever you do, don't try to organize and send your people out without first training them intensely. There are two parts of the initial training. First, there is the promoting truth training, as presented in this book. FA training will teach them how to become a friend and make a new disciple. So put your teams through a study of *Forcefully Advancing*. But there is another critical aspect to their training, and that is giving answers training. As we discussed in chapter nine, giving answers is not an optional part of promoting truth—it is vital. Therefore, your initial training should include a broad spectrum of giving-answers teaching as well. I recommend Evidence America's *Respond* DVD course for this portion of the training.[64]

arrange

A key part of accomplishing goals through a group is to organize. That's what this portion of the strategy is all about. In order to get the maximum return on our time and energy and make the most impact on the world around us, we must create a structure, develop action steps for our team members, and hold ourselves accountable to those commitments. This is accomplished by carrying out the following steps:

1. *Break the group into smaller units.* We need compact, efficient teams as the foundation of our larger group. I recommend teams have three to five people maximum with a single team leader (discussed next).

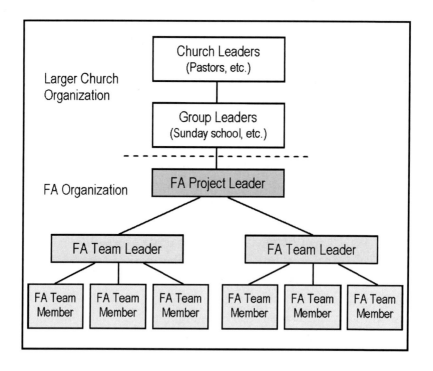

FAAS Organizational Structure

2. *Name leaders for the teams.* Each team needs a leader whose primary role is to facilitate the core functions of the team (such as goal development and accountability), communication within the team and to group leaders, and, in some limited way, shepherd the individuals on their team. Therefore, team leaders must be mature Christians who are gracious, organized, and responsible. Also, if you have multiple teams, you should also create an overall FA project leader. This person will be the liaison between the FA teams and group (like a Sunday school or life group leader) or church leaders (like a pastor). So in terms of hierarchy you would have, starting from the bottom, team members, team leader, project leader (if necessary), group leader, and church leaders. *Develop action plans for each team member.* This is where we formulate, with the help of our team leader, what we actually plan to do to impact the lost around us. An individual action plan should include at least three things. First, *a list of targets.* We should prayerfully develop a list of three to five people around us we can begin to reach. Then, *actions steps with time goals.* What exactly are we going to do and when? And, finally, *what resources do we need to accomplish our goals?* Is there anything I need from my group in order to accomplish these goals? If so, I need to communicate those to my team leader who will then communicate them to the project leader and then on to the group and/or church leaders.

3. *Set up a monthly debrief.* Let's be honest with ourselves. We are all busy people, and no matter how good our intentions, we typically only get done what we are in some way measured to accomplish. This is true of our outreach goals as well. Furthermore, we must keep in mind that the task of moving someone along the path of faith is a dynamic one; goals must be continually adjusted and new ones established as our friends progress along the road to genuine faith.

   Therefore, it is critical that we implement and voluntarily submit ourselves to a regular accountability and debriefing process. This process encourages us to accomplish previously set goals, helps us set new ones, and gives us the opportunity to get input and share needs. Here are some recommendations for your action debrief.

- *Perform the debrief on a monthly basis.* You can possibly stretch this out to two months, but I don't recommend it. You need to be moving the ball along on a monthly basis with your friends. You'll only do this if you are setting monthly goals.

- *The debrief should be between the team leader and the individual team member.* The debrief does not have to be a group thing. You may want to periodically have debriefs as a team exercise; but overall, especially since you want to do these on a monthly basis, setting them up separately will be easier.

- *Make it easy—do it over the phone.* Face-to-face debriefs are great, but give yourself the flexibility of simply talking over the phone.

- *Put your results in writing.* You need to keep a record of new goals and any issues or resources that are needed. Whether it's the team leader or the individual member, someone needs to summarize the results in writing and keep them for the next debrief.

- *Show brotherly concern and pray for each other.* Team leaders and members should inquire as to each other's well-being and pray for each other during the debrief. Our first command is to love one another, and this gives us an opportunity to do just that.

converge

This strategy element requires a periodic, regular meeting of the entire team. This meeting, which can be held in person or virtually through the Internet, benefits the team and kingdom by providing ongoing training, communication opportunities with other team members, and an opportunity to unite in prayer for those we are engaging. This meeting should accomplish three things.

First, each meeting should begin with a training segment (25–30 minutes). This element should focus on important promoting truth or giving answers teaching. Get the ideas for training subjects from the team members themselves; they are, after all, the ones engaging the lost on a day-to-day basis and, consequently, know firsthand what training they need. You can use DVD curricula during this time, work through books, or have a guest speaker give a short lesson and take questions. For a list of recommended resources, see Appendix 1.

Second, these meetings should give team members a chance to communicate openly with each other (25–30 minutes). Team leaders should facilitate this time and give the team a chance to share 1) successes and failures, 2) lessons learned, 3) ideas, 4) needs, and 5) questions. In reality, this is putting the concept of the body of Christ into practical use in promoting truth. There is so much wisdom among a gathered group of believers, and this portion of the strategy allows you to tap into that wisdom for the benefit of all.

Finally, these gatherings should give team members an opportunity to share prayer requests and pray for each other (25–30 minutes). Promoting truth puts us in the center of the spiritual struggle and places us in great need of God's help, strength, and activity on our behalf. In these times of prayer, the lost should be prayed for by name, as well as any difficulties team members are facing.

A couple of final thoughts. The total meeting time should run between one and one-fourth to one and one-half hours. If you make it too short, you can't cover what you need to, and if you make it too long, you'll lessen the impact. Also, to make the meetings easier to attend, you may consider hosting them over the Internet through a service such as Webex (www.webex. com). Not only can everyone view presentation material (like PowerPoint) at the same time and talk openly over the phone, but you can also record the entire meeting (presentation and audio) for others to view later.

tell

A very important aspect of the FAAS is providing feedback to church leaders regarding our efforts to promote truth. This feedback can help them manage resources, schedule events, give you much needed support, and, in general, get fired up about promoting truth as they see your efforts and success.

Before we review key areas to share with your leadership, let's mention a bit about the logistics of this feedback process. From the beginning you'll want to make it a regular, scheduled part of your activity. I recommend a quarterly meeting, at a minimum, with additional meetings when the situation warrants it. Further, this feedback doesn't need to come from each member. By polling team leaders and tracking important issues along the way, you can have only one leader, perhaps the primary group leader, share the necessary information with the church.

Here are several areas you'll want to review in your feedback meetings:

- *Successes.* Start the discussion with the positives. Share specific successes with your leaders. Give names and details. Remember to track successes as we discussed at the end of chapter six (friendships established, questions answered, gospel presentations made). And don't forget to share not only how *the community* is being influenced but also how *your people* are growing through this work.

- *Resources needed.* What problems are your people running into? Do they need more literature, larger meeting space, money to implement helpful technology? Whatever challenges emerge from your efforts, share them with your leaders, and ask for their help.

- *Events needed.* As I mentioned in chapter six, group gatherings aimed at overcoming a common objection, sharing the basics of the faith, or persuasively and clearly delivering the gospel can greatly benefit a person's efforts to promote truth to others. Whether you just don't think you can take the next step, or if you simply want the person to hear the message from someone besides you, having access to relevant, creative events sponsored by the church is a powerful thing. What our leaders lack many times is intel on what people in the community are dealing with, questioning, or need to know. You can provide that intel through this process.

Table 21

Action System Implementation Steps		
Letter	Name	Summary
R	Recruit	Generating interest and getting others to invest
E	Educate	Training for FA teams and leaders
A	Arrange	Organizing FA teams
C	Converge	Periodic, regular team meetings
T	Tell	Share information with church leaders

THOUGHTS FOR SUCCESS

As we close this part of our discussion, let's think for a moment about how best to make the FAAS a real success. The first thing I would suggest is to start small. If you are excited about what you are reading in this book, you probably want to go out and get everybody in your small group or church involved in FA—and that's great. Don't lose your passion, but temper it with a little reality. The church isn't used to having an organized approach to outreach. By and large, we think of promoting truth as something intentionally *un*organized.

Whatever the reason, getting Christians, small group leaders, and pastors to change the way they think, and eventually the way they act, will take some time. So start small in your efforts. If you are an average Joe, get some more of your average Joe Christian friends and start an FA team on your own; if you're a small group leader, start a team in your small group; if you're a pastor, present this plan to the evangelists in your congregation (you know who they are) and see if you can get them excited about it. Then when successes come, they'll fuel the passion of others.

There's one other thing I want you to remember, and it is something we all need to be reminded of as we endeavor to serve the

Lord: don't forget to *persevere*. Nobody ever said it would be easy; in fact, I'll go ahead and tell you right now—it won't be. As soon as you get your team off the ground, you'll have problems. Some will back out after a couple of months and others will get discouraged. You may not get the support you want from your pastor or small group leader. And who knows what else. But, if you persevere, you will see the fruit of your efforts because *Christ is for all of those who are for the Great Commission*. Set your mind now that no matter what problems come your way, quitting is not an option. If you do this, the battle will almost be won before it begins.

EVENTS THAT MATTER

Moving forward the FAAS is a critical element churches must implement to increase the effectiveness of their people in promoting truth. Another way the church can help is through the types of events it hosts.

No matter what kind of events you have now, the FA strategy will help make them better. You'll have people on the street who are engaging the lost every day and can invite those people to the events you already have scheduled. Furthermore, because of their knowledge of the questions people are asking and the needs of the local community, the FA teams can help you develop more relevant events from the start.

Whatever events you decide to put on, however, be sure they support your FA teams. The best way to do this is to make certain they reflect the stages of faith model from chapter six (cultivate, sow, and reap). Here are a few examples of events that follow this model:

1.*Cultivation Events*

Event Name: Friendship Development

Stages of Faith Category: These events can apply to all three stages of faith model categories, cultivate, sow, and reap, but are especially important for the first two.

Description: Friendship-development events are designed to give your people an opportunity to spend time with their lost friends in a fun, non-religious setting. Ball games, cookouts, bowling, and flag football are good examples of these events. Of course, your people will be scheduling activities on their own, but it is always helpful to have the church organize a larger event. Further, when the church hosts the event, it gives the lost person a chance to get to know more Christians in a comfortable setting. This will make them more likely to come to a small group meeting or larger church event down the road because they will know more people who will be there.

You want to make these events easy on the lost person, so you should avoid religious discussions and content, put no pressure on your guests to make any kind of commitment or decision, and stay away from events that take place at church facilities. This way they don't feel like they are going to "church" per se.

2. Sowing Events

Event Name: Giving Answers (Apologetics)

Stages of Faith Category: These events apply to the cultivating and sowing stages.

Description: During these events, you'll want to overcome objections that are common in your community. Using the feedback from your teams, develop group gatherings that answer the questions being posed in your area. You can have a small group meet for a few weeks to take on some specific questions or work through an applicable apologetics book on some key subject. Also, you could host a guest speaker on a Sunday morning or have a series devoted to critical issues. The options are endless.

Be sure to keep in mind the people you'll be inviting when you plan this event. If they are lifelong, hard-core atheists, you'll want to approach the location and content a little differently than if they were people who were not as hardened and had some Christianity in their background. Ask yourself this question as you develop the event: What is the best way to set up this event (location, content, group type) so that this person or group is most likely to attend? Your FA teams are critical here.

Event Name: Basics of Christianity

Stages of Faith Category: This type of event will apply mostly to the sowing stage but, under the right circumstances, could be helpful at both the cultivating or reaping stage.

Description: Sharing basic Christian teachings with the non-Christian is the purpose of these events. Keeping in mind that the culture is ignorant of biblical Christianity and is changing the meaning of key Christian terms—like sin, God, and Jesus—it is critical that we, as a precursor to reaping, teach the lost what Christianity really means. You can discuss the basics of God, Jesus, truth, the Bible, the gospel, heaven and hell, spirituality, or any other relevant teaching. Again, use small group or large group meetings to facilitate this type of event. Work through a book, tackle specific questions, or do a Sunday morning series. The options are wide open.

I would go easy on the gospel invitation here, depending on your audience. Remember, these folks are not necessarily ready to make a decision but are sifting through information, trying to make up their minds. Also, don't forget that many non-Christians avoid church services because inevitably they are put under pressure to believe. Certainly, asking someone to believe is not a bad thing, but keep in mind the larger purpose of this event and give the lost person their space. For sure, don't use any high-powered invitation that makes people feel uncomfortable or manipulated. Have faith in the Spirit's power.

3. Reaping Events

Event Name: Gospel Proclamation

Stages of Faith Category: This event applies almost exclusively to the reaping stage.

Description: Here the purpose is crystal clear: present the gospel with clarity and passion and invite the lost to receive it. Whereas in other types of events you are overcoming objections or educating about true Christianity and Christian teaching, here you are simply proclaiming the gospel in the power of God. Chapter ten provides some excellent content and applications for the gospel message; feel free to use the ideas presented there in your gospel presentations. You can approach this as a standard sermon and invitation or use a play or musical to share the gospel message.

Make sure your gospel presentation includes not only the benefits, root cause, and activating action, but also the requirements the gospel places on the lives of those who receive it. Jesus encouraged everyone who would follow him to count the cost (Luke 14:25–35), and we should never forget to include this in our presentations as well.

You don't have to have a walk-down-the-aisle type of invitation. This can make the lost feel very uncomfortable. Invite the person to respond, but don't necessarily make them feel like they have to come down in front of the entire crowd in order to be saved. Also, avoid manipulative or high-pressure methods—the message and the Spirit will apply all the pressure necessary.

one other idea: forcefully advancing day (fa day)

It would be very helpful to your FA teams to have a regular, reliable Sunday morning service (yes, *Sunday* morning) that they could invite their lost friends to on short notice. This is your regular Sunday morning service (same time and place), where the music, Scripture, and preaching are specially developed to prepare the lost for conversion. Songs would be selected whose content had to do with basic Christian teachings, the struggles of everyday people, faith questions (God's existence, Jesus' deity, creation, etc.), and salvation. The messages would not be on subjects that are distinctly "Christian" (like tithing, sanctification, predestination vs. free will, and the like), but those that address topics necessary for conversion (like the basics of Christianity, how to be saved, answers to faith questions, what it means to live the Christian life, and other key subjects).

Basically, we put ourselves in the shoes of the lost and turn all of our efforts for one Sunday a month to those things they need to be converted. We must think like them, reason like them, and understand our faith from their perspective. Of course, I'm not advocating softening or compromising God's Word to do this, but simply that we apply God's truth to them where they are in their relationship to God and Christ.

Why can't they just come to our regular service? Because they won't get it. The cultural and intellectual divide between biblical Christianity and the secular world is so wide (and getting wider every day) that the typical content of a Sunday morning service totally misses the lost person. They don't understand our language, our social structure, or our worldview. It's like speaking a foreign language to them. So we must—while maintaining a strong biblical stance—rewrite Sunday morning just for them.

Not only would this type of service provide a regular opportunity to invite the lost, it would also demonstrate to the church at large the importance of setting aside time for the Great Commission.

In terms of frequency, I recommend once a month; any longer intervals will not give your FA teams the flexibility they need. You can make this service a sowing or reaping event as mentioned in the previous section, or you can come up with something new. I recommend, however, that you work with your FA teams to develop the content and publish at least three months' worth of meeting topics in advance. Also, you may want to start this type of service about six months after you launch your FA teams; this will give them sufficient time to develop friendships that they can use to fill these meetings. Finally, do this every month without exception. Your teams must know they can count on this so they can use it to its maximum potential.

Table 22

Event Types
Cultivation Events
Sowing Events
Reaping Events
FA Day

WRAPPING IT UP

To fully take advantage of the FA strategy, we must go further than simple, once-per-year training; we must organize our people to set goals, communicate, and learn on a continual basis. The FAAS lays out a format for implementing this type of organizational system. Don't handicap your efforts to grow the kingdom and change the culture by leaving off this critical, final element.

GROUP DISCUSSION QUESTIONS

1. Do you think implementing an action system for promoting truth will help the church grow and change the culture? Why or why not?

2. What value do you see in the monthly debriefing as described in the chapter?

3. Why would ongoing training be important to us as we promote truth? Once you know the gospel, don't you know pretty much all you need to know?

4. How would the FA strategy improve church-wide events in your opinion?

CHAPTER 13

CARTER'S NEW VISION: A SECOND CHANCE FOR AMERICA AND AMERCAN CHRISTIANITY

L ight—blazing, white light—came from every direction, surrounding me, blinding me. I was paralyzed instantly, frozen in place like a statue. *What just happened?* I wondered. *Where am—?* But before I could finish the question, I knew the answer. *I think I'm back,* I cautiously informed myself. I listened for the blare of a horn, but found only silence—well, not really silence, but the peaceful melody of birds chirping and the hustle and bustle of small-town activity. The brightness this time was not a car racing toward me, but the power of a brilliant spring sun. As I lowered my eyes and took in the scene before me, I found myself in the middle of Center Street again, where my last vision began.

So what will I see now? What do I have to learn this time? And I wonder if J.R. will still be around? My mind came alive with questions.

First things first—I need to get out of the middle of the road. So

I turned left and headed for the sidewalk. Within a few steps, I saw the tracks on the right, perfectly level on their grassy hump, and I noticed the row of buildings ahead of me. The image, though brighter, matched my still strong memory from my first visit here.

Wow, what a gorgeous day; the sky is so blue and so clear. I searched for a cloud but spotted only a single thin puff just above a building in the distance. It was then I noticed the poles with telephone and electrical wires crisscrossing the road and the traffic lights at almost perfect intervals. The sidewalk was cleaner this time, littered only by the white pedals of neatly trimmed trees along the walkway.

"Why am I here *again?*" I asked out loud. The impact of my first visit had not been lost on me. Shocked, naïve, uncomfortable—these were the emotions that filled my mind after that experience. The things going on around me had incredible, long-term repercussions, but I was completely blind to them. Not anymore. God had given me a great gift. He had allowed me to see my nation in a few generations, and it had rocked me right out of my comfortable slumber.

Right away I started to educate myself on the tactics of my adversary. I read the books that criticized and undermined the Christian faith. I moved down the aisle in the bookstore, past the "Christian" section, where cultists and New Age pundits and overbearing atheists lined the shelves. I couldn't believe what was being written and taught. *No wonder people rejected the gospel. No wonder average Joe Christian—like me—was afraid to talk to his lost neighbor about God.*

As I watched the television and read the Web sites, I saw how much of this teaching had made it into the mainstream, right into the classrooms and hallways of our "good," local schools. If I had ever doubted my dream before, when I saw what was going on in the real world—my world—I didn't doubt anymore.

I shared my faith aggressively and continually. It was hard at first; I didn't really know what to say. Honestly, I was scared to death. But the more I did it, the better I got; and the more questions I got, the more I studied and the stronger I became.

Not the door-to-door kind of guy, I started with people I knew, people from work and my neighborhood. They were already people I would call friends, so they opened up to me right away. Somewhat to my surprise, I actually made a difference. It's only been five years, but I've helped people trust in Christ. I've helped them learn how to think biblically. I've answered their questions. I may not have reaped every soul—who does?—but I challenged them all, and, hopefully, made it possible for them to believe in the future.

And I didn't keep these lessons to myself. I shared with everyone. My Sunday school teacher, my pastor, my youth pastor, my Christian friends—all heard my story.

Some were open to my message. There is one Spirit, after all, and that same Spirit was telling others what he was telling me. There was such agreement and oneness of mind sometimes, it was like I was talking to myself. And then there were those who just didn't get it. What surprised me the most was that it was the *church leaders* who were the most resistant. Comfortable and satisfied, they just didn't want to make waves. Unbelievable.

Most importantly, I taught Jeff, my son. I realized I had been raising him to be naïve about the world around him and the spiritual war he would soon enter. I wasn't giving him the tools he needed to survive and be a powerful, culture-changer for the kingdom. But I turned that ship around quickly.

I taught him the tactics of our enemies and showed him his serious responsibility to push God's truth aggressively into the world around him. Whatever happened, my son was going to make a difference. It was during those times I realized how much I loved him, how special he was to me.

But lately, I have to admit, it had been getting harder. In spite of the success I'd had, the setbacks kept mounting. Many Christians, who were so in tune with me in the beginning, refused to do anything. They agreed with me, but they still didn't want to act, or maybe they just didn't have the time. And my own pastor, Jonathan, turned against me. At first he supported this message; he even let me speak in front of the church a couple of times. Not anymore. He got pretty upset with what he called the "harshness" of my message. The positives—I guess that's what he wants to focus on. But God's message isn't always positive.

The fact is, lately I'd been thinking about giving it a rest for a while. I felt so alone. Maybe God didn't want me telling everyone like I'd been doing. I just didn't know.

I continued walking. *Something is different,* I couldn't help but conclude. Yes, obviously, it was daylight now and spring, but something else had changed. There were people in the streets, but not the kind I'd seen before. No prostitutes flaunting themselves in the open, no addicts shooting up in plain sight, no drunks wandering the streets accosting passersby.

Not only were the people different, but the storefronts as well: an accounting firm, a bank, an Italian restaurant, a ministry center. *What—a ministry center? Right out in the open.* I stopped dead just past the window and backed up for a better view. The words *St. Mark's Ministry Center* covered my reflection in the door. Probably not twenty feet wide, the center took up just one slot in the parade of retail and office spaces. I couldn't help myself; I pulled the door open and walked in.

Right away it reminded me of J.R.'s place with its checkerboard tile and casual look. *But J.R.'s place was in a basement,* I remembered. *Maybe they've taken over the upstairs too?* There were kids there, teenagers, talking over open Bibles. Some were praying together. Some looked at me and smiled, welcoming me with cheerful faces. As I walked past them toward the back, I noticed an older black man working at a desk in the corner. For some reason I thought I'd seen him before. Then I knew: it was Ed. As if it had just been yesterday, an image of him popped into my mind—his grin as he joked about his condo at the beach and his beer breath as he asked me for money. But this wasn't the same Ed, not the drunk, homeless Ed I met.

His small, rectangular desk was cluttered with papers. Over reading glasses he stared intently at a computer screen, holding a yellow form in his hand. His head turned in my direction. "Can I help you, sir?" asked Ed, smiling widely.

"Yes," I said slowly, to buy some time. "Umm...how long have you guys been here, in this space, I mean?"

"Well, I think for about twelve years now. There was a salon in here before us. When they left, the landlord made us a great deal," he explained. "Why do you ask?"

Someone walked in through the back entrance, just behind Ed's desk. I looked at her and said hello. She passed quickly. "Well, I grew up around here and just didn't remember this place. It's been a while since I visited though," I continued. "How about you? How long have you been working here?"

"I've been here for probably eight years now," he answered. "I volunteer here with the kids three days a week and work at the substance abuse center the other two days, and sometimes on weekends." He leaned back in his chair.

"Substance abuse center?" I asked. The Ed I knew wouldn't be *working* there; he'd be *treated* there.

"Yes. It's a joint venture between St. Mark's and the town. It's called 'Simon's Place' after Simon the sorcerer in the book of Acts. Peter said Simon was a captive to sin, as are our addicts, but the power of God freed him. This is what we try to do at the center.

"The church had been running it alone for many years. Then the local town leadership, seeing all the benefit the center was producing for the community, offered to help fund it. The church retains control, but a lot of the money comes from the town treasury. The mayor mentions it frequently on the news," he finished.

I shook my head. "Unbelievable," I said, mostly to myself. "So the taxpayers don't protest this? Has anyone sued?"

"Well, I'm sure there are some who don't like it, but God has granted us great favor with these people, and their hearts are open to us. Besides, what's to complain about? Addicts are being freed and coming in off the streets. The whole town is a better place because of it. You're looking at living proof," he offered, spreading his arms wide.

I knew it! Yes! I tried not to act too anxious, but I had to know more. "You mean, you ... ?"

Ed admitted, "Yes, I was one of those addicts on the street."

I forced a surprised look on my face. "How did you get here, then?"

"You'll never believe it. It was by kids just like these." He motioned for me to take a seat. There was a lone, metal chair to my left.

I accepted his invitation. "Thanks."

"One morning I was recovering from a week of drinking and shooting up. I was hungry and so tired. And for the first time in all my years on the street, I really wanted out. But I didn't know how to get out. I had nowhere to go and no one to turn to. Right about that same time, these kids walked down the alley where I used to crash.

"Armed with sandwiches and some little booklets, they handed me one of each. One said to me, 'Are you tired of this yet? Would you like to be set free?' From the look on his face, I knew he cared for me, really cared; I didn't think anybody cared for me anymore. 'Yes,' I said, barely getting the words out. 'Come with us then,' he offered as he reached for my hand. 'There's someone we want you to meet.'

"I went with them to Simon's Place, though I didn't know the name at the time. That's when they introduced me to Jesus Christ and started me on the path of getting clean. As I slowly recovered, I knew what I had to do: help the kids that helped me and be Christ's instrument to deliver my friends from the street. So here I am."

What a beautiful story, my spirit spoke from within, *and what a contrast from before.* My heart was overflowing with joy for Ed and thankfulness to God. *This is book of Acts stuff, indeed. The government funding the center and nobody suing, and Christians freely walking the streets and rescuing addicts—unbelievable! I wonder what J.R. thinks of all this?*

"What a story, Ed. Beautiful. You have a lot to be thankful for."

"Indeed," he replied, nodding his head.

"I should introduce myself," I said. "I'm Carter Fitzgerald." I held out my hand.

A funny look appeared on his face, like he had seen a ghost or something. As he reached out for my hand, he made his introduction. "I'm Ed Jacobson. Nice to meet you, Carter."

"Ed, there's someone I'm trying to find, an old friend of mine. His name is J.R. Does he still work in this area?" I asked.

"Yeah, everybody knows J.R.," he answered quickly, with a grin. Then, as if he'd just remembered something bad, the grin disappeared.

"Do you know where I can find him?" I inquired. "I'd like to catch up to him today if I can."

"Yeah, he works at the big ministry center just around the block. Go down to Clay Street, take a left, go a few blocks, and make another left on Church. His place is at the corner of Church and Dover. You can't miss it. They'll be able to tell you about J.R. there," he explained.

Tell me about J.R.? That was a strange way to put it. Oh, well. In any case, I knew just where this was, or at least I knew the route. It was the same route I had taken before. My stomach tightened. *What will I see this time?* I wondered. Then I remembered the transformation I had seen in Ed, and I perked up. *Maybe God has invaded that area of this as well.*

"I appreciate all your help, Ed. Have a great afternoon," I said.

"You too, Carter."

I turned, walked out the front door, and headed for Clay Street.

As I approached the corner, I noticed the signs were gone, the ones about the girls and gay love. There weren't even any marks in the ground where they might have been, just green grass. I turned the corner and walked briskly down Clay. Again, there were people, but not like before. Whereas in my first visit they were gawking at prostitutes in store windows, this time they were sitting at tables having lunch in the warm sun and walking in and out of shops with their children. Order and decency described the scene.

As I got closer to the restaurant, I noticed a couple praying over their food, a young couple, no older than twenty. *Encouraging*, I thought.

I also saw a waiter cleaning a table, piling dishes and dropping forks and spoons into empty glasses. In the process, three bills were blown onto the sidewalk—his tip, I'm sure. The waiter, unaware, continued into the restaurant, while a teenager, who was just walking by, picked up the cash. As if wrestling with himself about what to do next, he paused.

Then he surprised me. Instead of stuffing it in his pocket, he backed up and walked into the restaurant. When I passed, he was talking to the waiter, holding out his hand with the money. *Righteousness—he's pursuing righteousness! Kids don't do that where I come from. Something powerful is going on here, something invisible, something profound,* I told myself. *What else am I going to see?*

By the time I reached my turn, I was walking on air. Everything God had showed me so far told me that things *were not destined to get worse* in America. There was still hope.

As I made my way down Church, I looked for the bulletin board from before. It wasn't exactly where I remembered, probably because of the light, but it was still there. I scanned it intently. "Yes, no Atheon!" I pumped my fist. *The temple to science may still exist, but it isn't coming to* this *town.*

Although there was no Atheon, there were plenty of ministry announcements posted: one for Simon's Place, inviting addicts to come in for help; one for an apologetics speaker coming to town to talk about truth; and one for a local soup kitchen. Of course, there were secular announcements as well, but it was obvious that God's people were making a measurable difference here.

As I continued toward the end of the block where J.R. worked, I passed a newspaper machine. Tall and thin, like a kiosk, with a flat touch screen at about eye level, it wasn't like any I had ever seen. Apparently, it still took coins and paper money, but instead of giving you a *paper* newspaper, it dispensed electronic pads instead. While I was studying it, someone walked up, put in a dollar, and walked away with a reader. I had to have one.

I reached into my pocket and found a dollar bill. After taking my money, a thin, lightweight reader about the size of a postcard was dispensed. Today's headlines were in hyperlinks on the screen. Entranced, I sat down on a nearby bench to have a look. Several of the headlines caught my attention. The first was entitled, "Town Council Votes to Restore Ten Commandments." With a touch of the finger, the article magically appeared.

The article reported—which was no surprise to me—that before the turn of the century, several humanist organizations had forced the removal of the display by persuading judges that their existence on public property violated the Constitution. Since then—to my utter shock—the tide had turned dramatically. Both the nation as a whole and the Supreme Court in particular now saw the value of God's law as the foundation of our society. The Council's vote was eight to two in favor. One council member was quoted as saying, "The Ten Commandments give shelter to all of our citizens, regardless of their religion, by encouraging the proper respect for our Creator and our fellow man. We are thankful today to be able to place them back in plain sight with the overwhelming support of our community."

"Overwhelming support of the community"—how could that be? It's hard to imagine people feeling this way. They are so antagonistic in my time.

I clicked "Return to Front Page" and continued through the headlines. Another article grabbed my attention: "Public Support Swells for Affirmation of Life Bill." *Oh, no*, I thought. *This sounds like a clever title for another abortion bill.* The article was filed by the Associated Press.

The opening paragraph said it all. "In spite of opposition from some small, pro-abortion groups, the Affirmation of Life Bill is scheduled to go before the full Senate next week. Polling shows 82 percent of Americans support the bill, which declares America's support of the right of all human beings to live, including unborn babies, invalids, and those presently considered for euthanasia. Thomas Jenkins, a local citizen and supporter of the bill, was interviewed outside of the Capitol Building on Tuesday. 'Americans recognize the ethical complexities that life and death bring,' he said, 'but as those made in the image of God, we must affirm and fight for life and not cheapen it through practices we've embraced in the past.' Jenkins's remarks echo the sentiments of the president and major congressional leaders from recent weeks."

This is amazing. I feel like I really am in a dream. It's almost too good to be true, I thought. *I need to walk for a minute and let this sink in. Plus, I'm dying to find J.R.'s place.* Back on my feet again, I slipped the reader into a cargo pocket in my pants leg and headed south.

In no time, I came to a small church building, Christ's Community Church. *They must be thriving now.* I imagined all the people in there worshipping God and praying, statues and idol worship removed. I ran up the steps with great anticipation. *Maybe Pastor Ken will still be here, or one of his sons. Wouldn't that be great!* I opened the door and was, once more, stopped cold.

This time it wasn't the incense or naked goddess that confused and stunned me; those didn't exist. But the pews were gone and in their place stood large displays with pictures and models. Just to my left a lady was standing behind a counter. "Would you like a ticket?" she asked politely. I scanned the counter. There were brochures and trinkets, souvenirs and maps. A sign was mounted below the counter: "Welcome to the Town Historical Museum." *Museum? That's weird.*

"No, thank you," I said, almost stuttering. "What happened to the church that was here?" I asked.

"It went under a number of years ago," she started to explain.

"Did they move somewhere else?"

"No, I don't think so. They just slowly lost their members. They kept to themselves for the most part. I think they brought in a young pastor at one point to try to grow the church, but he was gone within a year. Slowly the members died off, and eventually they had to sell the property. I only know because my mother used to go here."

"Oh, I see. Well, thanks anyway," I said as I backed out the front door. *How strange that God would show me all of this progress and then this too. I would expect there to be no more of this type of thing in a vision like this.* Now I was worried about J.R. and his folks. I figured I'd better go down there and check it out.

I finally arrived at what seemed to be the right location. Although I didn't remember the exact entrance to J.R.'s place from before—I was out cold at the time—this was where Ed said it would be. This wasn't a single, small office, however, like the other places along the strip. This place took up what would be six or eight of the individual spaces, more like an entire department store than anything else. I stepped back to see the sign mounted to the top, front of the building. "The Christian Life Center" it read. "I like that," I whispered to myself. "Good name."

I walked in the front door. There were signs directing visitors to different areas. One sign read "Worship Center" and pointed in one direction. Another read "Basketball Court" and a third, "Offices," told me where to go. At the end of the hallway, I came to an open space with some cubicles and small offices lining the room. A pleasant, older lady stepped out of one of the offices and greeted me. I recognized her instantly. It was Betty.

"Can I help you?" she asked, not recognizing me, of course.

"I'm looking for J.R. Is he around?" I replied.

With a confused look, she said, "Just a minute, please." She walked back into her office and picked up the phone. After about a minute, a tall, thin man stepped through a closed door and introduced himself. I recognized him from my first vision but never got his name.

"I'm John Fornelle," he offered with hand extended. "I'm the assistant director here." We shook hands. "J.R. is not in at the moment. Can I help you with something?"

"Do you know when he'll be back?" I inquired. "We're old friends, and I was hoping to catch up with him today."

"I'm really sorry, sir," he responded. "J.R. will not be back today. In fact, it will be very difficult for him to see you for some time."

"Why? Is he out of town or on vacation or something?" I couldn't leave without seeing J.R.

John paused. There was something he didn't want to tell me. I sensed it was something personal about J.R. Then he spoke, "You say you're an old friend of J.R.'s? When was the last time you saw or talked to him?"

"It's been several years now. Has something happened to him?" I asked emphatically.

"I'm sorry, sir," he responded. "I didn't get your name."

"I'm Carter Fitzgerald," I said.

John leaned back slightly and looked like ... well, like he had just seen a ghost. It was the same sort of look Ed gave me. Then, in a low and serious voice he said, "Mr. Fitzgerald, J.R. is in jail."

"For what?" I exclaimed.

"For hate crimes. He's awaiting trial. It starts in two weeks," he clarified.

"*Hate crimes?* What did he do?" I implored.

"There is an old statute on the books that makes it a crime to preach against homosexuality. It was passed some years ago, before the nation really started to change. We still have enemies out there, Mr. Fitzgerald, and they have used their power to take out J.R."

"Why?" I asked. "What has he done to them?"

"Why don't I let him explain that to you? I'm on my way to visit him now. He's at the local jail until he's transferred to Raleigh for his trial. Would you like to come?" he asked.

"Of course! Let's go," I said without even thinking.

On our short walk to the police station, I asked John, "How long has J.R. been in jail?"

"Overall, about a month I would say," he replied. "I'm surprised you hadn't heard about him already. It's been in all the local papers and even made the national news once or twice."

It was then I remembered my electronic newspaper. I reached down and pulled it out of my pocket. I touched the screen, and it lit up instantly. After scrolling through the headlines, I saw an article I must have missed before. "Local Boy's Trial Starts Next Week," was the title. I pulled it up and, sure enough, there was a picture of J.R. The caption read, "Jeffrey Renee (J.R.) Fitzgerald of Preston County awaits trial for hate crimes." *Jeffrey*

Renee Fitzgerald... but that's my son's name. Oh, God, is J.R.—?
He's about the right age, and he evens looks like my wife. I turned to
John for confirmation. "John, how long have you known J.R.?" I
asked instantly.

"I don't know; fifteen or twenty years, I guess."

"Did you ever meet his parents? What were their names?" I
asked in rapid fire.

We had just walked into the parking lot. He stopped, looked
at me with a knowing look, and said flatly, "Carter and Eileen
Fitzgerald."

I stood there, stunned. *God, what on earth are you doing?* I
prayed as I struggled to understand what was unfolding before
me.

J.R. is my son.

John didn't say another word, just headed toward the front
door. As we walked up to the main entrance, I noticed the cornerstone with the date "1939" carved into it. *This is one of the
first buildings I saw in my first vision.* Once inside, we signed in,
showed our IDs, and walked through the metal detectors.

At the end of the cold, bright hallway was a room marked
"Visitors." I walked in first, opening the door for John. On the
wall opposite the door were three panes of glass, with a small
countertop and chair in front of each. A microphone snaked up
from the tabletop. The panes had numbers, one through three,
printed over them. J.R. was already there, sitting behind counter
one. He smiled as he saw me, not as surprised as I had expected.
Unlike everyone else, he seemed to recognize me.

"You go ahead, Carter," said John. "I'll sit over here while you
two talk." He took a chair at the back of the room.

I slowly walked over to the chair and sat down. *I feel like I'm
in some kind of movie.*

"Hello, J.R." I started. "My name is—" But J.R. interrupted
my introduction.

"Carter," he said. "I know. I've been expecting you."

"Expecting me? How? Why?" I asked.

He waited just a moment and said, "Last night I had a dream.

In that dream I had a visitor here in this jail. That visitor was you. You introduced yourself. I wasn't sure when you would come, but I knew you would. I was just telling John about it when Betty buzzed in and said you were there," he explained. "I get one call a day, you know."

So that explains why J.R. wasn't surprised to see me and why John had that funny look on his face. But does he know I'm his father? I just didn't have the nerve to ask. "Wow, that's incredible," I said in a monotone voice. I was still processing. "You must be as amazed as I am with all of this."

"I guess you could say it's a first for me, for sure," he said seriously. "Why have you come?"

"Well, I guess there are two questions to start with. First, how'd you get in here? And second, what's happened to this town? I mean, since I was here last, there have been some big changes. Then it was headed straight to hell, if you'll pardon the expression. Now, it's like it has come back from the dead."

"Maybe I can answer both of those at once," he offered. "It all started about thirty years ago. The church was stagnant spiritually and shrinking in numbers quickly. We had all but given up on the Great Commission in our local communities and turned in on ourselves, sort of hiding from the world. As if that weren't enough, our enemies were making our faith out to be fairy tales and mythology in the culture, and we seemed too afraid or unsure to do anything about it."

"I know what you mean," I said.

"That was when God stepped in. He started a movement to reinvigorate his kingdom in America, calling a very special man to start this revolution. Although he didn't know it at the time, this man's pain at the state of the church and his passion to see it change would ignite Christians across the nation. We started to promote truth again—aggressively. We lost our fear and pushed ahead like Jesus and the apostles. We learned how to defend our faith and tear down the false arguments of the culture around us. We put politics on the back burner and, instead, focused on the gospel. We organized, sacrificed, overcame."

Someone else walked in to visit an inmate. A middle-aged man in a suit, looked like a lawyer. J.R. and I both turned to watch him sit down. Then J.R. continued.

"As the church started to change, so did the nation. When their hearts were won to the Lord, they changed the way they saw issues such as life and marriage and morality. We started to see the political issues change on their own because the people— the judges and politicians and voters—were starting to change. It was an amazing thing to see.

"But, don't get me wrong, we have not scored all the victories. Many churches are still on the brink, and evil still has its hold in many areas. You've probably noticed this too. The battle is far from over."

"Yes, I've noticed some things that seem out of place to me. But now that you put it like that, I'm not sure what I was expecting," I offered in a reflective tone.

"Anyway, about ten years ago, I took over for that man. He became ill and eventually passed away." His voice got a little lower at that point; he must have loved this man greatly.

He went on. "There were many leaders by then, of course. In fact, God had always had his men and women scattered through- out the land preparing for a counteroffensive. But my role was to take over where he left off and keep the momentum going, alongside my brothers and sisters elsewhere." The guard opened the door behind J.R. and brought in the other inmate. He sat down and started talking, oblivious to us.

"Of course, the enemies of the kingdom didn't like that. For some time now they've been trying to undermine and minimize me. I've felt a little like Nehemiah, to be honest. Finally, they were able to use this old statute against me, and here I am. But I don't fear them. This will work out to advance Christ too, in spite of their efforts."

It was funny. There he was sitting behind that glass—a pris- oner—and yet he was so confident, so full of trust in God. He was truly a man of faith. I was so proud of him.

But now I was also curious.

"Who was the man that started it all?" I asked. *Maybe when I get back, I can find him. Maybe I can even help in this effort.*

I could see tears well up in his eyes. He just looked at me for a minute, unable to speak. Then I understood.

"It was me," I whispered into the microphone.

He nodded his head slowly, his eyes focused on mine. "Yes, Dad, it was you."

I looked up but didn't need to say a word. "Dad." *He knew.* I can't explain how. Maybe God told him in his vision, or maybe he put it together on his own.

"Your first vision—the one you told me about again and again—that was what started it all. You thought it was just for you, but it wasn't. It was for all of us, the whole nation.

"I know there were times when you felt so alone. I know there were times when you thought no one was listening. But they were, Dad; they were. And whenever you feel that way, you must remember this experience and this moment. You must remember what you saw before, and you must remember what you have seen today. Remember this vision, Dad. Because you have a lot more to do. You're just getting started. Maybe that's why God has brought you back here to start with. The road ahead may be tough for you, and God is giving you strength to keep going. He will not leave you; he *is* using you."

The weight of his words was crushing me. *I never asked for this,* I thought. A few years ago, I was enjoying my life of ease, covered by the shadow of my ignorance. I didn't ask for that vision, and I didn't ask for this one either. Unlike most men, I didn't have the luxury of seeing my life unfold one day at a time anymore. Mine had just been laid out before me ... in thirty seconds. *I can't breathe.*

After a moment my spirit strengthened. *If this is God's will for me—that I must sacrifice and carry this weight—then so be it.* For some reason, Paul's words rang in my ears like divine megaphones. I kept repeating them to myself: *We must go through many hardships to enter the kingdom of God. We must go through many hardships to enter the kingdom of God. We must—*

J.R. broke in. "Dad, our time is short. You now know what you need to know, and it's almost time for you to go."

How does he know this? I wondered.

"There's just one more thing I need to tell you," he said. "I love you, Dad. You are a wonderful father and a great man. I'm so proud of you ... and I miss you, so much." He raised his hand to the glass.

As our hands met, separated only by the cold, clear glass between us, I said with trembling in my voice, "I love you, too, Son. I'll press on. I promise."

He smiled, relieved.

Oh, God, how good you are to a weak man such as me. Thank you for this encouragement.

As the thought left my mind, I looked at J.R. one last time. "See you again soon, Son."

"See you, Dad."

And then the bright light was back, and I was gone.

GROUP DISCUSSION QUESTIONS

1. Do you think the transformation Carter saw in America is actually possible? Why or why not? What would it take to bring about this transformation?

2. What is the significance of the losses Carter observed (closed churches and imprisoned saints) and J.R.'s words, "But, don't get me wrong, we have not scored all of the victories. Many churches are still on the brink, and evil still has its hold ... The battle is far from over"?

3. Do you think one person can make the difference Carter made? Elaborate.

4. Why is it significant to our efforts to hear Carter's frustration and see God, through this vision, encourage him to continue on? In other words, how does Carter's experience apply to us as we try to turn things around in America?

APPENDIX 1:
WHERE TO FIND ANSWERS

Barrier Category	Resource for Research
General Questions and Answers, DVD	*Respond: Apologetics Course[i]*, produced by Evidence America, www.evidenceamerica.org.
General Questions and Answers, Book	*The New Evidence that Demands a Verdict*, Josh McDowell, Nashville: Thomas Nelson, 1999. *Reasons We Believe: 50 Lines of Evidence that Confirm the Christian Faith*, Nathan Busenitz, Wheaton, IL: Crossway Books, 2008. *Baker Encyclopedia of Christian Apologetics,* Norman Geisler, Grand Rapids: Baker Books, 1999. *The Evidence Bible*, Ray Comfort, Orlando: Bridge-logos, 2003.
Science and Evolution	Answers in Genesis Ministries: www.answersingenesis.org. *The New Answers Book*, Ken Ham, editor, Green Forest, AK: Master Books, 2006. *The New Answers Book 2*, Ken Ham, editor, Green Forest, AK: Master Books, 2008. *Refuting Evolution*, Jonathan Sarfati, Green Forest, AK: Master Books, 1999.
Document Issues	*The Da Vinci Deception*, Erwin Lutzer, Carol Stream, IL: Tyndale House, 2004. *The Case for Christ*, Lee Strobel, Grand Rapids: Zondervan, 1998. *Baker Encyclopedia of Christian Apologetics,* Norman Geisler, Grand Rapids: Baker Books, 1999.
God Questions	*World's Apart: A Handbook on Worldviews*, Norman Geisler and William D. Watkins, Grand Rapids: Baker, 1989. *Baker Encyclopedia of Christian Apologetics,* Norman Geisler, Grand Rapids: Baker Books, 1999. *The God Question: An Invitation to a Life of Meaning*, J. P. Moreland, Eugene, OR: Harvest House, 2009. *Discovering the God Who Is*, R. C. Sproul, Ventura, CA: Gospel Light, 2008.

Bible Questions	*When Skeptics Ask: A Handbook on Christian Evidences*, Norman Geisler and Norman Brooks, Grand Rapids: Baker Books, 2008. *When Critiques Ask: A Popular Handbook on Bible Difficulties*, Norman Geisler and Thomas Howe, USA: Victor Books.
Jesus Questions	*Jesus Among Other Gods*, Ravi Zacharias, Nashville: Thomas Nelson, 2000. . *The Case for Christ*, Lee Strobel, Grand Rapids: Zondervan, 1998. *The Case for the Resurrection of Jesus*, Gary Habermas and Michael Licona, Grand Rapids: Kregel, 2004.
Truth Questions	*How do you know you're not wrong?* Paul Copan, Grand Rapids, Baker: 2005 *The New Evidence that Demands a Verdict*, Josh McDowell, Nashville: Thomas Nelson, 1999. *Introduction to Philosophy: A Christian Perspectivpe,* Norman Geisler and Paul Feinberg, Grand Rapids: Baker, 1980.
Christianity vs. Other Faith Systems	*Handbook of Today's Religions*, Josh McDowell and Don Stewart, Nashville: Thomas Nelson, 1993. *The Kingdom of the Cults*, Walter Martin, Minneapolis: Bethany Books, 2003. *Answering Islam: The Crescent in Light of the Cross*, Norman Geisler and Abdul Saleeb, Grand Rapids, Baker: 2002. *Oprah, Miracles, and the New Earth: A Critique*, Erwin Lutzer, Chicago: Moody, 2009.
Websites	Evidence America, www.evidenceamerica.org Answers in Genesis, www.answersingenesis.org Norman Geisler, www.normangeisler.net Gary Habermas, www.garyhabermas.com Erwin Lutzer, www.moodychurch.org/radio Ravi Zacharias, www.rzim.org Lee Strobel, www.leestrobel.com

---

[i] This is an 11-lesson DVD curriculum for small groups that covers basic questions asked in the culture today. Topics include truth, death and suffering, God's existence, evolution, hypocrisy, the Bible, and Jesus.

APPENDIX 2:
BARRIER CATEGORIES AND STRATEGIES

SCIENCE AND EVOLUTION

Typical Key Issues

- Starting assumptions/bias: People are so inundated with evolution's message, they believe it without even thinking about it. They start with the assumption that it's true and the Bible is false. Because of this, they interpret all evidence to prove evolution.

- Two types of science: Not all science is the same. There's *observational science,* which is based on the scientific method, is repeatable and testable, and applies to the present only. There's also *origins science,* which is not directly based on the scientific method, is not repeatable or testable, and applies to the past. Origins science is a scientist's way of explaining the past with present facts; it's about history and is highly biased to the scientist's worldview. Evolution and creation are both origins science, not observational.

- Key science topics: Mutations, natural selection, dating methods, and the fossil record.

- Weaknesses of scientific theory: The science supposedly confirming evolutionary theory is very weak. The actual facts support the Bible's history much better (the straightforward six-day model).

Basic Approach
A good, basic approach here is as follows:

- Educate your friend about the reality of their starting assumptions/bias.
- Teach them about the two types of science, highlighting the limitations of origins science.
- Explain the key topics to them and their fundamental weaknesses.[66]
- Show how the Bible's history explains the facts better.

DOCUMENT ISSUES

Typical Key Issues

- Starting assumptions/bias: People are so inundated with false teachings about the Bible's documents, they believe them without thinking about it. They start with the assumption that the Bible's documents are corrupted and the final canon is a result of a great conspiracy.

- The copying process: How does an ancient document make it to our modern world? First, the original document is written, and then copies are made in the original language for distribution. Later, translations are made from early copies into other languages. In the case of the Bible, we get our modern translations from the earliest copies in the original language.

- Errors in manuscripts: The manuscripts from which we translate our modern Bibles have errors in them, copying mistakes introduced through the centuries. However, the vast majority of these "errors" are insignificant. Furthermore, the tremendous number of copies available help to ensure an accurate recreation of the original writing.

- Gospels included: Not all "gospels" were included in the final version of the Bible. The Gnostic gospels, such as Thomas, Mary, and Judas, were excluded. The church used reasonable, honest criteria to do this: 1) the book must have been written by an apostle or close associate (eyewitness requirement), and 2) the book's teaching had to be consistent with teaching of books already received.

Basic Approach
A good, basic approach here is as follows:

1. Educate your friend about the reality of their starting assumptions/bias.

2. Educate your friend about the copying process, explaining how we get our Bibles today.

3. Explain to them the types of errors in the manuscripts and the vast number of manuscripts we have of the Bible in its original languages.

4. Review with them the process the church used to select documents for the New Testament.

5. Explain how, contrary to what is taught in the culture, the Bible is the most well-preserved, ancient book in the world.

TRUTH QUESTIONS

Typical Key Issues

- Starting assumptions/bias: Even with the issue of truth, the average nonbeliever has heard the world's message so long—

there is no truth, it's all relative—that they take it for granted and start with a bias against the truth claims of the Bible.

- Truth defined: Truth is that which conforms to reality and is different from a belief. A belief is a person's conviction about that reality. If my belief is consistent with reality, then it is true; if not, it is false. Truth about reality doesn't change. However, my convictions or beliefs about truth can change. And, my beliefs about reality do not change reality.

- Knowing truth: How can I know what is true about reality? Truth can be known in many ways. Norman Geisler notes several in his writings: authority, experience, rationalism, and pragmatism are examples.[67] These are often used in chorus to come to a conclusion about truth.

- Relative truth: Truth changes with time, culture, or situation, or from person to person. There is no truth that doesn't change or that is absolute for all people at all times. This claim is self-defeating because the claim itself is absolute. Among other things, a great weakness of this view is that no one can live it out. We all hold to certain moral principles, for example, that we judge as absolute. Most consider murder, rape, genocide, and pedophilia as immoral no matter what the situation.

- Possibility versus probability: Many people want to know with *absolute certainty* when few things, if any, can be proven *without the possibility* of another explanation. Requiring absolute certainty for a belief has many weaknesses. We can be sure of something without being absolutely certain. The Bible takes this for granted.

Basic Approach
A good, basic approach here is as follows:

1. Educate your friend about the reality of their starting assumptions/bias.
2. Share with them the definition of truth and some ways they can come to know it.
3. Ask them questions to point out that they hold

absolute truth convictions now, like the truth that there is no absolute truth or convictions regarding moral issues.

4. Teach them that they can be sure of something without being absolutely sure (sure without the possibility of another explanation).

5. Show them how the Bible takes truth for granted and promises we can know truth with certainty.

GOD QUESTIONS

Typical Key Issues

- Starting assumptions/bias: From the classroom to the boardroom, atheistic and agnostic arguments prevail in our culture. Like the leaning Tower of Pisa, many start with the assumption that God does not exist or that he is not knowable.

- God's existence: How can we know God exists? What proof is there of his reality? Many convincing arguments exist to demonstrate this, from moral law to the existence of the universe, to the argument of design and the resurrection of Jesus Christ.

- God's knowability: If there is a God, can I know anything about him? Is he personal, or is he an "it"? Is he separate from me or a part of all of us? God can be known, generally from his creation and most specifically from his Word. He has communicated with us so that we can know him.

- God's will: What does God want from me? What does he approve of or disprove of? This cannot be known through reason or the created world, but only if God told us himself. The Bible claims to be just this: God's communication to man.

Basic Approach
A good, basic approach here is as follows:

1. Educate your friend about the reality of their starting assumptions/bias.

2. Show them how they can know God exists.

3. Share with them how they can know who God is (by studying his creation and his Word).

4. Explain how the Bible is the only place to know for sure what God desires for mankind in general and for each of us specifically.

BIBLE QUESTIONS

Typical Key Issues

*   Starting assumptions/bias: The Bible is attacked every day in every conceivable way. The average man on the street could name four or five Bible difficulties without taking a breath. For this reason, your typical lost friend will doubt your claims about the Bible from the word go. The pressure will be on you to show him that what he's heard all his life is wrong.

*   Contradictions/inconsistencies: From the perspective of the lost, the Bible has a long list of inconsistencies and downright contradictions. From Cain's wife (where did she come from, anyway?) to differing gospel accounts, there is a lot of explaining to do. Reasonable, fact-based arguments exist for every challenge.

*   Scientific inconsistencies: Modern science and the Bible don't mix, and the world knows it. There are solid answers that uphold the Bible and discredit science. See previous discussion above on science/evolution.

*   Interpretation: Everybody has their own interpretation of the Bible; therefore, I can have my own or just reject the whole

thing from the start. However, when we study how we understand language in general—from its context—the meaning of Scripture has much less variability.

- Miracles: Are they possible? In most cases, those who argue miracles are impossible have already stacked the deck by holding that either God doesn't exist or he doesn't act in his world. When those assumptions are overcome, the possibility of miracles comes alive again.

- Claim of divine authorship: How can I know the Bible is what it claims to be: the Word of God himself? There are many ways to test this claim, including historical, archeological, and scientific tests.

Basic Approach

A good, basic approach here is as follows:

1. Educate your friend about the reality of their starting assumptions/bias.

2. Based on their issue, explain the apparent contradiction or inconsistency, show them how to understand language in general and apply that to the Bible, analyze why most reject miracles and how they are not illogical, or work through some of the confirmations of the Bible's claim of divine authorship.

3. Share how each time the Bible is put to the test, it passes. It can be trusted, especially about what is says regarding salvation.

JESUS QUESTIONS

Typical Key Issues

- Starting assumptions/bias: Misrepresentations, distortions, and outright lies about Jesus permeate pop culture today. Everybody wants to know who the real Jesus is. He is everything from a good man to a spirit-presence to a fairy tale. Whatever he is, he certainly is not what the Bible claims he is—this is the belief of your neighbors, coworkers, and friends.

- The disciples: What did they really believe about Jesus? Did they think he was God, or did they just make it up? There is a mountain of evidence supporting their conviction that he really was God.

- The church: Did the church manipulate the gospels to make Jesus divine when he really wasn't? The church used reasonable requirements to select the gospels. Jesus' divinity was a settled belief within the Christian community from the earliest days.

- Jesus himself: Did he believe he was divine? Did he ever say this? What did he prove himself to be? Jesus made many clear claims that he believed he was God in the flesh, and he confirmed his claim through his miracles and resurrection.

- The Resurrection: Is there any proof of the resurrection? Couldn't the disciples have faked it or hidden the body? Was Jesus really dead? Each possible objection to the resurrection fails utterly under the weight of the evidence. There is only one conclusion: Jesus was raised from the dead, just as the Scriptures claim.

Basic Approach

A good, basic approach here is as follows:

1. Educate your friend about the reality of their starting assumptions/bias.

2. Take your friend through a step-by-step analysis of each group involved in Jesus' claim of deity (the disciples, church, and Jesus himself), demonstrating that the only valid conclusion is that he was who he said he was: God in the flesh.

3. Analyze the objections to his resurrection (he never died, the disciples stole the body, the disciples made

up the story, and so on), and show the fatal weaknesses of each criticism.

4. Ask your friend what it means if Jesus really was resurrected. Tell them how it confirms all he said and did, including his redemptive message.

CHRISTIANITY VS. OTHER FAITH SYSTEMS

Typical Key Issues

- Starting assumptions/bias: Even most Christians today believe that all religions are basically the same. It is a belief that makes sense to the average person and one they hear over and over again. It is the default paradigm of our culture.

- Law of noncontradiction: This law states that something cannot be both *A* and non-*A* at the same time and in the same relationship. My boss cannot be both my boss and not my boss at the same time and in the same relationship. That is a contradiction. No contradiction can be true. We live by this rule every day; it is universally accepted and known, even by those who cannot articulate it.

- Teachings: What are the central teachings of the world's major religions (Christianity, Judaism, Islam, Hinduism, and Buddhism)? Each, though possibly containing some similar teachings, is radically different—and contradictory—in its core beliefs. Therefore, they cannot all be true. Either they all are false, or one is true and the others are false.

- Christianity: If all cannot be true, can Christianity demonstrate that it is? Christianity is the most logical, reasonable, fact-based, confirmable religion on earth.

Basic Approach
A good, basic approach here is as follows:

1. Educate your friend about the reality of their starting assumptions/bias.

2. Explain to them the law of noncontradiction, and show how they use it in everyday life.

3. Review the central teachings of the world religions in question and show the contradictions that exist.

4. Work through the proof of Christianity, including, among others, the Bible's reliability and the resurrection of Jesus Christ.

5. Ask your friend if they have heard the Bible's message of salvation. Explain the cross to them.

APPENDIX 3:
WHAT TO DO WHEN THEY BELIEVE

S o someone says yes to Jesus. You're pumped; you want to run out in the street and jump up and down and scream, "Praise the Lord!" Though you weren't sure at first, now you're so happy that God gave you the desire and courage to step out and push his Word forward. You've done it. Now it's time to move on to the next lost soul ... or is it?

I've often wondered what happened to the seed that fell on the path, rocky places, and thorns in Mark 4:3–20. You remember the parable Jesus told about how the same seed (the Word) can produce different effects based on the type of soil (the people) into which it is sown. The first three places—along the path, rocky places, and thorns—bear no fruit. But why? The text itself gives us the direct causes: Satan, trouble and persecution, and "worries of this life, the deceitfulness of wealth and the desires for other things."

But I wonder if it isn't possible that underlying these direct causes is the failure of the sower to continue his work after his seed was sown. In other words, is it possible that the disciple who converts the lost person can help prevent these fruitless responses by taking on some of the task of their initial discipling? I believe it is.

Let us be reminded that the Great Commission has two parts. There is the making of the new disciple, called *promoting truth*. Then, after the event of baptism, there's the ongoing, lifelong training of that new disciple, called *discipleship*. Jesus' command includes both with equal emphasis. We must guard against an imbalance toward either side. The trend today is to leave off promoting truth and focus only on discipleship; this is wrong and reflects a misguided understanding of the Great Commission. However, equally misguided is when those of us who have a passion for promoting truth carry on as if as soon as a person trusts Christ our job is finished and complete. Wrong. In fact, in some ways this is our most important hour.

Our job is not done until the new believer is on the path of true, lifelong discipleship. We must take responsibility for them up until this point. If we don't, who will? So, after our friends take the step of faith, there is still critical work for us to do, work that cannot be left to chance, or our labors may prove to be in vain (as well as their faith).

FIVE THINGS TO TEACH THEM AFTER THEY BELIEVE

Much of your role thus far has been to educate your friend. You've helped him understand the basics of the faith, given him answers to his questions, and taught him about Jesus and his work of salvation. Now, after he's put his trust in Christ, there are new things your friend must learn, things that can make the difference between his being a fruitful disciple or one who, like a shooting star, burns brightly and then disappears.

Although there are limitless issues you could address, here are five I believe are critical and basic to being a genuine follower of Jesus.

1. *Baptism.* After his or her conversion, one of the first things your new disciple needs to learn about is baptism. In the New Testament, every person who expressed faith in Christ was baptized in his name. This is the first act of obedience and

a vital step in the discipleship process. Among other things, baptism is an open expression of faith in the death, burial, and resurrection of Jesus, the belief we one day will experience the same, and the conviction that we count ourselves "dead to sin but alive to God in Christ Jesus" (Romans 6:1–11). In essence, it is incarnating our faith in a single, rich, powerful act.

Educate your friend on the basics of baptism and encourage him to be baptized as soon as he can. Help facilitate this by contacting your church leadership to schedule a baptism service.

2. *Prayer and devotion.* One of the first Christian disciplines every new disciple must learn is the discipline of prayer and devotion. One of the ultimate ends of salvation, after all, is to know and be near to God. This is the time we set aside to talk to God in prayer and hear from him through his Word. New disciples should begin to cultivate this activity as soon as they are converted. Show your friend examples from Jesus' life where he spent time with God in solitary prayer and how he knew God's Word intimately. Encourage him to set aside time in his weekly activities for prayer and Bible reading. A good place to start would be three times a week for fifteen to twenty minutes each time. Help your friend develop a simple prayer list and share a good Bible reading plan with him.[68]

3. *Spiritual education.* As I've noted before, a disciple is a learner. In the biblical sense, a disciple of Jesus is one who continually learns about him, his teachings, and his will, and over time becomes more like him (more about this last element in just a moment). On one occasion, Jesus expressed it this way: "Come to me, all you who are weary and burdened, and I will give you rest. Take my yoke upon you and *learn from me,* for I am gentle and humble in heart, and you will find rest for your souls" (Matthew 11:28–29).

Your new disciple needs to understand how critical it is that he begin his Christian education right away. Although he's learned much from you, there is much more to learn, and it is God's will for your friend to start on this new journey as soon as he can. Christ has much to teach him, and his chosen instrument for this education, primarily, is his Word and the local church. To this end, encourage your friend 1) to attend a Bible-centered local church, 2) get into a Christian class or small group for new Christians, 3) read all he can of the Bible, and 4) read Christian literature on basic discipleship topics.

4. *Life change.* Don't forget this: True salvation eventually produces life change. God accepts us as we are but never leaves us there. He begins to change us from the moment we are saved. He lives in us and works through us (Philippians 2:13). As I've hinted at thus far, God's ultimate purpose is to make us into Christ's moral image. Paul said it this way in Romans 8:29: "For those God foreknew he also predestined *to be conformed to the image of his Son,* that he might be the firstborn among many brothers." God desires and demands moral holiness in his people. And, with God's help, we must constantly identify areas of our lives that do not meet his requirements and work with him to change them. From the very beginning, train your new disciple to seek moral holiness and Christ's likeness.

5. *Promoting truth to others.* We are saved to save others. When we cross the line to Christ's side, we do not enter a vacation paradise where we rest and wait for the cruise ship of eternal life to dock. Far from that, we enter a spiritual war where the eternal lives of our friends are at stake; we, who were once captives to the enemy, now return to the battle as deliverers. Don't let your new disciple fall into the trap so many have in American Christianity. Don't let your friend receive Jesus' salvation only to disappear into the Christian subculture. He is now Christ's instruments in his circle of life and influence. Teach him right away the need to share the good message with others. Give him a copy of this book, and encourage him to start spreading the gospel right away.

CONCLUSION

After your friend believes, your work is not over. There is still a lot to teach them. Follow these simple guidelines, and more of the seed you sow will end up producing fruit instead of being lost along the path, in the rocky places, or among the thorns.

ENDNOTES

1. Aubrey Malphurs, *Developing a Vision for Ministry in the 21ˢᵗ Century* (Grand Rapids: Baker Books, 1999), 13.

2. Southern Baptist Convention, Southern Baptist Council on Family Life, 2002 Annual Meeting, Report on Family Life in America, 12 June 2002, available from www.sbcannualmeeting.net/sbc02/newsroom/newspage.asp?ID=261; Internet; accessed 6 December 2007.

3. 1972 Gay Rights Platform, available at http://www.afa.net/Homosexual_Agenda/ha1972.htm; accessed 7 April 2009. These goals, as listed on the AFA website, are listed in the same way on many homosexual sites.

4. I strongly oppose the homosexual movement and homosexual marriage or unions in any form. Further, I believe homosexuality, both the desire and the act, to be sin before God. But at the same time, we who hold these righteous positions should not participate in or condone oppression or mistreatment of homosexuals, prostitutes, transvestites, and others who practice sexual perversions.

5. Adelle M. Banks, "Iowa Supreme Court Approves Gay Marriage," 7 April 2009, available from www.crosswalk.com/news/commentary/11601879; accessed 7 April 2009.

6. Paul Boutin, "The Atheon—a 'Temple of Science'—coming to Berkeley," 5 September 2008, available from http://gawker.com/5046144/the-atheon-a-temple-of-science-coming-to-berkeley; accessed 7 April 2009.

7. Albert Mohler, "Marvelous Suicide and Beneficial Abortion: Worldviews Matter," 6 April 2009, available from www.crosswalk.com/news/commentary/11601737; accessed 7 April 2009.

8. *Strong's Greek Lexicon* in *Online Bible Edition,* Version 1.42 (Ontario: Online Bible Foundation, 2004).

9. *Ibid.*

10. D. A. Carson, "Commentary on Matthew" in *The Expositor's Bible Commentary,* Volume 8, Frank E. Gaebelein, editor (Grand Rapids: Zondervan, 1984), 266.

11. *Strong's Greek Lexicon* in *Online Bible Edition,* Version 1.42 (Ontario: Online Bible Foundation, 2004).

12. *Ibid.*

13. *Ibid.*

14. *Ibid.*

15. Everett F. Harrison, "Commentary on Romans" in *Expositor's Bible Commentary,* Volume 10, Frank E. Gaebelein, editor (Grand Rapids: Zondervan, 1984), page 157.

16. For further proof, you may want to look up Jesus' many references to hell (Matthew 10:28 is a good example) and his references to condemnation (like John 3:18), both topics the modern world abhors.

17. *Strong's Greek Lexicon* in *Online Bible Edition,* Version 1.42 (Ontario: Online Bible Foundation, 2004).

18. *Ibid.*

19. J. H. Bratt, "Salt," in *Zondervan Pictorial Encyclopedia of the Bible,* Vol. 5, Merrill C. Tenney, editor (Grand Rapids: Zondervan), 220.

20. *Strong's Greek Lexicon* in *Online Bible Edition*, Version 1.42 (Ontario: Online Bible Foundation, 2004).

21. *Ibid.*

22. For examples, see his comments in Matthew 6:1, 5, 16; 7:1–2, 3–5, and 21–23.

23. *Strong's Greek Lexicon* in *Online Bible Edition*, Version 1.42 (Ontario: Online Bible Foundation, 2004).

24. *Ibid.*

25. D. James Kennedy and Jerry Newcombe, *What if Jesus had never been born?* (Nashville: Nelson, 1994), 221.

26. The Barna Group, "Survey Shows How Christians Share Their Faith," 31 January 2005, available from http://www.barna.org/barna-update/article/5-barna-update/186-survey-shows-how-christians-share-their-faith; accessed 7 April 2009.

27. Let me say here that my purpose is not to criticize The Barna Group. They are a wonderful Christian organization doing a great work. I read and recommend their material frequently. My purpose is to show that the numbers reflected here do not reflect what is really going on in the church, not through any fault of Barna, but due to the factors I will list here.

28. *Strong's Greek Lexicon* in *Online Bible Edition*, Version 1.42 (Ontario: Online Bible Foundation, 2004).

29. *Ibid.*

30. *Ibid.*

31. Chuck Colson, "The Witness of Jack Kemp: A Life's Testimony," available at http://www.crosswalk.com/news/commentary/11603591/; accessed 15 May 2009.

32. If you feel led to a more direct approach, I strongly recommend The Way of the Master Ministries, www.wotm.org.

33. The Barna Group, "A New Generation Expresses its Skepticism and Frustration with Christianity," 24 September

2007, available at http://www.barna.org/barna-update/article/16-teensnext-gen/94-a-new-generation-expresses-its-skepticism-and-frustration-with-christianity; accessed 8 April 2009.

34. Ibid.

35. By the way, the fourth most common negative perception was that Christianity was "too involved in politics," 75 percent—see chapter three.

36. *Strong's Greek Lexicon* in *Online Bible Edition*, Version 1.42 (Ontario: Online Bible Foundation, 2004).

37. Here are a few references you can look up to get an idea of his disdain for hypocrisy: Matthew 6:2, 5, 16; 7:5; 15:7; 16:3; 22:18; and 23:13–29.

38. *Strong's Greek Lexicon* in *Online Bible Edition*, Version 1.42 (Ontario: Online Bible Foundation, 2004).

39. *Ibid.*

40. Peter T. O'Brien, *The Letter to the Ephesians, The Pillar New Testament Commentary* series, D. A. Carson, General Editor (Grand Rapids: William B. Eerdmans Publishing, 1999), 361.

41. *Strong's Greek Lexicon* in *Online Bible Edition*, Version 1.42 (Ontario: Online Bible Foundation, 2004).

42. D. A. Caron, "Commentary on Matthew" in *The Expositor's Bible Commentary*, Volume 8, Frank E. Gaebelein, General Editor (Grand Rapids: Zondervan, 1984), 293.

43. By this I do not mean that we sacrifice our biblical priorities of God, family, and rest. But with these things in balance, we show the world the value of a Christian worker and, in so doing, the glory of the Christian God.

44. *Strong's Greek Lexicon* in *Online Bible Edition*, Version 1.42 (Ontario: Online Bible Foundation, 2004).

45. O'Brien, 327.

46. Geoffrey W. Bromiley, editor, *Theological Dictionary of the*

New Testament, Abridged Edition (Grand Rapids: Eerdmans, 1985), 918.

47. Pornography. (n.d.). Dictionary.com Unabridged (v 1.1). Retrieved June 01, 2009, from Dictionary.com website: http:dictionary.classic.reference.com/browse/pornography.

48. Bromiley, 339.

49. *Strong's Greek Lexicon* in *Online Bible Edition,* Version 1.42 (Ontario: Online Bible Foundation, 2004).

50. For direction on biblical conflict principles, I recommend Peacemaker Ministries at www.peacemaker.net.

51. Please keep in mind, I'm not saying that fellowship and discipleship gatherings are not important to Christian development. Of course they are. The point I'm trying to make is that there may be an imbalance in some places. Furthermore, promoting truth is an excellent forum for Christian development.

52. As a sidebar, whenever you're going to invite someone to church, make sure you know who is speaking and the subject of the message. The last thing you want to do is have someone come to church with you the day your pastor is preaching on tithing or when you've got some less than adequate guest speaker. Take the time to ensure the message and speaker are right.

53. God can use us to influence strangers or mere acquaintances. He does this on a regular basis and there are several excellent training programs for this type of situation. My proposition here is that you may be able to do more long-term good from the position as a friend, than as a stranger or new acquaintance, especially in the antagonistic spiritual environment of modern America. Given this, the training provided in this book will focus on friendship building.

54. *Strong's Greek Lexicon* in *Online Bible Edition,* Version 1.42 (Ontario: Online Bible Foundation, 2004).

55. Kenneth S. Wuest, *The New Testament: An Expanded*

Translation (Grand Rapids: Eerdmans, 1961), 189.

56. This system is pronounced like the word "buddy" and is based broadly on the recommendations given in Joe Aldrich's book, *Lifestyle Evangelism* (Sisters, OR: Multnomah Publishers, 1993), 175–189. The BUDDI acronym was developed by this author.

57. *Strong's Greek Lexicon* in *Online Bible Edition*, Version 1.42 (Ontario: Online Bible Foundation, 2004).

58. *Ibid.*

59. Starting assumptions are also called presuppositions. This entire concept comes from Ken Ham at Answers in Genesis, www.answersingenesis.org.

60. Peter Galling, "Do Creationists Reject Science?" 04 February 2008, available from www.answersingenesis.org/articles/2008/02/04/do-creationists-reject-science; Internet; accessed 7 February 2008.

61. Of course the Bible teaches that God cares for all of mankind, even those who do not believe in him. For examples in Scripture see Acts 17:24–29, Romans 10:12, and John 3:16.

62. H. Buis, "Hell," in *Zondervan Pictorial Encyclopedia of the Bible*, Volume 3, Merrill C. Tenney, ed., (Grand Rapids: Zondervan), 1976.

63. Ibid.

64. Evidence America's *Respond* course is an excellent DVD-based group study program that gives answers to key questions raised in the culture. For more information, visit our website at www.evidenceamerica.org. You also could work through a book on an important topic. See the appendix for recommendations.

65. This is an 11-lesson DVD curriculum for small groups that covers basic questions asked in the culture today. Topics include truth, death, and suffering, God's existence, evolution, hypocrisy, the Bible, and Jesus.

66. You may think you have to be a PhD scientist to do this, but you don't. The basics of these four topics are very easy to understand. Also, you may assume your friend knows a lot about these subjects, but in most cases they only know what they've heard on television. If you understand the basics, you'll know more than they do.

67. Norman Geisler and Paul Feinberg, *Introduction to Philosophy: A Christian Perspective* (Grand Rapids: Baker Book House, 1980) in Libronix Digial Library System 3.0b CD-ROM, 2000–2006, by Libronix Corporation.

68. A common plan I like is to read one gospel, then the book of Acts, and then the remainder of the New Testament. When this is complete, go back, pick a different gospel, and read Acts and the rest of the New Testament again.

LIVE

listen|imagine|view|experience

AUDIO BOOK DOWNLOAD INCLUDED WITH THIS BOOK!

In your hands you hold a complete digital entertainment package. In addition to the paper version, you receive a free download of the audio version of this book. Simply use the code listed below when visiting our website. Once downloaded to your computer, you can listen to the book through your computer's speakers, burn it to an audio CD or save the file to your portable music device (such as Apple's popular iPod) and listen on the go!

How to get your free audio book digital download:

1. Visit www.tatepublishing.com and click on the e|LIVE logo on the home page.
2. Enter the following coupon code:
   fad0-68a5-3c71-6386-1ee3-9b53-fec0-1a28
3. Download the audio book from your e|LIVE digital locker and begin enjoying your new digital entertainment package today!